OXFORD MONOGRAPHS IN
INTERNATIONAL LAW

General Editors: Professor Ian Brownlie CBE, QC, FBA
Former Chichele Professor of Public International Law in the
University of Oxford and Member of the International Law Commission, and
Professor Vaughan Lowe, *Chichele Professor of Public International Law in the*
University of Oxford and Fellow of All Souls College, Oxford

INTERNATIONAL ORGANIZATIONS
AND THEIR EXERCISE OF
SOVEREIGN POWERS

OXFORD MONOGRAPHS IN
INTERNATIONAL LAW

The aim of this series is to publish important and original pieces of research on all aspects of international law. Topics that are given particular prominence are those which, while of interest to the academic lawyer, also have important bearing on issues which touch upon the actual conduct of international relations. Nonetheless, the series is wide in scope and includes monographs on the history and philosophical foundations of international law.

RECENT TITLES IN THE SERIES

Just War or Just Peace?
Humanitarian Intervention and International Law
Simon Chesterman

State Responsibility for Transboundary Air
Pollution in International Law
Phoebe Okowa

The Responsibility of States for International Crimes
Nina H. B. Jørgensen

The Law of International Watercourses: Non-navigational Uses
Stephen C. McCaffrey

International Justice and the International Criminal Court:
Between Sovereignty and the Rule of Law
Bruce Broomhall

Human Rights in International Criminal Proceedings
Salvatore Zappalà

Universal Jurisdiction: International and
Municipal Legal Perspectives
Luc Reydams

INTERNATIONAL ORGANIZATIONS AND THEIR EXERCISE OF SOVEREIGN POWERS

DAN SAROOSHI

Herbert Smith Reader in International Law, University of Oxford
Fellow, The Queen's College, Oxford

OXFORD
UNIVERSITY PRESS

OXFORD

UNIVERSITY PRESS

Great Clarendon Street, Oxford OX2 6DP

Oxford University Press is a department of the University of Oxford.
It furthers the University's objective of excellence in research, scholarship,
and education by publishing worldwide in

Oxford New York

Auckland Cape Town Dar es Salaam Hong Kong Karachi
Kuala Lumpur Madrid Melbourne Mexico City Nairobi
New Delhi Shanghai Taipei Toronto

With offices in

Argentina Austria Brazil Chile Czech Republic France Greece
Guatemala Hungary Italy Japan Poland Portugal Singapore
South Korea Switzerland Thailand Turkey Ukraine Vietnam

Oxford is a registered trade mark of Oxford University Press
in the UK and in certain other countries

Published in the United States
by Oxford University Press Inc., New York

© D. Sarooshi, 2005

The moral rights of the author have been asserted

Crown copyright material is reproduced under Class Licence
Number C01P0000148 with the permission of HMSO
and the Queen's Printer for Scotland

Database right Oxford University Press (maker)

First published 2005

British Library Cataloguing in Publication Data

Data available

Library of Congress Cataloging-in-Publication Data

Data available

ISBN 0–19–928325–7   978–0–19–928325–5

1 3 5 7 9 10 8 6 4 2

Typeset by Newgen Imaging Systems (P) Ltd., Chennai, India
Printed in Great Britain
on acid-free paper by
Biddles Ltd., King's Lynn

This work is dedicated to my wife, Mary, for her continual love, friendship, and constant encouragement

General Editors' Preface

The rise of international organizations such as the EU, and the increasing tendency of States to collaborate in international activities under the auspices of bodies such as the UN Security Council and NATO, bring to the fore the question of the respective rights and duties of these bodies and of the States that use them. Among the issues are the nature of the relationship between the States and the international body, the responsibility of the body and of the States for actions taken in the name of the body, and the rights of States against organizations on which they have conferred powers. Dr Sarooshi distinguishes between different types of conferrals of powers on international organizations, including transfers and delegations of powers and agency relationships. The clarity and thoroughness of his analysis provides a firm foundation for the development of the law in this important area.

IB
AVL

Foreword

Dr. Sarooshi's earlier study, *The United Nations and the Development of Collective Security*, provided an intellectual framework for ascertaining the permitted parameters of delegation of powers by the Security Council to States. The starting point was the identification in the Charter of the United Nations of functions to be performed by the Security Council and the assignment to it of powers necessary for that purpose. This book received well-merited favourable attention.

In this new study, Dr. Sarooshi deals with issues that are to an extent related, but conceptually anterior in time—the exercise by international organizations themselves of powers that have been conferred on them by States—powers that, when exercised by States, are commonly referred to as 'sovereign powers'. He observes that the very nature of these powers—executive, legislative and judicial—has led domestic political and judicial actors to question both the constitutionality and the propriety of such broad powers having been passed. He believes such debates would be better informed by a clearer understanding of the powers conferred, and to that end contributes a typology. He is able to move our understanding of legal phenomena in the world of international organizations from 'stuff happens' to a conceptual picture within which we are given the tools correctly to place future events.

Just as, in his earlier work, Dr. Sarooshi was able to show that delegation of powers held by international organizations (back) to States are not all of a kind, so here he effectively demonstrates that the powers initially transferred by States to international organizations vary in character and exist along a spectrum of possibilities. At one end of the spectrum lies a conferral of powers in which the international organization effectively acts as agent of the States concerned. Definitionally, such conferrals of powers are revocable. The author provides a detailed and extended analysis, of considerable interest, of agency relationships between States and international organizations, in which he skilfully weaves together theory, the relevant literature, case law of international courts and other examples in international State practice. At the other end of the spectrum lie full and non-revocable transfers of powers.

There may be different perceptions, both by the protagonists themselves and by third parties, as to how any particular power exercised by an international organization is to be characterized. Where redress is sought against States members of an international organization for the default of the organization itself, this question assumes more than academic interest, as the International Tin Council litigation of the 80s has shown. As Dr Sarooshi demonstrates, issues of fiduciary duty and of international responsibility depend for their proper resolution upon an understanding of precisely what type of powers have been transferred and the character of their exercise by the organization concerned.

Dr. Sarooshi provides a series of tests to identify the nature of the conferral of a particular power. Among these, in his view the role of States in the exercise of control over the exercise of powers by an organization is central to this exercise. He perceptively notes the underlying tension to this reality—that the greater the powers of control over decision-making which are transferred to an organization, the more States seek still themselves to exercise control over organizational decisions—often as a result of increased domestic political pressures. Of particular interest in this context is the current phenomenon of concurrent competences exercised by States and by the international organization concerned. A short analysis of this practice within the EU is followed by an absorbing, more detailed study of the phenomenon in the United States' relationship with the WTO.

The reader will here find an analysis of the issues that draws on very wide source materials and evidences an ability to set both practice and writings within the intellectual framework of analysis that the author has chosen for his book. This intellectual framework, within which Dr Sarooshi deploys his typology and examination of practice thereunder, is one which identifies international organizations as 'a forum for the contestation of sovereignty'. He draws on recent and current philosophy on the concept of sovereignty, including its normative character, and sees these contrasting perceptions being played out within this overarching relationship between States and the organizations of which they are members.

This study confirms Dr Sarooshi as a leading writer today in the field of international organizations—a field in which he has immersed himself and taken on the challenge of its ever expanding and deepening nature. As with *The United Nations and the Development of Collective Security*, he has married impressive knowledge of detail with original conceptual thinking. The result is a book that is at once informative and challenging.

Judge Rosalyn Higgins
International Court of Justice
Peace Palace, The Hague

Acknowledgments

This study would not have been produced without the constant guidance, assistance, inspiration, and personal friendship of Judge Dame Rosalyn Higgins QC and Professor Vaughan Lowe.

I wish also to single out and acknowledge the essential contribution that has been made by Professor Georges Abi-Saab, Dapo Akande, Professor Philip Alston, Professor Sir Franklin Berman QC, Professor Ian Brownlie QC, Nicholas Bamforth, Sir Alan Budd, Judge Lucius Caflisch, Professor Paul Craig QC, Professor James Crawford SC, Professor Malgosia Fitzmaurice, Richard Gardiner, Professor Guy Goodwin-Gill, Professor Vera Gowlland-Debbas, Professor Christopher Greenwood QC, Professor John Jackson, Professor Jeffrey Jowell QC, Dr Peter Khan, Professor Frederic Kirgis, Professor Maurice Mendelson QC, Professor Alain Pellet, Professor Michael Reisman, Professor Sir Adam Roberts, Professor Malcolm Shaw QC, Dr Stefan Talmon, Professor Colin Warbrick, Professor Joseph Weiler, Professor Karel Wellens, Professor Derrick Wyatt QC, and Sir Michael Wood, who—by providing valuable assistance during different stages of writing and in a number of cases comments on certain chapters—have each made their unique contribution to this work.

Many thanks go to my wider family—the Sarooshis and the Huddlestons—for all of their love and support. Many thanks also to my research assistant Jason Evans, but particular thanks must go to my research assistant Veronika Fikfak for her excellent work at the final stages in assisting with bibliographical research and chasing recalcitrant footnotes.

Finally, I would like to thank John Louth and the Delegates of Oxford University Press.

DS
The Queen's College, Oxford

Contents–Summary

Introduction   1

1. International Organizations as a Forum for the Contestation of Sovereignty   3

2. The Processes by which States Confer Powers on International Organizations   18

3. Conferrals by States of Powers on International Organizations: a Typology   28

4. Agency Relationships between States and International Organizations   33

5. Delegations of Powers to International Organizations   54

6. Transfers of Powers to International Organizations   65

7. Measures a State can take against an International Organization on which it has Conferred Powers   108

Concluding Remarks   121

Bibliography   123

Index   145

Contents

INTRODUCTION	**1**
1. INTERNATIONAL ORGANIZATIONS AS A FORUM FOR THE CONTESTATION OF SOVEREIGNTY	**3**
I. Sovereignty as an Essentially Contested Concept and International Organizations	3
1. Sovereignty as an 'essentially contested concept'	3
2. The nation-State as 'exemplar'	5
3. Sovereignty and international organizations	6
4. The normative character of sovereignty and the question of values	9
5. The ontological function of sovereignty	11
II. The Prima Facie Application of Domestic Public and Administrative Law Principles to International Organizations	14
2. THE PROCESSES BY WHICH STATES CONFER POWERS ON INTERNATIONAL ORGANIZATIONS	**18**
I. Conferrals of Powers by Constituent Treaty	18
II. Conferrals of Powers on an Ad Hoc Basis	19
1. The role of an organization's reaction to conferrals of powers	20
3. CONFERRALS BY STATES OF POWERS ON INTERNATIONAL ORGANIZATIONS: A TYPOLOGY	**28**
I. A Spectrum of Conferrals: Agency Relationships, Delegations, and Transfers	29
II. The Measurement of the Degree to which Powers have been given away by States	29
1. The blunt instrument of revocability	29
2. Control by States over the organization	30
3. An exclusive or concurrent competence to exercise conferred powers	31
4. AGENCY RELATIONSHIPS BETWEEN STATES AND INTERNATIONAL ORGANIZATIONS	**33**
I. Principal and Agent as Separate Legal Entities	34
II. The Existence of Consent and the Issue of Revocability	35

1. Consent as prerequisite for agency relationships 35
2. Implied consent: the role of State control 37
3. Consent and the revocability of agency relationships 41

III. The Establishment of Agency Relationships between
States and International Organizations 42

1. Member States 43
2. Non-member States 49
3. Consequences of the establishment of agency relationships 50
   (i) An agent can change certain legal relations of
its principal 50
   (ii) The responsibility of a principal for the acts of
its agent 50
   (iii) The fiduciary duty of the agent to act in the
interests of its principal 51

**5. DELEGATIONS OF POWERS TO INTERNATIONAL
ORGANIZATIONS 54**

I. The Revocable Nature of Delegations of Powers 54
II. The State's Competence to Exercise Delegated Powers
Concurrently with that of the Organization 58
III. Consequences of Delegations of Powers for the
State-Organization Relationship 62

1. Fiduciary issues 62
2. Issues of responsibility 63

**6. TRANSFERS OF POWERS TO INTERNATIONAL
ORGANIZATIONS 65**

I. The Irrevocable Nature of Transfers of Powers 66
II. A State's Consent to be Bound by Obligations that Flow
from an Organization's Exercise of Conferred Powers:
'Partial Transfers' and 'Full Transfers' of Powers 69

1. The contestation of sovereign values by domestic courts:
the case of the 'full transfer' of powers to the EC 72
2. The contestation of sovereign values by domestic
legislatures: the case of the 'partial transfer' by the US
of powers to the WTO 76
   (i) The US Congress and transfers of powers to
international organizations 76
   (ii) The 'partial transfer' by the US of powers to the WTO 78

(a) Economic autonomy as a value of US sovereignty 79
(b) The contestation of economic sovereignty within
   the US: the Congress-Executive relationship and
   trade policy control 82
(c) The US Congress and efforts to project observance
   of corporate economic autonomy 91
(d) The US Congress and the establishment of the
   WTO dispute settlement system 95
(e) Why did the US push for the establishment of the
   WTO dispute settlement system? 98

III. Consequences of Transfers of Powers for the
State-Organization Relationship 100

1. Fiduciary issues 100
2. Issues of responsibility 101
   (i) Partial transfers of powers 102
   (ii) Full transfers of powers 104

7. **MEASURES A STATE CAN TAKE AGAINST AN
INTERNATIONAL ORGANIZATION ON WHICH IT HAS
CONFERRED POWERS** **108**

I. Agency Relationships 109
II. Delegations of Powers 110

1. Treaty amendment 110
2. Unilateral financial measures 111
3. Termination of conferrals 114
4. Persistent objection 115

III. Transfers of Powers 116

1. Treaty amendment 117
2. Unilateral financial measures 117
3. Termination of conferrals 117
4. Persistent objection 118

IV. The Future 118

CONCLUDING REMARKS **121**
Bibliography **123**
Index **145**

Introduction

'O ye the elected representatives of the people in every land! Take ye counsel together, and let your concern be only for that which profiteth mankind and bettereth the condition thereof. . . .'

Bahá'u'lláh, in a Tablet to Queen Victoria, 1867

This book provides a conceptual and legal analysis of the exercise by international organizations of sovereign powers. These powers have been conferred by States on organizations and include the full range of executive, legislative, and judicial powers of the State.[1]

The broad range of measures being taken by international organizations in the exercise of these powers has led a variety of domestic political and judicial actors and commentators to question the constitutionality and propriety of conferring these broad powers on organizations. There is, however, a considerable lack of clarity in discussion of these issues. The labels used to describe particular conferrals of powers are often used uncritically to refer to different types of conferrals. Failure to distinguish between different types of conferrals of powers confuses analysis of the differing legal consequences of these conferrals and obfuscates the domestic policy debates that surround their conferral. In order to provide clarity in this area, Chapter 3 provides a typology of the different types of conferrals by States of powers on international organizations: cases of agency relationships,[2] 'delegations of powers',[3] and 'transfers of powers'.[4] The classification of these different types of conferrals depends on a measurement of the degree to which States have given away their powers to international organizations. This typology is used in subsequent chapters to clarify a number of important legal consequences that flow from these differing types of conferrals. These include: When an international organization exercises conferred powers, does it do so on its own behalf or on behalf of the State? Whose legal relations are changed by the exercise of powers: the State's or the organization's? In the case where the State has retained the right to exercise powers it has conferred on an organization, whose interpretation of the powers will prevail in the case of a conflict that

[1] It should be made clear that this is a wholly different enquiry from earlier work by this writer which examined the delegation (back) to States of powers previously conferred on an organization: D. Sarooshi, *The United Nations and the Development of Collective Security: the Delegation by the UN Security Council of its Chapter VII Powers* (1999).
[2] See Chapter 4.   [3] See Chapter 5.   [4] See Chapter 6.

arises from the concurrent exercise of powers? And who is responsible for breaches of international law that may occur as a result of the organization's exercise of conferred powers: the State or the organization or both? These issues lead on to a consideration in Chapter 7 of the measures available to a State under international law when it wants to try and change the way that an organization is exercising conferred powers.

However none of these issues are the central problem that arises when international organizations exercise sovereign powers of government. The main problem is the conceptual one of what sovereign values should international organizations seek to *achieve and use* when they exercise sovereign powers. Sovereign values play a dual role in this question because they not only provide objectives for, but at the same time provide normative constraints on, the exercise of sovereign powers.

It is in Chapter 1 that a detailed exploration of the nature and value content of sovereignty is undertaken and a conceptual framework is established. This framework is then brought to bear in subsequent chapters on a number of different types of conferrals of sovereign powers on international organizations (for example, the United Nations, World Trade Organization, and the European Communities) in order to understand more precisely the relationship between an organization and its member States in the processes of formulation and application of sovereign values on the international plane.

1

International Organizations as a Forum for the Contestation of Sovereignty

The meaning of the concept of sovereignty is largely contingent upon the text in which it figures. There is no objective concept that is universally applicable[1] and yet it is of fundamental importance to the concept of a State and indeed of modern political knowledge. Much of the literature on sovereignty in international legal journals has been devoted to discussing the relationship between sovereignty and international law and organizations and the limitations that are said to flow therefrom for the exercise by the sovereign State of its governmental powers within, and external to, its territory. This approach has often led to international organizations being viewed with suspicion, and as being problematic, from the perspective of the State, since certain domestic commentators consider that these organizations involve the 'loss' of a State's sovereignty.[2] The response in legal journals by supporters of international organizations has been too narrow, technical, and often simply reaffirms the fears of the domestic commentators by focusing on the binding nature and scope of obligations that are imposed on States as a result of the organization's exercise of conferred powers.

The approach adopted herein is different. It involves a focus on sovereignty as an essentially contested concept and contends that this characterization of sovereignty has a number of important consequences for our discussion of the exercise by international organizations of conferred powers of government. A number of these consequences are set out in this chapter and demonstrated in a number of the chapters that follow.

I. SOVEREIGNTY AS AN ESSENTIALLY CONTESTED CONCEPT AND INTERNATIONAL ORGANIZATIONS

1. Sovereignty as an 'essentially contested concept'

The precise meaning and scope of the application of sovereignty in different contexts remains unclear. Stephen Krasner has provided a useful typology of the

---

[1] Cf. A. James, *Sovereign Statehood: The Basis of International Society* (1986), pp.14–22; and J.S. Barkin and B. Cronin, 'The State and the Nation: Changing Norms and the Rules of Sovereignty in International Relations', 48(1) *International Organization* (1994), p.107.

[2] This was, for example, the view of Republican Senate Leader Robert Dole who considered that the US joining the World Trade Organization would involve a loss of US sovereignty: see J. Jackson, 'The Great 1994 Sovereignty Debate: United States Acceptance and Implementation of the Uruguay Round Results', 36 *Columbia Journal of Transnational Law* (1998), p.157 at p.186.

concept, and yet there are still different ways of approaching, giving content to, and using the concept. In addition to domestic sovereignty, interdependence sovereignty, international legal sovereignty, and Westphalian sovereignty,[3] the concept of sovereignty, as the ultimate and supreme power of decision, can be both analysed and qualified from the perspective of what can be called its 'contested elements': such elements as legal *v* political sovereignty, external *v* internal sovereignty, indivisible *v* divisible sovereignty, and governmental *v* popular sovereignty.[4] These elements of sovereignty have always been contested within polities and the outcome of these contests at a particular point in time has established where sovereignty can be said to rest on a number of different spectra where these contested elements represent points of extremity. However the specific locus of decision-making within polities resulting from these contestations through history is almost secondary to the importance of sovereignty as an essentially contested concept.[5] Being used here is the notion of an essentially contested concept as it is used in the philosophy of language.[6] Samantha Besson provides a useful meaning of this notion when she states:

[an essentially contested concept] *is a concept that not only expresses a normative standard and whose conceptions differ from one person to the other, but whose correct application is to create disagreement over its correct application or, in other words, over what the concept is itself. . . .* To claim that a concept is [essentially] *contestable* is to make the analytical claim that debates about the criteria of correct application of a concept are inconclusive. . . . disputes about the meaning of the concept go to the heart of the matter and can generate *rival paradigms and criteria of application* and that . . . it is part of the *very nature* of the concept to be contested and to raise questions as to its nature.[7]

This is central to sovereignty's contribution: that the very existence of the concept of sovereignty generates continual arguments as to its core criteria.

---

[3] S. Krasner, *Sovereignty: Organized Hypocrisy* (1999), p.9.

[4] S. Besson, 'Sovereignty in Conflict', 8(15) *European Integration online Papers* (2004), http://eiop.or.at/eiop/texte/2004-015.htm, Sections 3.2.1.1–3.2.1.5.

[5] On sovereignty as an essentially contested concept, see G. Sorensen, 'Sovereignty: Change and Continuity in a Fundamental Institution', 47 *Political Studies* (1999), p.590 at p.604; and, importantly, for detailed consideration of how the concept of sovereignty fulfils the three preconditions for a concept to be considered as being essentially contested (the concept must be normative, intrinsically complex, and lacking any immutable minimal criteria of correct application), see Besson, *supra* n.4, Sections 3.1–3.3.

[6] For the original promulgation of the idea of essentially contested concepts, see W.B. Gallie, 'Essentially Contested Concepts', LVI *Proceedings of the Aristotelian Society* (1956), p.167; and for its subsequent development and application in varying contexts, see, for example, J. Kekes, 'Essentially Contested Concepts: A Reconsideration', 10(2) *Philosophy and Rhetoric* (1977), p.71; J. Gray, 'On the Contestability of Social and Political Concepts', 5(3) *Political Theory* (1977), p.331; W. Connolly, *The Terms of Political Discourse* (1993, 3rd edn), p.10 *et seq*; J. Gray, 'On the Contestability of Social and Political Concepts', 5(3) *Political Theory* (1977), p.331; and J. Waldron, 'Is the rule of law an essentially contested concept?', 21(2) *Law and Philosophy* (2002), p.137.

[7] Besson, *supra* n.4, Section 2.1. Original emphasis. For a similar view, see J. Gray, 'On the Contestability of Social and Political Concepts', 5(3) *Political Theory* (1977), p.331 at p.344.

For example: What are the conditions for the existence and exercise of sovereignty? Who should exercise sovereignty and what form should these entities take?

2. The nation-State as 'exemplar'

An important element of W.B. Gallie's original formulation in 1956 of an essentially contested concept is that its contestation proceeds by a process of imitation and adaptation from an 'exemplar'.[8] Jeremy Waldron has added an important and useful qualifier to this element when, in a discussion of the Rule of Law as an essentially contested concept, he states:

> In Gallie's original exposition, essential contestability was associated with the existence of an original exemplar, whose achievement the rival conceptions sought to characterize and develop.... But I am suggesting, now, that *reference back to the achievement of an exemplar* may be too narrow an account of what gives unity to a contested concept. Perhaps there is no exemplar of the Rule of Law, but just a problem that has preoccupied us for 2,500 years: *how can we make law rule?* On this account, the Rule of Law is a solution-concept, rather than an achievement-concept; it is the concept of a solution to a problem we're not sure how to solve; and rival conceptions are rival proposals for solving it or rival proposals for doing the best we can in this regard given that the problem is insoluble.[9]

This approach is useful since it provides a constant touchstone for the essentially contested concept in question, which brings those contesting the concept always back to the reason for the concept's existence or, put differently, back to the problem that the concept was in the first place invented to try and solve. This does not in any way detract from the dynamic and lively contestation of the core criteria that arguably make up a complex concept like sovereignty. But the identification of the central issue does provide a general conceptual framework within which these contestations can take place and, moreover, provides a basis for distinguishing the relevant from the irrelevant during contestation. What then is the central problem of sovereignty about which there is continual contestation? It is suggested that it is the following: what are powers reserved to government; who exercises which of them; and how should they be exercised? As such, the contours of the conceptual framework generated by this core problem clearly allow us to speak of the concept of sovereignty within the context of international organizations exercising conferred powers of government.

---

[8] Gallie, *supra* n.6, pp.176–177. Cf. Garver who states: '...Gallie is right to say that an exemplar can give unity to an essentially contested concept, but it can do so only because an exemplar is a kind of essentially contested argument. It is not the fact that there was a Roman Republic that gave unity to disputes about sovereignty in the eighteenth century, but the fact that the Roman Republic [itself an essentially contested concept] was appealed to and recognized as authoritative.' (E. Garver, 'Rhetoric and Essentially Contested Arguments', 11(3) *Philosophy and Rhetoric* (1978), p.156 at p.162.)   [9] Waldron, *supra* n.6, pp.157–158.

However, to dispense entirely with Gallie's notion of an 'exemplar', as implicitly suggested above by Jeremy Waldron, may detract somewhat from the explanatory power of an essentially contested concept. The obvious 'exemplar' in the case of contestations of sovereignty within international organizations is the nation-State. Instead, however, of characterizing the nation-State as an 'exemplar' it may be more accurate to describe it as being a reference point since it does not provide the desired end-point but rather the starting point for the contestation of sovereignty within international organizations.

The contestation of the concept of sovereignty has always moved to a more transcendent level of human institution: from the tribe to the city-state to the region to the institution of independent and sovereign nation-States and now, finally, to international organizations. The initial content of the concept of sovereignty to be contested at each new, higher level has usually taken as its starting point of reference the position attained within the lower level. In this regard the contestation of sovereignty on the international plane is no different: the nation-State is the starting point of reference for the concept of sovereignty to be contested within international organizations. It is for this reason in large part that the debate, for example, about the legitimacy of the exercise by international organizations of governmental powers (the so-called 'democratic deficit') is largely framed by reference back to the exercise of these powers within the nation-State. Moreover, as explained below in Section II, with conferrals by States of governmental powers on international organizations, the general starting point for the limitations on the exercise of these powers are largely those that attach to the use of the powers within the national polity.

This approach that the sovereignty of States is only the starting point of reference for contestation within international organizations, does not, it should be emphasized, mitigate the important role of States *as actors* in contesting sovereignty within international organizations. The lower level of government has in history always played an active and important role as a safeguard against the capacity of the more recently established, higher, level of government to establish and enforce problematic conceptions of sovereignty. This is particularly relevant in the context of global institutions where maintaining the system of national autonomy is so essential if the evils of excessive centralization are to be avoided.

3. Sovereignty and international organizations

The characterization of sovereignty as an essentially contested concept has an important real-world manifestation in relation to international organizations. The concept of sovereignty being inherently unstable and in a constant state of having its core criteria subject to contestation and change has the consequence that there is no single, or indeed authoritative, definition that can be given to the concept. This has two important implications. First, it necessarily admits that the concept of sovereignty can legitimately be contested in other fora and, for our purposes, this includes international organizations that exercise conferred powers of government. Second, it does not privilege conceptions of sovereignty determined within States as opposed to those decided upon within international organizations. As a matter of positive law within a State, the decision of a particular domestic arm of government in the exercise of its powers may of course be authoritative, but even these decisions will be subject to contestation domestically and in the case where States have conferred powers on international organizations these may well be subject to contestation within these organizations.

The contestation of sovereignty within an international organization has inherent within it causation that runs both ways between States and the organization: States and their representatives contest conceptions of sovereignty put forward by other States during the organization's exercise of governmental powers, but this contestation and its outcome on the international plane inevitably affect domestic conceptions of sovereignty.[10] A good example of this is provided by the debate within the UK on the constitutional basis of judicial review of Acts of Parliament for their conformity with EC Law and whether indeed such review can be justified by domestic interpretations of the constitutional relationship between democracy and sovereignty.[11]

When considering the contestation by a State of the exercise by international organizations of sovereign powers it is important not to treat the State in this context as being a unitary rational actor with a one-dimensional set of preferences. The contestations of sovereignty which continue to take place on the domestic plane between domestic arms of government remain important, even where an organization has been given a binding power of decision in the exercise of conferred powers.[12] It is an important part of the thesis being advanced in this work that the contestations of sovereignty which have been, and are still, occurring within nation-States are often the very same contestations that are now taking place within international organizations. They are about the central problem of sovereignty: what are powers reserved to government; who exercises which of them, and how should they be exercised?

---

[10] As Harold Koh has observed more generally: 'Once nations begin to interact, a complex process occurs, whereby international legal norms seep into, are internalized, and become embedded in domestic legal and political processes.' (H.H. Koh, 'Transnational Legal Process', 75 *Nebraska Law Review* (1996), p.181 at p.205.)

[11] W. Wade, 'Sovereignty—Revolution or Evolution?', 112 *Law Quarterly Review* (1996), p.568; but cf. T. Allan, 'Parliamentary Sovereignty: Law, Politics, and Revolution', 113 *Law Quarterly Review* (1997), p.443.

[12] International organizations possess such binding powers of decision in cases where States have 'transferred' powers to organizations: on the elements of transfers of powers, see Section I in Chapter 3 and Chapter 6.

And it is largely for this reason that the domestic arms of government seek to engage in the contestation of sovereignty within international organizations that exercise governmental powers. This is demonstrated in the case of a number of international organizations in Chapters 5–6, below.

Moreover, the extent to which the domestic arms of government contest sovereignty domestically is arguably a reliable indicator of the extent to which they may seek to contest the exercise of sovereign powers by an organization. This will in turn depend on a number of legal and political constraints that operate within a State. For example, the extent to which the judiciary within a State contests conceptions of sovereignty will largely depend on whether there is a constitutional court that has compulsory jurisdiction to exercise judicial review of legislative and executive acts. Similarly in the case of the legislature of a State, the degree to which it may contest the exercise of sovereign powers domestically, and also within international organizations, may be said to depend on such factors as the degree to which it is controlled by the government (where, for example, the legislative process is not autonomous), the extent to which the legislature is circumscribed by constitutional limitations from engaging in such contestation, or indeed the extent to which the legislature has delegated its powers to the government.[13] These issues are considered below in Chapter 6.[14]

This emphasis on the essentially contested nature of sovereignty does not discredit realist explanations. To the contrary, in the process of contesting conceptions of sovereignty on the international plane it is likely that more powerful States will be able to project their approach to specific values to a much greater degree than will less powerful States. A good example of this is provided by the US projection onto other States of the value of 'corporate economic autonomy' through first the General Agreement on Tariffs and Trade ('GATT') and then the World Trade Organization ('WTO'), an issue considered in detail in Chapter 6.[15]

This brings us to the important question of sovereign values.

[13] In a number of States the legislature delegates to the executive certain legislative powers in order to implement domestically the obligations flowing from membership of international organizations. For example, within Spain the legislature has delegated powers to the government for the purpose of applying European Community law and the Spanish government has, pursuant to these delegated powers in Act 47/1985, enacted delegated legislation for the adjustment of Spanish law to Community requirements: see E. Garcia de Enterria and L. Ortega, 'European influences on the national administrative laws from the point of view of the Member States: Spanish Report' in J. Schwarze, ed., *Administrative Law under European Influence: on the Convergence of the Administrative Law of the EU Member States* (1996), p.695 at pp.697–698.

[14] In the case of contestation by a State's judicial arms of government, see Section II(1) in Chapter 6; and in the case of contestation by a State's legislature, see Section II(2) in Chapter 6.

[15] For extended consideration of this value and its projection by the US, see Section II(2)(ii) in Chapter 6.

4. The normative character of sovereignty and the question of values

The concept of sovereignty has always been associated with an entitlement to exercise governmental powers in the internal and external domain, but this has always been subject to sovereign values that have conditioned its exercise. Put in more conceptual terms, sovereignty possesses an important normative character. As Samantha Besson observes more generally:

As a normative concept, the concept of sovereignty expresses and incorporates one or many values that it seeks to implement in practice and according to which political situations should be evaluated. These values are diverse and include, among others, democracy, human rights, equality and self-determination. Concept determination amounts therefore to more than a mere description of the concept's core application criteria; it implies an evaluation of a state of affairs on the basis of sovereignty's incorporated values. What lies behind the prima facie categorical use of central political and legal concepts like sovereignty are not facts that should be established, but conceptions and interpretations that should be evaluated and maybe amended in order to account better for the values encompassed by these concepts. It follows therefore that the determination of the concept of sovereignty cannot be distinguished from the values it entails and from the normative discussion that generally prevails about it.[16]

An early starting point for the concept of sovereignty focused mainly on paradigms involving the formulation and application of such statal values as exclusive control by a State of its territory and non-intervention in the internal affairs of other States.[17] Today, however, through a process of contestation the concept in the Western liberal tradition has arguably been broadened both to include other actors and also to contain values such as legitimacy, autonomy, self-determination, freedom, accountability, security, and equality that are core to a modern conception. This is not a static or exhaustive[18]—and some may even say accurate—list and indeed based on what has been said earlier it could not be: it is continually subject to contestation and change. The point is though that these, or indeed other, values do provide sovereignty with a normative character which can be used to evaluate a state of affairs within a society or, in our case of an international organization, between societies.

To take Besson's work one step further, the incorporation of these values as an integral part of the concept of sovereignty allows the argument to be made that the exercise of public powers of government can only be considered an

[16] Besson, *supra* n.4, Section 3.1. For the normative character of essentially contested concepts, see also W. Connolly, *The Terms of Political Discourse* (1993, 3rd edn), p.22 and Waldron, *supra* n.6, pp.149–150.

[17] But cf. the fascinating analysis of the period 1870–1914 in M. Koskenniemi, *The Gentle Civilizer of Nations: The Rise and Fall of International Law 1870–1960* (2001), pp.98–178.

[18] Cf. Joseph Weiler's proposed sovereign principle or value of 'constitutional tolerance' within the EU: see J.H.H. Weiler, 'Federalism Without Constitutionalism: Europe's *Sonderweg*' in K. Nicoladis and R. Howse, eds., *The Federal Vision: Legitimacy and Levels of Governance in the United States and the European Union* (2001), p.54 at pp.62–70.

exercise of *sovereign* powers when this is in accord with sovereign values, otherwise the exercise of public powers is something entirely distinct from the exercise of sovereign powers and can even be considered as a violation of sovereignty. As Michael Reisman has stated in relation to this limiting—but also implicitly evaluative—characteristic of one of his proposed sovereign values:

> International law is still concerned with the protection of sovereignty, but, in its modern sense, *the object of protection is* not the power base of the tyrant who rules directly by naked power or through the apparatus of a totalitarian political order, but *the continuing capacity of a population freely to express and effect choices about the identities and policies of its governors.* In modern international law, the "unilateral declaration of independence" by the Smith Government in Rhodesia *was not an exercise of national sovereignty but a violation of the sovereignty of the people* of Zimbabwe. The Chinese Government's massacre in Tiananmen Square to maintain an oligarchy against the wishes of the people was a *violation of Chinese sovereignty.* The Ceausescu dictatorship was a *violation of Romanian sovereignty....* Fidel Castro *violates Cuban sovereignty* by mock elections that insult the people whose fundamental human rights are being denied, no less than the intelligence of the rest of the human race.[19]

This feature of sovereign values being an integral part of the concept of sovereignty is of particular importance to our discussion of conferrals by States of sovereign powers—which include the full range of executive, legislative, and judicial powers of the State[20]—on international organizations, since in order for an organization to be said to exercise *sovereign* powers then it must ensure that this is in accord with sovereign values. A practical consequence of this approach for international organizations is set out in Section II below. This approach to sovereign values does raise a potential problem though at one level, for the internationalist, since so long as different societies possess differing approaches to these core values of sovereignty then a truly shared sense of sovereignty—and the ability and legitimacy of an international organization to exercise sovereign powers—becomes problematic.[21] It is in part

---

[19] W.M. Reisman, 'Sovereignty and Human Rights in Contemporary International Law', 84 *AJIL* (1990), p.866 at p.872. Emphasis added.

[20] See J. Alvarez, 'The New Treaty Makers', 25 *B.C. Int'l & Comp. L. Rev.* (2002), p.213; T. Franck, 'Can the United States Delegate Aspects of Sovereignty to International Regimes?' in T. Franck, ed., *Delegating State Powers: The Effect of Treaty Regimes on Democracy and Sovereignty* (2000), pp.4–5; P. Sands and P. Klein, eds., *Bowett's Law of International Institutions* (2001, 5th edn), p.275 *et seq*; J. Klabbers, *An Introduction to International Institutional Law* (2002), pp.91, 205; D. Anderson, 'Law-Making Process in the UN System', 2 *Max Planck Yearbook of United Nations Law* (1998), p.23; and Chayes and Chayes, *The New Sovereignty*, pp.226–227.

[21] But maybe this is to overstate the actual position, since there would seem to be identifiable commonalities that exist within 'world culture': Katzenstein, Keohane, and Krasner cite work by sociologists, led by John Meyer, who have demonstrated a large degree of similarity in formal national practices relating to issues as diverse as censuses, social security, education, and science despite significant variations in national socio-economic and ideological characteristics. (P. Katzenstein, R. Keohane, and S. Krasner, '*International Organization* at Its Golden

this issue that led the German Constitutional Court to retain for itself the competence to decide whether the exercise by the European Community of conferred powers are in conformity with German fundamental rights. This controversial approach is considered in more detail in Chapter 6.[22] But, to reiterate for present purposes, it is precisely the stimulation of this kind of debate—what are sovereign values and how are they to be reconciled in the case of conflict—which is the vital, and indeed unique, contribution that is made by the essentially contested concept of sovereignty. This understanding of sovereignty's role together with its important ontological function provide a cogent counter-argument[23] against those who advocate its abolition.[24]

5. The ontological function of sovereignty

The process of contestation of the concept of sovereignty involves, in almost circular fashion, a set of ontological and legitimating decisions. The first is ethical: deciding who *We* are: who is a friend, who is an enemy, and who is a stranger.[25] The other is metahistorical: where *We* came from, how *We* became friends, how *We* got here, where *We* are, and where *We* are going in the future.[26] It is obvious as such that the concept of sovereignty is inextricably intertwined with identity and history. But to put the point differently, the essentially contested nature of the concept of sovereignty means that it continually generates discussion on, and contributes to the formulation, formation, and identification with, the concept of a community. Sovereignty has been used to constitute societies but also to exclude from societies. History is replete with decisions that give identity to the *We* as opposed to the *Other* by focusing on geographical or other perceived differences between parts of humanity based on such factors as ethnicity, language, tribe, and even, it must be said with a degree of ironic circularity, nationality. This stimulation of ontological decisions by the essentially contested nature of sovereignty poses, according to some, an inherent conflict at the core of modern conceptions of

Anniversary' in P. Katzenstein, R. Keohane, and S. Krasner, eds., *Exploration and Contestation in the Study of World Politics: A Special Issue of International Organization* (1999), p.1 at p.35.) For a similar approach, see R. Goodman and D. Jinks, 'Toward an Institutional Theory of Sovereignty', 55 *Stanford Law Review* (2003), p.1749 at pp.1752–1753.

[22] See Section II(1) in Chapter 6.

[23] Another argument in favour of retaining the concept of sovereignty is because of its important role in the management of inequality between States, see B. Kingsbury, 'Sovereignty and Inequality', 9 *EJIL* (1998), p.599.

[24] See N. MacCormick, *Questioning Sovereignty* (1999), Chapter 8. However, even MacCormick's approach to, and critique of, sovereignty seems dependent on a particular conception of sovereignty (see H. Lindahl, 'Sovereignty and the Institutionalization of Normative Order', 21 *Oxford Journal of Legal Studies* (2001), p.165 at p.166 at p.175) and as such he is engaged in the process of contestation of the concept.

[25] J. Bartelson, *A genealogy of sovereignty* (1995), p.6.   [26] *Ibid*, p.6.

the concept. Jens Bartelson, for example, observes:

Man, as the hero of modernity, made the state out of conflict, but out of the state inevitably arises a new state of conflict; man, in his quest for sovereignty, has pushed the tragedy of his political predicament out of his hands by making the Other the condition of possibility of his essential sameness within the state. From Rosseau on, early-modern strategies of peace have no option left save to proceed by domestic analogy when it comes to international transformation; at the same time, the dialectic of conflict can only constitute harmony out of conflict by the logic of sublimation; as Hegel remarked on the possibility of a federative solution to the problem of transcendence: 'even if a number of states join together as a family, this league, in its individuality, must generate opposition and create an enemy.' Thus, it appears as if the modern promise of transcendence is based upon an ontology whose inherent dialectic continuously pours cold water on the hope of its immanent fulfilment.[27]

Is it possible that the next stage of contestations of sovereignty may, ontologically, focus on the constitution of communities based on the extent to which different persons accept and apply values as opposed to differences based on, for example, tribe, ethnicity, and nationality? And the next question is: can international organizations provide an institutional forum for the contestation and formulation of such values?[28]

It is the first claim being advanced in this chapter that the very existence of international organizations performs an important ontological function since these organizations provide a forum, transcendental to the State, where conceptions of sovereignty—and more specifically the content of sovereign values—can be contested and formulated on the international plane. This is demonstrated below in Chapter 6. This is, moreover, arguably a positive development since simply transposing domestic conceptions of sovereignty onto the international plane is not always appropriate and indeed on the international plane the value may be developed more extensively than is possible at the national level. In the case of one of our types of conferrals of powers—'transfers' by States of powers to international organizations[29]—this has often been taken further by the provision within the organization of a dispute settlement body which is given the authority to render binding interpretations of the organization's constituent treaty and the scope of obligations thereunder

[27] J. Bartelson, *A genealogy of sovereignty* (1995), p.232.

[28] This certainly seems to be the approach adopted—but only in part (a State still must be 'European')—by the Draft Treaty Establishing a Constitution for Europe which provides in Article 1(2) as follows: 'The Union shall be open to all European States which respect its values and are committed to promoting them together.' Article 2 of the Draft Treaty goes on to provide: 'The Union's values. The Union is founded on the values of respect for human dignity, liberty, democracy, equality, the rule of law and respect for human rights. These values are common to the Member States in a society of pluralism, tolerance, justice, solidarity and non-discrimination.' This does not, however, mean that there are not significant problems with this Draft Constitution and indeed with the EU's human rights policies: see *infra* nn.37–38 and corresponding text in Chapter 6.   [29] On transfers of powers, see Chapter 6.

for member States. These decisions represent in substance a determination by a dispute settlement body of the values that underlie the sovereign powers being conferred by States on organizations. A good example of this is provided by the case of the WTO dispute settlement system, considered in more detail in Chapter 6.[30] However, suffice to note that even these decisions of the WTO dispute settlement body remain at a political level subject to contestation within the WTO[31] and also within member States. An example of the latter is provided by the approach of the US Congress to the WTO dispute settlement system: that it is only the US Congress that can decide how it will, if at all, change US law to comply with a specific panel or Appellate Body decision in a case.[32]

There is, however, an additional layer of complexity that exists when international organizations perform this ontological function. The very existence of international organizations as necessarily a forum for contestation may lead to the solidification of conceptions of sovereignty within a State in response to this *Other*. This may on the one hand seem to compromise the contribution of that State and its peoples to the formation of a common approach to an issue since it may have forced them to adopt, sometimes prematurely, a position on an issue in response to its being raised within the context of an international organization (for example, the UK 'opt-outs' from various EU issues such as European Monetary Union). But on the other hand the very consideration of an issue at the international level requires a State to have to formulate its approach or response to an issue (having to make up its mind: will it participate in EMU) and even a decision not to participate represents a contribution to the process of contestation of sovereignty on the international plane. Such an approach to sovereignty exemplifies the virtue encapsulated in the concept of unity in diversity: peoples are free to identify themselves as members of a community by virtue of their acceptance of certain values, but what is often more important than the actual content of the values is their common acceptance of a process of contesting these values, thereby allowing the members of the same community to place differing emphasis on the content of even the same value.

The second claim being advanced in this opening chapter is that the extent to which a State can contest sovereign values within the context of an international organization will depend largely on the degree (or type) of conferrals of powers that have been made to the organization. A detailed typology of conferrals of powers and the consequences of these different types of conferrals for the State-organization relationship is set out in Chapter 3. These types of conferrals also affect the extent to which a State is free to reject within its

---

[30] See Section II(2)(ii) in Chapter 6.
[31] See *infra* n.53 and corresponding text in Chapter 6.
[32] For extended consideration of the contestation by the US Congress of values being applied by the WTO, see Section II(2) in Chapter 6.

domestic legal order the outcome of the process of contestation that has taken place within an international organization.

The third, and final, claim made in this chapter is that domestic public and administrative law principles are prima facie applicable to the exercise by international organizations of conferred sovereign powers.

II. THE PRIMA FACIE APPLICATION OF DOMESTIC PUBLIC AND ADMINISTRATIVE LAW PRINCIPLES TO INTERNATIONAL ORGANIZATIONS

It is the inextricable link between domestic public law and the activity of governing[33] that mandates in general terms the application of domestic public law principles to those international organizations that exercise conferred powers of government.

Moreover, the contestation of sovereignty within a large number of States has led to the development of values that, to varying degrees, impose constraints on the exercise of sovereign powers at the domestic level. Consider, for example, the value of accountability. In most States this value has come to be regarded as being inextricably interlinked with the exercise of sovereign powers at the domestic level[34] through a long and arduous process of contestation, and the value is often reflected in constitutional and other public law constraints on the exercise of such powers.[35] The conferrals by States of their powers on international organizations free from the normative limitations that constrain the exercise of these powers at the national level is to dispense with, by the stroke of a pen, the limitations on governmental tyranny that peoples have fought hard to win within their domestic polity. But more fundamentally, it may be recalled from above that an international organization can only be said to exercise *sovereign* powers when this is in accord with their underlying sovereign values.[36] The incorporation of these values in domestic public and administrative law principles is another reason that mandates in general terms the application of these principles to the

---

[33] As Martin Loughlin states: 'public law . . . must be conceived as an assemblage of rules, principles, canon, maxims, customs, usages, and manners that condition and sustain the activity of governing.' (M. Loughlin, *The Idea of Public Law* (2003), p.30.)

[34] Cf. N. MacCormick, *Questioning Sovereignty: Law, State, and Nation in the European Commonwealth* (1999), p.25.

[35] A possible reason why accountability for the exercise of governmental powers has emerged as an important sovereign value is that it appears to contribute to the quality of governance within a polity. See, for example, Adsera, Boix, and Payne who contend, based in part on statistical analysis, that the quality of government hinges on the extent to which citizens can make their politicians accountable for their actions: A. Adsera, C. Boix, and M. Payne, 'Are You Being Served? Political Accountability and Quality of Government', 19(2) *The Journal of Law, Economics, & Organization* (2003), p.445.   [36] See *supra* Section I(4).

exercise by international organizations of conferred sovereign powers.[37] It is the governmental nature of these powers that allows us to distinguish between the types of domestic law that prove useful as a source of analogy. In particular, domestic private law which regulates private rights and powers will not generally be suitable for transplantation to the law of international organizations.[38] An example of this is provided in our discussion in Chapter 4 of the private law relating to agency and its potential application to the relationship between an organization and States.[39]

Conferrals by States of powers on international organizations often affect, arguably even undermine, the separation of powers within States, especially between the executive and legislative branches of government since it is the executive branch which represents the State in the organization when decisions are being made concerning the use of powers that may otherwise have been the prerogative of the legislature. This provides at least a partial explanation of why the German Constitutional Court—the *Bundesverfassungsgericht*—in its *Maastricht* decision sought to ensure that the German legislature (the Bundestag and Bundesrat) exercised control over the content of the powers being conferred by Germany on the EU by giving the legislature the competence to specify by statute the powers being conferred.[40] In this respect, the view being advanced here that domestic public and administrative law principles are of general application to the exercise by international organizations of sovereign powers is important, since it allows the participation, albeit indirectly, by domestic legislatures in the process of contestation of sovereignty on the international plane—an issue considered in detail in Chapter 6.[41] This participation by domestic legislatures is of crucial importance if international organizations—as an emerging additional layer of government—are to engage in a deeper, and thus more meaningful, contestation of the concept of sovereignty within their respective spheres of concern.

---

[37] See, for example, the jurisprudence of the European Court of Justice which has had recourse by analogy to the domestic public law systems of EC Member States in order to ascertain the relevant principle which should apply in particular cases: see T. Tridimas, *The General Principles of EC Law* (1999), p.4 *et seq*; and M. Aznar-Gomez, 'The 1996 Nuclear Weapons Advisory Opinion and *Non Liquet* in International Law', 48 *ICLQ* (1999), p.3 at p.6. For more general support for this kind of approach, see I. Brownlie, *The Rule of Law in International Affairs: International Law at the Fiftieth Anniversary of the United Nations* (1998), p.213.

[38] On the inappropriateness of applying private law analogies to international organizations more generally, see R. Higgins, 'Final Report of the Legal Consequences for Member States of the Non-Fulfilment by International Organizations of their Obligations Towards Third Parties', *Report of the Institut de droit International, Annuaire de l'Institut de Droit International*, (66-I, 1995), p.251 at p.287, and E. Raftopoulos, *The Inadequacy of the Contractual Analogy in the Law of Treaties* (1990), p.201 *et seq*.   [39] See *infra* n.9 in Chapter 4.

[40] Judgment of 12 October 1993, (*Maastricht*), 89 *BverfGE* 155, paras.438–439 as translated and contained in A. Oppenheimer, ed., *The Relationship between European Community Law and National Law: The Cases*, (1994), p.526 at p.556.

[41] See Section II(2) in Chapter 6.

All of this, however, raises the key question: *to what extent* is it appropriate to employ domestic public and administrative law principles when constructing the normative framework that governs the exercise of sovereign powers by international organizations?[42] The general applicability of domestic public and administrative law principles to international organizations does not, of course, mean that these principles apply automatically to the exercise of conferred powers by an organization. There are two reasons for this.

First, when States establish an international organization they are agreeing to be bound by certain common obligations which flow from the treaty: as such, there cannot be a presumption that the treaty is to be applied in a different way to member States depending on their domestic public or administrative law systems and the way in which the conferred governmental power or an analogous power is treated under these various systems. A domestic public or administrative law principle is arguably only applicable to the exercise by an international organization of governmental power where this principle can be identified as applying to the particular power within the domestic public and administrative law systems of a number of member States, since only then can it be considered as a general principle of law[43] and thus a formal source of law applicable to international organizations:[44] otherwise the domestic law analogy can only be of gentle persuasive value.[45]

Second, the constituent treaty itself will specify certain competences and institutional and other limitations which attach to the exercise of the power in question, and these may be of such a nature that it is inappropriate to use a domestic law analogy. For example, it was by engaging in this type of enquiry that Jackson and Croley found that WTO Panels and the Appellate Body should not have recourse by analogy to the US administrative law

---

[42] The general importance of this type of enquiry has recently been highlighted by Sir Robert Jennings: see R. Jennings, 'Book review of *The Spirit of International Law*', 97 *AJIL* (2003), p.725 at p.727.

[43] A legal principle does not, however, need to be universally recognized to constitute a 'general principle of law': M. Mendelson, 'The Subjective Element in Customary International Law', 66 *BYBIL* (1995), p.177 at p.191.

[44] General principles of law, as a source of international law, are applicable to international organizations: see H. Thirlway, 'The Law and Procedure of the International Court of Justice 1960–1989, Part Eight', 67 *BYBIL* (1996), p.1 at p.13; and H. Schermers and N. Blokker, *International Institutional Law*, (2003, 4th edn), p.997. This approach assumes however that international organizations are subject more generally to international law: on this, see *Interpretation of the Agreement of 25 March 1951 between the WHO and Egypt, ICJ Reports*, 1980, p.72 at pp.89–90 (para.37); and R. Higgins, *Problems and Process: International Law and How We Use It* (1994), p.46.

[45] For exposition of the more general role of analogical reasoning in the context of international law, see V. Lowe, 'The Politics of Law-Making: Are the Method and Character of Norm Creation Changing?' in M. Byers, ed., *The Role of Law in International Politics* (2000), p.207 at p.210; and, in a judicial context, see J. Raz, *The Authority of Law* (1979), pp.201–206.

concept of judicial deference to agency decisions[46] when determining the scope or standard of review to be afforded national court decisions.[47]

An example of a case where a domestic public law principle can, arguably, be applied to international organizations is when ascertaining the contours of the normative framework that governs an organization's competence to sub-delegate its powers.[48] Such a limitation, however, is arguably relevant only in the case where States have 'delegated' powers to an organization, a category whose contours are clarified below in our typology of conferrals by States of powers on international organizations.[49]

[46] In particular, the decision of the US Supreme Court in the case of *Chevron USA Inc. v. Natural Resources Defence Council, Inc.*, 467 *U.S.* 837 (1984) where the Court decided that US Government agency interpretations of the Statutes they administer are to be accepted by the US Courts as binding in certain cases. For comment on this decision, see for example: D. Barron and E. Kagan, 'Chevron's Nondelegation Doctrine', 2001 *Sup. Ct. Rev.* (2001), p.201; R. Anthony, 'Which Agency Interpretations Should Bind Citizens and the Courts?', 7 *Yale Journal on Regulation* (1990), p.1 at p.3; R. Pierce, '*Chevron* and its Aftermath: Judicial Review of Agency Interpretations of Statutory Provisions', 41 *Vanderbilt Law Review* (1988), p.301; T. Merrill, 'Judicial Deference to Executive Precedent', 101 *Yale Law Journal* (1992), p.969; and D. Spulber and D. Besanko, 'Delegation, Commitment, and the Regulatory Mandate', 8 *Journal of Law, Economics, and Organization* (1992), p.126 at pp.132–133, 144–146.

[47] John Jackson and Steven Croley state: 'In stark contrast to administrative agencies, GATT/WTO members are not specifically charged with carrying out the GATT/WTO. To be sure, members are obligated to fulfil their responsibilities under the WTO Agreement. In that limited sense, GATT/WTO members are charged with administering the GATT/WTO. But no country or combination of countries was ever delegated the responsibility of implementing the WTO Agreement in the way that administrative agencies are charged with implementing their statutes. Countries party to an antidumping dispute are not delegates whose technical expertise specially qualifies them to make authoritative interpretive decisions. They are, rather, interested parties whose own (national) interests may not always sustain a necessary fidelity to the terms of international agreements. Thus, while there may well be reasons for panels to defer to an authority's permissible interpretation of the WTO Agreement, expertise of parties to a panel dispute is probably not among them. The same is true for the argument from democracy. Indeed, this argument cuts in the opposite direction from *Chevron*, once transplanted to the GATT/WTO context. Unlike agencies, national authorities that are parties to an antidumping dispute are not accountable to the GATT/WTO membership at large. GATT/WTO panels, not disputing parties, are the membership's delegates.... The argument in *Chevron* that judges should defer to the interpretive decisions made by those accountable to the citizenry's representatives simply has no analogue in the GATT/WTO anti-dumping context.' (S. Croley and J. Jackson, 'WTO Dispute Procedures, Standard of Review, and Deference to National Governments', 90 *AJIL* (1996), p.193 at p.209.)

[48] See D. Sarooshi, *The United Nations and the Development of Collective Security* (1999), Chapter 1.

[49] On the elements of delegations of powers as delineated in our typology, see Section I in Chapter 3.

2

The Processes by which States Confer Powers on International Organizations

International law does not prevent a State from conferring its sovereign powers of government on international organizations, and it may even be an important part of a State's sovereignty that it has the competence to give away its powers of government.[1] But the processes by which States confer powers on organizations do raise a number of issues under international law.

The main way States confer powers on international organizations is by concluding treaties that provide for such conferrals. This obligation does not necessarily mean, however, that States are precluded from being able to exercise these powers in an individual capacity, nor that States are necessarily bound by the organization's exercise of conferred powers, nor indeed that these conferrals are irrevocable by States. These aspects of conferrals depend on the *types* of conferrals of powers, a matter that will be considered in our typology of conferrals in Chapter 3. At this stage in our discussion, however, it is necessary to consider the two main treaty mechanisms by which one or more States can confer powers on international organizations: by use of a constituent treaty or on a more ad hoc basis by use of a treaty that is separate from the constituent treaty.

I. CONFERRALS OF POWERS BY CONSTITUENT TREATY

The International Court of Justice has affirmed that a constituent treaty can act as a mechanism for conferrals by States of express powers on an organization. In the *WHO Advisory Opinion* case, the Court observed: 'The powers conferred on international organizations are normally the subject of an express statement in their constituent instruments.'[2] A constituent treaty is, however, a complex instrument and its function is not only to serve as a mechanism for conferrals by States of express powers on an organization. This complexity does not prevent the constituent treaty from being characterized

---

[1] See also Jessup, P., *A Modern Law of Nations* (1968), pp.18–19.

This is, however, only the position under international law. The competence of a State under its constitution to confer powers on an organization may indeed be considerably more limited. Although a number of constitutions of States provide in express terms for conferrals of powers on international organizations, the scope and operation of this competence remains, however, a vigorously contested issue. On a number of such contestations, see, in particular, Chapter 6.

[2] *Legality of the Threat or Use of Nuclear Weapons, Advisory Opinion, ICJ Reports*, 1996, p.64 at p.79 (para.25).

as a mechanism for conferrals of powers, but it does mean that international organizations and their constituent treaties cannot be analysed in a comprehensive fashion by focusing only on conferrals by States of express powers on organizations.[3]

One or more States may also purport to confer additional powers on an organization on an ad hoc basis by use of a treaty that is separate from the constituent treaty. In the case of such purported conferrals of powers, the main issue that arises is whether the treaty actually contains substantive conferrals of powers. This enquiry is necessary since a treaty purporting to confer powers on an ad hoc basis may in substance represent nothing more than either a request to the organization to exercise its existing powers in a particular situation or the proffering of consent by the State in cases where such consent is necessary for the organization to be able to exercise express or implied powers that it already possesses.

II. CONFERRALS OF POWERS ON AN AD HOC BASIS

There have been a number of cases where a group of States have concluded a treaty between themselves providing for conferrals of powers on an organization on an ad hoc basis.[4] When States ratify such a treaty they bind themselves

---

[3] Two examples suffice to illustrate the point. First, the constituent treaty of an organization may exhibit certain constitutional characteristics which do not result directly from the conferrals of express powers by States. See, for example, T. Sato, *Evolving Constitutions of International Organizations* (1996), p.230; J. Crawford, 'The Charter of the United Nations as a Constitution' in H. Fox, ed., *The Changing Constitution of the United Nations* (1997), p.3; B. Simma, 'From Bilateralism to Community Interest in International Law', 250 *Recueil des cours* (1994-VI), p.217 at pp.258–262; W.M. Reisman, 'The Constitutional Crisis in the United Nations', 87 *AJIL* (1993), p.83; and B. Fassbender, *UN Security Council Reform and the Right of Veto: A Constitutional Perspective* (1998). But cf. G. Arangio-Ruiz, ' "The Federal Analogy" and UN Charter Interpretation: A Crucial Issue', 8 *EJIL* (1997), p.1. Our second example is that the powers of an international organization are not restricted to those which are expressly conferred by member States, since the generally accepted view is that international organizations also possess implied powers. See *Reparation for Injuries Suffered in the Service of the United Nations* case, *ICJ Reports*, 1949, p.174 at pp.180, 182; and, from the voluminous literature, see J. Klabbers, *An Introduction to International Institutional Law* (2002), pp.67–75, H. Schermers and N. Blokker, *International Institutional Law* (1995, 3rd edn), pp.158–163; and N. White, *The Law of International Organisations* (1996), pp.128–131.

[4] Consider, for example, the Peace Treaty between Italy and the UK, US, France, and the Former USSR (the latter four States being known as the 'Four Powers') that conferred on the Four Powers the power to decide on the future of the Italian Colonies in Africa, but which in Annex XI(3) provided that if the Four Powers could not agree within one year of the entry into force of the Treaty then the power of decision was to be given to the UN General Assembly: 49 *UNTS*, p.3 at p.215. In the event the Four Powers could not agree and the conferrals of power were accepted by the General Assembly when it adopted the following resolutions concerning the territories: 289 (IV) of 21 Nov. 1949; 387 (V) of 17 Nov. 1950 (Libya); 390 (V) of 2 Dec. 1950 (Eritrea); 442 (V) of 2 Dec. 1950 (Somalia); 515 (VI) of 1 Feb. 1952 (Libya); 617 (VII) of 17 Dec. 1952 (Eritrea); and 1418 (XIV) of 5 Dec. 1959 (Somalia). For a convenient summary of the discussion which took place in the UN concerning the use of the power, see: *UNYB, 1948–1949*, pp.256–279; *UNYB, 1950*, pp.345–373; and, specifically, in the cases of Libya

to confer the stipulated powers on the organization. However the organization is not usually a party to such treaties and this raises the issue of the acceptance by an organization of conferred powers, an issue which is part of the broader question of when can substantive conferrals of powers on an ad hoc basis be said to have taken place.

1. The role of an organization's reaction to conferrals of powers

It is a requirement that an international organization must accept purported conferrals of powers by States for the conferrals to have legal effect. Article 34 of the 1969 Vienna Convention on the Law of Treaties provides that a 'treaty [between States] does not create either obligations or rights for a third State without its consent.' This general rule is applicable *mutatis mutandis* to the case of an international organization which is a third party to a treaty between States, since the rule exists as part of customary international law[5] and as such is applicable to international organizations.[6] Application of this general rule in our case means that a treaty between States which purports to confer powers on an organization does not have this effect without the consent of the organization.[7] The expression of this consent by the international organization may take a variety of forms depending on the type of organ of the organization which accepts the conferral.[8] For example, in the case of a deliberative

(*UNYB, 1951*, pp.266–277) and Eritrea (*UNYB, 1951*, pp.277–285, and *UNYB, 1952*, pp.262–266). For analysis of the conferrals of powers see J. Crawford, *The Creation of States in International Law* (1979), pp.330–332, F. Vallat, 'The Competence of the United Nations General Assembly', 97 *Recueil des cours* (1959-II), p.203 at pp.229–230, and B. Sloan, 'General Assembly Resolutions Revisited (Forty Years Later)', 58 *BYBIL* (1987), p.39 at pp.61–62; and for a review and analysis of much of the State practice of ad hoc conferrals of a power of territorial disposition onto international organizations and the competence of, in particular, the UN to exercise these powers, see Crawford, *ibid*, pp.323–333. For examples of cases where States conferred such a power of disposition on the League of Nations Council, see the *Treaty of Lausanne (Frontier between Turkey and Iraq) case, PCIJ, Series B No.12* (1925) at pp.27–28. See also the ad hoc conferrals of governmental powers on the UN by treaty in the cases of Western Sahara and Cambodia (see *infra* nn.9, 22–28, respectively).

[5] On the customary nature of the principle in Article 34 see R. Jennings and A. Watts, *Oppenheim's International Law* (1992, 9th edn), pp.1260–1261 and the citations to International Court of Justice decisions and the ILC debates contained in n.3.

[6] On the general application of international law (including, for our purposes, custom) to international organizations, see *supra* n.44 in Chapter 1. On the applicability of Article 34 to international organizations see C. Chinkin, *Third Parties in International Law* (1993), pp.11–12. This view is, moreover, supported by the reproduction of the rule, *mutatis mutandis*, in Article 34 of the 1986 Vienna Convention on the Law of Treaties between States and International Organizations or between International Organizations.

[7] However, this requirement of consent does not exist in the case of the constituent treaty of an international organization even though the organization is in law a third party to the constituent treaty (Chinkin, *supra* n.6, p.12) due to the nature of the special relationship of the organization to its constituent treaty (Chinkin, *ibid*, p.12; and A. McNair, *The Law of Treaties* (1961), pp.259–271.)

[8] Cf., however, Article 36 which stipulates that in the case of conferrals by treaty of rights on a third State, the assent of the third State 'shall be presumed so long as the contrary is not indicated,

organ the adoption of a resolution accepting the conferrals may be appropriate;[9] while in the case of the Secretariat (usually represented by a Secretary-General) a unilateral act or declaration[10] may be more appropriate.[11] In any case, however, it is not the form that is decisive, but rather the indication of a clear intention by the organ concerned that it has accepted the conferrals of powers in order for the conferral to have prima facie legal effect.

However, even where an organization may seem to have accepted purported conferrals of powers, this does not mean that substantive conferrals will always have taken place. The reason for this is that the powers the States are purporting to confer by treaty on an ad hoc basis may already be those an organization possesses under its constituent treaty. Put differently, substantive conferrals on an ad hoc basis only take place when the powers purporting to be conferred are those which the organization does not otherwise possess under its constituent treaty. The determination as to whether this is the case will largely depend on the reaction of the organ on whom powers are purportedly

unless the treaty otherwise provides'. If conferrals by States of *powers* on an international organization can be equated, by analogy, with conferrals by States of *rights* on a third party—a proposition about which this author is at best uncertain due to the necessary conflation of powers with rights—then it could alternatively be argued that there is no need for the indication of a clear intention by an organ of an organization that it has accepted the conferrals of powers.

[9] Consider the following three examples: First, the acceptance by the UN General Assembly in its resolutions of the delegation of power concerning the Italian colonies in Africa (see *supra* n.4). Second, the acceptance by the UN Security Council in resolution 745 of the delegation of power from the Paris Peace Accords concerning Cambodia (see text following *infra* n.24). Third, the acceptance by the UN Security Council of the conferrals by Morocco and the Frente POLISARIO (although of course the only State involved was Morocco) of governmental powers on the UN Secretary-General and his Special Representative in order to conduct a referendum in Western Sahara. The exercise of these powers was carried out with the approval and support of the UN Security Council which adopted the following resolutions: 621 (1988), 658 (1990), 690 (1991), 725 (1991), 809 (1993), 907 (1994), 973 (1995), 995 (1995), 1002 (1995), 1017 (1995), 1042 (1996), 1056 (1996), 1084 (1996), 1108 (1997), 1131 (1997), 1133 (1997), 1148 (1998), 1163 (1998), 1185 (1998), 1198 (1998), 1204 (1998), 1215 (1998), 1224 (1998), 1228 (1998), 1232 (1999), 1235 (1999), and 1238 (1999).

[10] There is no reason why an international organization—which like a State often possesses international legal personality and the competence to accept binding obligations under international law—should not be bound by unilateral declarations. Moreover, the reason why such unilateral declarations bind a State is equally applicable to the case of an international organization. In the context of a State, the International Court in the *Nuclear Tests* cases held: 'One of the basic principles governing the creation and performance of legal obligations, whatever their source, is the principle of good faith. . . . Just as the very rule of *pacta sunt servanda* in the law of treaties is based on good faith, so also is the binding character of an international obligation assumed by unilateral declaration. Thus interested States may take cognizance of unilateral declarations and place confidence in them, and are entitled to require that the obligation thus created be respected.' (*Nuclear Tests (New Zealand v. France), ICJ Reports*, 1974, p.268 (para.46).)

For an interesting application of this type of approach, see V. Lowe, 'Can the European Community Bind the Member States on Questions of Customary International Law?' in M. Koskenniemi, ed., *International Law Aspects of the European Union* (1998), p.149.

[11] In both cases, however, the relevant organ of the organization would need to possess the required competence under its constituent treaty in order to adopt such decisions.

being conferred. For example, an organ may make it clear in responding to conferrals that it is being given a power that it did not otherwise possess under its constituent treaty. This determination by an organ of the scope of its powers will, in the absence of review by a body which has jurisdiction to decide such a matter, certainly prevail over the interpretation of States purporting to confer powers on an organ of an organization. This locus of authoritative decision-making within an organization flows from the principle expounded by the International Court in the *Expenses* case that 'each organ must, in the first place at least, determine its own jurisdiction'.[12]

This issue of the proper characterization of purported conferrals of powers is of practical importance, since where there are substantive ad hoc conferrals then the conferring States can arguably impose constraints on the organization's exercise of conferred powers. While in the case where there are no substantive conferrals on an ad hoc basis then the States parties to the treaty in question cannot seek to control or impose any limitations on the exercise by the organization of its powers, since this is a matter governed solely by the constituent treaty.

This important difference can be illustrated, for example, by reference to cases where the response of the UN Security Council to purported ad hoc conferrals was to utilize its own powers under Chapter VII of the Charter rather than taking up the purported conferrals that were on offer. This occurred, for example,[13] in the case where the UN Security Council—more

---

[12] *Expenses* case, *ICJ Reports*, 1962, p.151 at p.168.

[13] Another example of this is provided by the Dayton Peace Agreement that was concluded between three States of the former Yugoslavia and which appeared, at least arguably, to confer powers on the UN Security Council in order to ensure the implementation of the terms of the Agreement. Article 1(1)(a) of Annex 1-A to the Dayton Peace Agreement *invited* the Security Council, 'to adopt a resolution by which it will authorise Member States or regional organisations and arrangements to establish a multinational military Implementation Force (hereinafter 'IFOR'). The Parties understand and agree that this Implementation Force may be composed of ground, air and maritime units from NATO and non-NATO nations, deployed to Bosnia and Herzegovina to help ensure compliance with the provisions of this Agreement (hereinafter 'Annex'). . . .' The Security Council accepted the invitation of the Parties to establish a force (IFOR) to ensure implementation of the Agreement when, in resolution 1031, the Council, acting under Chapter VII of the Charter, decided to authorize 'the Member States acting through or in cooperation with the organization referred to in Annex 1-A of the Peace Agreement [NATO] to establish a multinational implementation force (IFOR) under unified command and control in order to fulfil the role specified in Annex 1-A and Annex 2 of the Peace Agreement'. The resolution then stated that the Council '[a]uthorizes the Member States acting under paragraph 14 above to take all necessary measures to effect the implementation of and to ensure compliance with Annex 1-A of the Peace Agreement, stresses that the parties shall be held equally responsible for compliance with that Annex, and shall be equally subject to such enforcement action by IFOR as may be necessary to ensure implementation of that Annex and the protection of IFOR, and takes note that the parties have consented to IFOR's taking such measures'.

Article 1 of Annex 1-A stipulates that the objectives of the Peace Agreement are to establish a durable cessation of hostilities; provide for the 'support and authorization of the IFOR and in particular to authorize the IFOR to take such actions as required, including the use of necessary force, to ensure compliance with this Annex, and to ensure its own protection'; and to establish lasting security and arms control measures as outlined in Annex 1-B to the General Framework

specifically a UN subsidiary organ established by the Council, the UN Transitional Authority for Eastern Slavonia, Baranja and Western Sirmium—exercised governmental powers over these areas of the territory of the Republic of Croatia.

An agreement (the 'Basic Agreement') was signed between the Government of the Republic of Croatia and the local authorities of Serbian ethnic origin in Eastern Slavonia on 12 November 1995[14] with the intention of providing for the peaceful re-integration of the region comprising Eastern Slavonia, Baranja, and Western Sirmium into the Croatian legal and constitutional system following four years of armed conflict between the Croatian Government and the local Serbs.[15] The parties agreed in paragraph 2 of the Basic Agreement that during a transitional period, initially of 12 months, a UN Transitional Authority would govern the region in the interest of persons resident in or returning to the region.[16] Moreover, the parties requested that the Transitional Authority seek to achieve the following specific objectives: to demilitarize the parties which 'shall include all military forces, weapons and police, except for the international force and for police operating under the supervision of, or with the consent of, the Transitional Administration'; to facilitate the 'return of refugees and displaced persons to their homes of origin'; to 'take the steps necessary to re-establish the normal functioning of all public services in the region without delay'; to 'establish and train temporary police

Agreement. The objectives for which IFOR could use force against the parties to the Agreement subsequently became, however, the point of contention between Russia and other members of the Security Council. The Russian representative stated in the Council that the member States participating in IFOR were authorized to do only what the parties had agreed to. (S/PV.3607, p.25.) This position conceives of the States parties to the Dayton Agreement as conferring on the Council—and its delegate, IFOR—the power to take military enforcement action against them when one of their number breaches the obligations specified in the Agreement. This is, however, a clear misconception of the legal position. The Security Council possesses under Article 42 of the Charter a power to order military enforcement to be taken against a State or an entity within a State; obviously without the need for the consent of those who are to be subject to such action. In the case of the Dayton Agreement, it was clear that once the Security Council had adopted, 'acting under Chapter VII of the Charter', resolution 1031, then the Council considered that it was exercising its own powers and not a power conferred by the States parties to the Agreement. As such, the Council was not constrained 'to do only what the Bosnian sides agreed to', since the authority of the Council did not derive from the Agreement but from its own powers under Chapter VII of the Charter which in the area of military enforcement action does not require the consent of a target State. Accordingly, the inclusion of the reference in resolution 1031 to the 'parties have consented to IFOR's taking such measures' was for political not legal reasons. The mention of State consent in the resolution was of no legal consequence.

[14] Contained in S/1995/951, Annex.

[15] See 'Report of the Secretary-General pursuant to Security Council resolutions 981 (1995), 982 (1995) and 983 (1995)', S/1995/987, para.29; and 'Report of the Secretary-General pursuant to Security Council resolution 1025 (1995)', S/1995/1028, para.6.

[16] See S/1995/951, Annex, p.2. For a useful analysis of the exercise of a power of arrest by the UN Transitional Administration (UNTAES) to assist the work of the International Criminal Tribunal for the former Yugoslavia, see S. Lamb, 'The Powers of Arrest of the International Criminal Tribunal for the former Yugoslavia', 70 *BYBIL* (1999), p.165 at pp.181–186.

forces'; and to organize 'elections for all local government bodies, including for municipalities, districts and counties'.[17]

The parties provided that the Basic Agreement would enter into force 'upon the adoption by the UN Security Council of a resolution responding affirmatively to the requests made in this agreement'. The Security Council in resolution 1037 'acting under Chapter VII of the Charter of the United Nations,' decided 'to establish for an initial period of 12 months a United Nations peace-keeping operation for the Region referred to in the Basic Agreement, with both military and civilian components, under the name "United Nations Transitional Administration for Eastern Slavonia, Baranja and Western Sirmium" (UNTAES)' and further 'Request[ed] the Secretary-General to appoint, in consultation with the parties and with the Security Council, a Transitional Administrator, who will have overall authority over the civilian and military components of UNTAES, and who will exercise the authority given to the Transitional Administration in the Basic Agreement'. The express reference by the Council to its Chapter VII powers is important, since it means that the Council is exercising governmental powers over parts of Croatian territory using its Charter powers, and not as a consequence of governmental powers being conferred on it by the Republic of Croatia—the only party to the Basic Agreement which was a State.

This characterization of the legal basis for the exercise of powers was to prove controversial but important when determining whether it was Croatia or the UN Security Council that had the power to terminate the activities being carried out by UNTAES.

Following the successful holding of elections in the region by UNTAES, the UN Transitional Administrator developed a two-phase 'exit strategy' which was described by the UN Secretary-General in the following terms:

> In the first phase, the Transitional Administrator would devolve to Croatia executive responsibility for the major part of civil administration of the region while maintaining his authority and ability to intervene and overrule decisions should the situation deteriorate and the achievements of UNTAES be threatened. The pace of devolution would be commensurate with Croatia's demonstrated ability to reassure the Serb population and successfully complete peaceful reintegration. In the second phase, and subject to satisfactory Croatian performance, remaining executive functions would be devolved, with Croatia assuming responsibility for the continued demilitarization of the region and the gradual integration of the Transitional Police Force into the Croatian police force.[18]

This position was endorsed in express terms by the Security Council in resolution 1120. The Council, moreover, decided in this resolution, adopted on 14 July 1997, to extend the mandate of UNTAES for a further six months until 15 January 1998. This resolution was adopted despite the strong objections of

---

[17] S/1995/951, Annex, p.2.
[18] S/1997/487, 23 June 1997, para.48. See also S/1997/767, 2 October 1997, para.3.

Croatia who argued that UNTAES should at this time be immediately terminated and that powers of government be resumed immediately by Croatia. The fact of its adoption by the Security Council confirmed that the establishment and operation of UNTAES was an exercise by the Council of its own Chapter VII powers and not pursuant to the exercise of powers conferred by Croatia on an ad hoc basis. This control by the Council was further reiterated when it decided in resolution 1145 of 15 January 1998 to terminate UNTAES, the Council alone having decided that UNTAES had now fulfilled its mandate.[19]

To conclude, a treaty that purports to confer powers on an organization which it already possesses under its constituent treaty will not, in general terms,[20] have the intended legal effect. Such a treaty may usefully be characterized as a request to the organization to exercise its powers in a particular situation or even as the proffering of consent by the State in cases where such consent is necessary for the organization to be able to exercise its powers, but it should not, in general terms, be characterized as substantive conferrals of powers.[21] In the example discussed above, however, even this consent was not needed, since the UN Security Council does not require the consent of States to exercise its Chapter VII powers. As such, the Basic Agreement represented no more than a request to the Council to exercise its Chapter VII powers.

There is, however, a possible exception to this general position that substantive conferrals of powers only take place when the powers purporting to be conferred are those which the organization does not possess under its constituent treaty. This exception is where the organ of an organization, although possessing the powers being conferred, chooses instead to take up the conferrals using a general competence to do so under its constituent treaty rather than treating the purported conferrals as an invitation to use its existing,

[19] See the statement by the President of the Security Council on behalf of the Council: S/PRST/1998/3, 13 February 1998.

[20] Cf. the exceptional case at *infra* n.22 and corresponding text.

[21] Similar issues arise concerning the role that State consent plays in the establishment and utilization by the Security Council of UN peace-keeping forces. The establishment and utilization of such forces by the UN Security Council represents the exercise by the Council of an implied power under Chapter VII of the Charter (D. Sarooshi, 'The Role of the United Nations Secretary-General in United Nations Peace-Keeping Operations', 20 *Australian Yearbook of International Law* (1999), p.279 at pp.280–282) and not the exercise of a power conferred on it by States. However, the ICJ in the *Expenses* case held that UN peace-keeping operations are not military enforcement 'action' within the terms of Chapter VII. The consequence of this being that the deployment and utilization of a UN peace-keeping force is conditional on the consent of both the States contributing troops to the force and the host State where the force is to be deployed. (*Expenses case, ICJ Reports*, 1962, p.165. See also on consent the report of the SG, A/3302, contained in R. Higgins, *United Nations Peacekeeping 1946–1967* (vol.1, 1969), pp.263–264.) It is important, however, not to confuse this consent requirement of States to contribute troops to a UN peace-keeping force (as contained in a Status of Forces Agreement) and of States to have the force stationed on their territory as being conferrals of powers on the UN such that the States concerned can seek to control or specify limits on the use by the Council of its implied powers once their consent has been given. Cf. those cases where States have tried to exercise such control in the case of UN peace-keeping, see Sarooshi, *ibid*, pp.288, 290–291, 295.

express, powers.[22] This choice is not simply a matter of semantics. It may have the important practical consequence that the conferring States can impose constraints on the exercise of powers by the organization. A good example of this is provided by the practice of the UN Security Council where it has in certain cases chosen to accept conferrals of powers that would seem to fall within the scope of its powers under Chapter VII thereby constraining itself to exercise the powers subject to the terms and conditions of the particular conferral.

A specific instance of this occurred in relation to the case of Cambodia where there were ad hoc conferrals of broad powers of internal governance on the UN through the Paris Peace Accords (the 'Accords').[23]

The Accords created a Supreme National Council that was defined as the 'unique legitimate body and source of authority in which, throughout the transitional period, the sovereignty, independence and unity of Cambodia are enshrined'.[24] The Accords went on to stipulate that the Supreme National Council 'delegates to the United Nations all powers necessary to ensure the implementation of this Agreement'.[25] Accordingly, Article 2 of the Accords invited the Security Council to create the United Nations Transitional Authority in Cambodia (UNTAC) 'with civilian and military components under the direct responsibility of the Secretary-General of the United Nations,' 'to provide UNTAC with the mandate set forth in this Agreement,' and 'to keep its implementation under continuing review'.[26] The Security Council accepted these conferrals of powers and established UNTAC by resolution 745 in 1992. The Security Council in establishing UNTAC was, arguably, exercising powers conferred on it by the Paris Peace Accords and was not acting pursuant to its own Chapter VII powers, since there was no express reference in resolution 745 to Chapter VII and it is the consistent practice of the Council to make such a reference in cases where it is using its Chapter VII powers. Moreover as Ratner, in the case of Cambodia, has observed:

If the United Nations were to administer Cambodia, under generally accepted interpretations of the Charter an entity authorized to represent Cambodia would need to

---

[22] On the concept of a general competence, see P. Bekker, *The Legal Position of Intergovernmental Organizations: A Functional Necessity Analysis of Their Legal Status and Immunities*, (1994), p.75; and, for its role in the establishment of UN subsidiary organs, see D. Sarooshi, 'The Legal Framework Governing United Nations Subsidiary Organs', 67 *BYBIL* (1996), p.413 at pp.427–431.

[23] The Paris Conference concluded the following four Accords: the Final Act of the Paris Conference on Cambodia (31 *ILM* (1992), p.180); the Agreement on a Comprehensive Political Settlement of the Cambodia Conflict (31 *ILM* (1992), p.183); the Agreement Concerning the Sovereignty, Independence, Territorial Integrity and Inviolability, Neutrality and National Unity of Cambodia (31 *ILM* (1992), p.200); and the Declaration on the Rehabilitation and Reconstruction of Cambodia (31 *ILM* (1992), p.203).)

[24] The Agreement on a Comprehensive Political Settlement of the Cambodia Conflict (Comprehensive Settlement Agreement, *ibid*), Articles 3 and 5, *ibid*. Security Council resolution 668 (1990) confirmed this sovereign nature of the Supreme National Council.

[25] Comprehensive Settlement Agreement, *ibid*, Article 6.   [26] *Ibid*, Article 2.

delegate power to the Organization or otherwise indicate Cambodia's consent to the operation; or, alternatively, the Security Council would have to approve enforcement action under chapter VII to restore international peace and security in Southeast Asia. The latter option, however, never received serious consideration owing to the Council's unwillingness to impose a large UN presence on Cambodia without any agreement by the factions, especially in view of the Council's reluctance to invoke chapter VII before the Persian Gulf war. In the absence of a single government accepted by all states as politically legitimate and legally able to delegate power, the idea emerged of a Supreme National Council that would include representatives from all the factions and serve as a unique and legitimate source of authority.[27]

As such, the Security Council was always careful to ensure that UNTAC did not exceed the mandate conferred on it by the Paris Peace Accords: thus, for example, in resolution 840 the Council requested UNTAC to 'continue to play its role in conjunction with the Supreme National Council during the transitional period in accordance with the Paris Agreements'. Moreover, UNTAC was required to comply with certain directions (what was inaccurately termed as 'advice') of the Supreme National Council. As Ratner has observed:

the body of the Agreement and the annex include details on the authority of UNTAC, with respect to its relationships to the SNC [Supreme National Council] and the governments in place and to the tasks that it should perform, i.e., the depth and breadth of its power. The depth of UNTAC's authority is described in the annex by the following scheme: UNTAC must comply with any advice from the SNC on any aspect of the settlement if (1) the SNC is acting unanimously when it gives its views or, in the absence of unanimity, Prince Sihanouk, as President of the Council, provides the advice on the Council's behalf, 'taking fully into account' its members' views; and (2) the advice is 'consistent with the objectives of the present Agreement' as determined by the chief of UNTAC, the Secretary-General's Special Representative.[28]

Moreover, Matheson has stated that the exercise of governmental authority delegated by the Supreme National Council to UNTAC was 'limited by the requirement that UNTAC follow any "advice" approved by a consensus of the factions represented in the Supreme National Council, to the extent that it did not conflict with the Agreement.'[29]

Having considered the processes by which States confer powers on international organizations, let us now turn to consider in the next chapter our typology of the different types of conferrals.

---

[27] S. Ratner, 'The Cambodia Settlement Agreements', 87 *AJIL* (1993), p.1 at pp.9–10.

[28] Ratner, *ibid*, p.12.

[29] M. Matheson, 'United Nations Governance of Postconflict Societies', 95 *AJIL* (2001), p.76 at p.77.) On UN territorial administration more generally, see F. Kirgis, 'Security Council Governance of Postconflict Societies: A Plea for Good Faith and Informed Decision Making', 95 *AJIL* (2001), p.579; and R. Wilde, 'From Danzig to East Timor and Beyond: the Role of International Territorial Administration', 95 *AJIL* (2001), p.583.

3

Conferrals by States of Powers on International Organizations: a Typology

There is a considerable lack of clarity and consistent usage in the conceptual labels used to describe different types of conferrals by States of powers on international organizations. Such terms as 'ceding', 'alienation', 'transfer', 'delegation', and 'authorization' are used interchangeably by international and domestic courts as well as by commentators, often to refer to the same type of conferrals of powers[1] or the same conceptual label is used in a general way to refer to different types of conferrals.[2] However not all conferrals of powers are the same, and there are important differences that flow from the types of conferrals for the legal relationship that is thereby established between States conferring powers and organizations. Moreover, the conflation of these differing types of conferrals of powers obfuscates the domestic policy debates that surround the conferrals of powers.[3]

---

[1] See, for example, just in the case of conferrals by States of powers onto the European Community the wide variety of concepts used (eg. delegation, transfer, and cession) in the following: M. Martin Martinez, *National Sovereignty and International Organizations* (1996); C. Ku and H. Jacobson, 'Using military forces under international auspices and democratic accountability', 1 *International Relations of the Asia-Pacific* (2001), p.21; C. Bradley, 'The Treaty Power and American Federalism', 97 *Michigan Law Review* (1997–1998), p.390; T. Schilling, 'The Autonomy of the Community Legal Order: An Analysis of Possible Foundations', 37 *Harvard International Law Journal* (1996), p.389; A. Cassese, 'Modern Constitutions and International Law', 192 *Recueil des cours* (1985-III), p.331 at p.415; P. Lindseth, 'Democratic Legitimacy and the Administrative Character of Supranationalism: the example of the European Community', 99 *Columbia Law Review* (1999), p.628 at pp.631, 633, 637, 639, & 645; J. Kingston, 'External Relations of the European Community—External Capacity Versus Internal Competence', 44 *ICLQ* (1995), p.659; and P. Tangney, 'The New Internationalism: The Cession of Sovereign Competences to Supranational Organizations and Constitutional Change in the United States and Germany', 21 *Yale Journal of International Law* (1996), p.395.
See also, more generally, the confused usage of concepts to describe conferrals between States of sovereign powers: eg., *Customs Régime between Germany and Austria, PCIJ Reports, Series A/B No.41*, 1931, p.37 at pp.46, 58–59, 77.

[2] Ku, for example, states: 'The constitutional issues implicated in these relationships [between the United States and international organizations] are most usefully understood as international delegations. An international delegation is the transfer of constitutionally-assigned federal powers—treaty-making, legislative, executive, and judicial powers—to an international organization.' (J. Ku, 'The Delegation of Federal Power to International Organizations: New Problems with Old Solutions', 85 *Minnesota Law Review* (2000–2001), p.71 at p.72.) See also, for example, uses of the conceptual label of 'delegation' to refer to different types of conferrals of powers: F. Seyersted, 'Is the International Personality of Intergovernmental Organizations valid *vis-à-vis* Non-members?', 4 *Indian Journal of International Law* (1964), p.233 at p.247; E. Denza, 'Two Legal Orders: Divergent or Convergent?', 48 *ICLQ* (1999), p.257 at pp.259–260; and K. Zemanek, 'The Legal Foundations of the International System: General Course on Public International Law', 266 *Recueil des Cours* (1997), p.9 at pp.90–91.

[3] See for examples of this confusion S. McBride, 'Dispute Settlement in the WTO: Backbone of the Global Trading System or Delegation of Awesome Power', 32 *Law & Pol'y Int'l Bus.* (2001),

I. A SPECTRUM OF CONFERRALS: AGENCY RELATIONSHIPS, DELEGATIONS, AND TRANSFERS

In order to provide clarity it may be useful to consider these conferrals of powers as being on a spectrum that at one end has conferrals that establish an agency relationship between the State and the organization and at the other extremity has conferrals that involve transfers of powers to the organization. In between these two positions can be said to lie the category of delegations of powers. The locus of particular conferrals of powers on this spectrum depends on the degree to which a State has given away its powers to the organization. It should, however, be made clear that conferrals of powers do not usually contain only one type of conferrals: they often contain both delegations of certain powers and transfers of others to an international organization. This has the consequence that an organization will often have a complex web of differing relationships with conferring States depending on the particular type of conferrals involved.

II. THE MEASUREMENT OF THE DEGREE TO WHICH POWERS HAVE BEEN GIVEN AWAY BY STATES

There are three characteristics of conferrals that can be used to ascertain the degree to which powers have been given away by a State, and thus within which category a particular conferral of powers can be placed. First is the question of revocability. Second is the degree to which States retain control over the exercise of powers by the organization. And our third is to determine whether the organization possesses the sole right to exercise conferred powers or whether States have retained the right to exercise powers concurrently with the organization.

1. The blunt instrument of revocability

First then the question of revocability. In the cases of agency and delegations in our typology the conferrals of powers are clearly revocable;[4] while in the case of transfers the conferrals will generally be irrevocable.[5]

In practice, however, it would seem that conferrals of powers are always revocable so long as the State has retained its independent legal personality

---

p.643 at p.644; and M. Presley, 'Sovereignty and Delegation Issues Regarding U.S. Commitment to the World Trade Organization's Dispute Settlement Process', 8 *J. Transnat'l L. & Pol'y* (1998), p.173.

[4] In the case of agency, see Section II(3) in Chapter 4; and for the case of delegations, see Section I in Chapter 5.

[5] See Section I in Chapter 6; but cf. the important category of exceptions to this general position: *infra* nn. 8–9 and corresponding text.

and not merged its powers and personality into a larger political unit. Of course the actual revocation of conferrals does not mean that this is lawful. States may even take into account, inter alia, the issue of the legality of a proposed revocation when deciding whether it is in its interest to withdraw, for example, from an organization (thereby revoking its conferrals of powers).[6] The likelihood of legality being at least one of the factors to be taken into account by States when deciding an issue of withdrawal from an organization allows us to use the competence of a State to revoke lawfully its conferrals in a particular case as providing evidence of the extent to which a State considers that it has given away its powers to an organization. Where a revocation is clearly lawful then the State can easily reclaim its powers and can thus be presumed to have given away its powers less than in the case where there may be obvious legal difficulties relating to revocation. This view is supported, for example, by the importance attached in debates in the US Congress to the express provision in the WTO Charter which provides for termination of membership as a safeguard against abuse by the WTO of conferred powers.[7]

However, the legality of States being able to withdraw unilaterally from a treaty conferring powers remains, by itself, too blunt an instrument to measure accurately the degree of conferrals of powers on an organization.[8] What are more sensitive as instruments of measurement are our second and third characteristics of conferrals of powers. It is for this reason that there is a category of conferrals which are revocable but which still fall within the category of transfers since they strongly exhibit the second and third characteristics of transfers of powers.[9]

2. Control by States over the organization

Our second characteristic is the degree to which States retain control over the exercise of powers by the organization. This issue of control is multilayered. At one level it involves questions of direct control by States over the organization's exercise of powers. But at another level it involves issues relating to control by States over the implementation of the organization's decisions within their domestic legal orders. This latter issue is considered in the context of our third characteristic since it forms part of the broader issue of whether the organization possesses the sole right to exercise conferred powers

[6] For consideration of the policy reasons which militate in general terms against withdrawal by States from a constituent treaty that confers powers on international organizations, see Section II(3) in Chapter 7.

[7] See J. Jackson, 'The Great 1994 Sovereignty Debate: United States Acceptance and Implementation of the Uruguay Round Results', 36 *Columbia Journal of Transnational Law* (1998), p.157 at p.172. Nonetheless, there have been serious attempts made by the US Congress at least to consider withdrawal: see *infra* nn.127–130 and corresponding text in Chapter 6.

[8] See J.H.H. Weiler, *The Constitution of Europe* (1999), p.18.

[9] See, for example, the case of the WTO dispute settlement system: *infra* nn.13–17 and corresponding text in Chapter 6.

or whether States have retained the right to exercise conferred powers concurrently with the organization.[10]

In terms of direct control, as one moves along our spectrum—from one extremity of an agency position through to the other extremity of a transfer of powers—the degree of direct control that a State can exercise over the organization's use of power markedly decreases. In the case of agency relationships, States can exert direct control over the organization's exercise of powers;[11] while they cannot in our categories of delegations and transfers.[12]

The clarification of the issue of control in our typology reveals an inherent conflict between law and politics at the heart of the practice of States conferring governmental powers on international organizations. It is part of the thesis of this work, to be demonstrated in subsequent chapters, that the greater the degree or extent of conferrals by States of powers on an international organization, the less is the degree of direct control that States are allowed to exert over the organization's exercise of powers outside the confines of the organization's decision-making processes; and yet, as a State confers powers to a greater degree on an organization there will often be more pressure exerted by the State—often as a result of increased domestic political pressures—to try and control the organization's decisions. This attempt to try and exercise greater control over the organization's decisions is not only actively pursued by the State's executive branch, but also by the legislative[13] and judicial branches[14] of a State who may seek either to direct the executive in its representation of the State in the organization[15] or more simply threaten to exercise their own powers on the domestic plane to block the organization's decisions from having an effect within the State's legal system. This represents an attempt by these arms of government to participate in, and influence, the contestation of sovereign values that are being formulated and applied by international organizations. This issue is considered at length in Chapter 6 in the context of transfers by States of powers to the European Union and the World Trade Organization.

3. An exclusive or concurrent competence to exercise conferred powers

Our third and final characteristic of conferrals that can be used to ascertain the degree to which powers have been given away by States is to determine whether the organization possesses the sole right to exercise conferred powers

---

[10] See *infra* Section II(3).   [11] See Section II in Chapter 4.

[12] In the case of delegations, see the introductory *chapeau* in Chapter 5; and in the case of transfers, see the introductory *chapeau* in Chapter 6.   [13] See Section II(2) in Chapter 6.

[14] See Section II(1) in Chapter 6.

[15] This is often problematic due to the scope of foreign affairs discretion which most executive arms of government enjoy. See, for example, Weiler, *supra* n.8, p.38. But cf. the vigorous attempts by the US Congress to control the US Government when it acts on behalf of the US in the WTO: see Section II(2)(ii)(b) in Chapter 6.

or whether States have retained the right to exercise powers concurrently with the organization. In the cases of agency relationships and delegations, States retain the right to exercise powers concurrent with, and independent of, the organization's exercise of powers;[16] while in the case of transfers the organization is the sole place for the lawful exercise of conferred powers.[17] This third characteristic will largely depend on the extent to which States have accepted to be bound—in both their internal legal systems and on the international plane—by obligations that flow from an organization's exercise of powers. This characteristic of conferrals of powers is particularly useful in gauging the extent to which States have given away powers (or, in other words, to what extent they have retained powers for themselves) since it reflects the extent to which States may simply ignore directives from the organization and, moreover, the extent to which the decisions of an organization in the exercise of conferred powers should be implemented in practice within States.

The classification of all conferrals within one of our categories cannot, however, always be precise since the boundaries between these categories are not definitively fixed and there may be cases that contain elements common to two categories that are adjacent on our spectrum. The categories in our typology do provide, nonetheless, a useful analytical tool since the classification of particular conferrals of powers as mainly being within one of the categories on our spectrum helps clarify the legal consequences that result from these conferrals. These legal consequences include the following: When an international organization exercises conferred powers, does it do so on its own behalf or on behalf of the State? Whose legal relations are changed by the exercise of powers: the State's or the organization's? In the case where the State has retained the right to exercise powers it has conferred on an organization, whose interpretation of the powers will prevail in the case of a conflict that arises from the concurrent exercise of powers? And who is responsible for breaches of international law that may occur as a result of the organization's exercise of conferred powers: the State or the organization or both?

Let us now turn in the next chapter to examine the starting point on our spectrum and the first category in our typology: those conferrals that establish agency relationships between States and organizations.

---

[16] In the case of agency relationships, see Section III(3) in Chapter 4; and in the case of delegations, see the introductory *chapeau* in Chapter 5.   [17] See Section II in Chapter 6.

4

Agency Relationships between States and International Organizations

An agency relationship is the only category in our typology that also exists as a distinct legal concept under international law. The existence of agency relationships under international law has been recognized by the International Court of Justice,[1] the International Law Commission,[2] and authoritative commentators[3] in a number of different cases where, in general, a principal has empowered an agent to act on its behalf to change certain of its rights and duties.[4] What emerges from these cases is that international law recognizes the existence of an agency relationship, our specific form of empowerment, where two conditions are fulfilled. The first is where a principal and agent are separate legal entities; while the second is a dual consent requirement, both principal and agent have consented to conferrals on an agent of powers to act on the principal's behalf. After examining these two conditions, this chapter turns to consider the establishment of agency relationships between States and international organizations and what consequences flow from such relationships for the organization and States concerned.

---

[1] See *infra* n.4 and *infra* nn.16–17, 23 and corresponding text.

[2] See *infra* nn.12–15, 21–22 and corresponding text.

[3] A number of authoritative commentators have argued that organizations can act as an 'agent' on behalf of member States and other States. See, for example, J. Crawford, as part of the work of the Commission of the Institut de Droit International, contained in 'Report by Rosalyn Higgins', 66-I *Annuaire de l'Institut de Droit International* (*'AIDI'*) (1995), p.334; I. Brownlie, *Principles of Public International Law* (2003, 6th edn), p.659; C. Chinkin, *Third Parties in International Law* (1993), p.115; and C. Amerasinghe in 'Report by Rosalyn Higgins', 66-I *AIDI* (1995), p.353.

[4] Consider, by way of illustration, the following two examples: First, there is the case of international agency that exists between Switzerland and Liechtenstein where, under a series of treaties concluded after World War I, Switzerland assumed responsibility for the diplomatic and consular representation of Liechtenstein, the protection of its borders, and the regulation of its customs (Treaty between Principality of Liechtenstein and Switzerland concerning the Union of the latter with the Swiss Customs Territory, signed at Berne on 29 March 1923, contained in Vol.XXI *League of Nations Treaty Series* (1923–1924), p.243.) As Eduardo Jimenez de Aréchaga stated in the ILC: 'The 1923 Treaty between Switzerland and Liechtenstein ... seemed to constitute a case of agency, in which one State entrusted another with the power to represent it not only for the purpose of concluding certain treaties, but also for the purpose of claiming rights under those treaties.' (*YBILC*, vol.1, 1964, 732nd mtg., p.56 (para.37).) Cf., however, the amendment on 2 November 1994 of the Customs Treaty dated 29 March 1923 between Liechtenstein and Switzerland in order to allow the participation of Liechtenstein in the EEA. (See Decision of the EEA Council No 1/95 of 10 March 1995 on the entry into force of the Agreement on the European Economic Area for the Principality of Liechtenstein, *Official Journal L 086*, 20/04/1995 pp.0058–0084.)

Second, the International Court of Justice in the *Rights of United States Nationals in Morocco* case found the existence of international agency as a result of conferrals of powers. The Court

I. PRINCIPAL AND AGENT AS SEPARATE LEGAL ENTITIES

An important condition for the existence of an agency relationship in both international and domestic law[5] is that the principal and agent are separate legal entities.[6] This flows from the principle of representation inherent in an agency relationship: that an agent acts on behalf of its principal to change certain of its rights and obligations. In our case of a potential relationship of agency between an international organization and one or more States, if the organization does not possess a separate legal personality then the organization constitutes nothing more than an extension of the States concerned and thus when the organization acts it is nothing more than the States themselves acting.[7] It was this type of scenario that existed, for example, in the case of the 'Administering Authority' in relation to Nauru, as expressly recognized by the International Court of Justice in the *Case concerning Certain Phosphate Lands in Nauru* when it stated that 'this Authority did not have an international legal personality distinct from those of the States thus designated'.[8]

held: 'The rights of France in Morocco are defined by the Protectorate Treaty of 1912... Under this Treaty, Morocco remained a sovereign State but it made an arrangement of a contractual character whereby France undertook to exercise certain sovereign powers in the name and on behalf of Morocco, and, in principle, all of the international relations of Morocco . . .' (*Case Concerning Rights of Nationals of United States of America in Morocco (France v. USA), ICJ Reports*, 1952, p.176 at pp.185, 188.)

[5] See, for example, *Williams v The Shipping Corporation of India*, US District Court, Eastern District Virginia, 10 March 1980, 63 *ILR*, p.363 at p.368; *Edlow International Co. v Nuklearna Elektrarna Krsko,* US District Court, District of Columbia, 7 December 1977, 63 *ILR*, p.100 at p.103; and *Dayton v Czechoslovak Socialist Republic and others*, US District Court, District of Columbia, 19 December 1986, 79 *ILR*, p.590 at p.596; and *The Attorney-General of Israel v Kamiar*, Supreme Court of Israel sitting as the Court of Criminal Appeals, 9 June 1968, 44 *ILR*, p.197 at p.249.

[6] The separate identity of principal and agent does not mean, however, that in the case of an agency relationship between one or more States and an international organization that the former can be considered as having 'loaned' organs to the States concerned. An international organization with separate legal personality will continue, at least in formal terms (cf. the case of *de facto* control: *infra* n.22 and corresponding text *et seq*), to use its processes of decision-making even when it acts as an agent for States and exercises conferred powers. See J. Crawford, First Report on State Responsibility, A/CN.4/490/Add.5, pp.27–28 (para.231).

[7] The likelihood of this scenario occurring is not as remote as may at first appear the case for the reason that relatively few constituent treaties provide explicitly for the international legal personality of organizations, (J. Klabbers, *An Introduction to International Institutional Law* (2002), p.53) and that even where they do, as Klabbers notes, '[a]t best, the provisions are ambiguous, providing quite simply that the organization concerned "shall have legal personality" or similar terms'. (Klabbers, *ibid*, p.53 (n.41).) In cases where there is no express provision for the separate legal personality of an organization then it will be necessary to employ the functional test adopted by the International Court in the *Reparations* case where it ascertained the existence of the UN's separate legal personality from that of its Member States. (*Reparations for Injuries Suffered in the Service of the United Nations* case, *ICJ Reports*, 1949, p.174.)

[8] *Case Concerning Certain Phosphate Lands in Nauru (Nauru v. Australia), ICJ Reports*, 1992, p.240 at p.258 (para.47). This has the important consequence, as explained by ILC Special Rapporteur Crawford, that the issue of responsibility did not involve the acts of an international organization, but only those acts of 'the three States (Australia, New Zealand, United Kingdom) which together constituted the Administering Authority for the Trust Territory of Nauru.' (Second Report on State responsibility, A/CN.4/498 Add. 1, p.4 (para.160).)

II. THE EXISTENCE OF CONSENT AND THE ISSUE OF REVOCABILITY

1. Consent as prerequisite for agency relationships

The necessity for, and emphasis on, consent as a prerequisite for the establishment of an agency relationship exists to a much greater extent in international law than it does in domestic legal systems.[9] In domestic legal systems, the operation of the law may remove the need for the consent of the principal to the establishment of certain agency relationships.[10] However, international law by contrast places more importance on the role of States consenting to their obligations.[11]

The essential role that a State's consent plays in establishing an agency relationship was highlighted by the work of the International Law Commission (ILC) on the Law of Treaties when it considered the possibility of one State acting as agent for, and concluding a treaty on behalf of, another State. This agency approach attracted criticism from within the ILC by Grigory Tunkin who argued that the concept of agency 'had in fact been used mainly in colonial practice, in connexion with protectorates',[12] and as such should be omitted from the ILC's Draft.[13] There was, however, strong opposition voiced

---

[9] There are similarities between the international law concept of agency and its domestic law counterpart, but agency in international law cannot solely be equated with, or constructed by analogy from, its domestic counterpart for two main reasons. First, the domestic law of agency is in the main concerned with conferrals of private law powers; while in the context of international organizations it is public law powers being conferred by States on an organization. This limitation of the use of private law analogies has also been recognized by some domestic public law systems. For example, in the English courts it was held in the case of *Town Investments Ltd. v Environment Secretary* that the relationship between 'the Crown' and 'Ministers of the Crown' had to be analysed in public law terms and not by using private law concepts of agency and trust. (*Town Investments Ltd. v Environment Secretary*, [1978] AC 359.) Second, the domestic law of agency is largely directed at allocating, or rather balancing, commercial risk between business actors and thus its transplantation to public international law which concerns relations between sovereign States is problematic.

These problems do not, however, prohibit in general terms recourse to the domestic law of agency, but they do mean that the concept as it appears in public international law may differ in content. For example, the notion of an undisclosed principal in the domestic law of agency has no application in the context of public international law, since, as Chinkin states, 'any such claim should be dismissed as contrary to the principle of openness in international relations, and the right of States to select their treaty partners.' (Chinkin, *supra* n.3, p.66.)

[10] See A. Sereni, 'Agency in International Law', 34 *AJIL* (1940), p.638 at p.645. Nonetheless, the general approach also in domestic law is that both the agent and the principal must consent to the establishment of the agency relationship. See W. Gregory, *The Law of Agency and Partnership* (2001, 3rd edn), p.97; F. Reynolds, *Bowstead and Reynolds on Agency* (2001, 17th edn), Article 1; G. Fridman, *The Law of Agency* (1996, 7th edn), pp.14–21; and W. Seavey, 'The Rationale of Agency', 29 *Yale Law Journal* (1919–1920), p.859 at p.868.

[11] See I. Brownlie, *Principles of Public International Law* (2003, 6th edn), p.643; and B. Cheng, *General Principles of Law as applied by International Courts and Tribunals* (1987), pp.213–214. [12] *YBILC*, 1964, vol.1, 732nd meeting, p.58 (para.53).

[13] A lot of the discussion that ensued on this point was strongly affected by the fact that most of the examples concerned protectorates, and decolonization was in full flow at the time.

by a number of ILC members in response to this critique. The ILC Chairman, Roberto Ago, held an opposing view:

45. . . . *as the agency relationship was freely established between two States,* the Commission should not express a favourable or an unfavourable opinion on that practice.[14]

Moreover, Eduardo Jimenez de Arechaga also stated in the ILC debates:

The Commission should not adopt a negative attitude to the legitimate institution of agency merely because it might have been used in the past to set up protectorates. . . . It should be remembered that representation by the operation of law did not exist in international law; the only form of representation was by virtue of a treaty. Any agency relationship which might be established would therefore be subject to the rules in Parts I and II of the draft articles. Such rules as those relating to free consent, nullity on grounds of coercion, *jus cogens*, the power of denunciation in certain circumstances, and determination for change of circumstances would apply in all cases. There would thus be ample safeguards to ensure that no State would in future, as had happened in the past, use the method of agency by treaty to set up a protectorate regime against the free will of the State represented.[15]

Both these statements emphasize the necessity of a State having to consent freely to an agency relationship in international law. This is the context within which the statement by Eduardo Jimenez de Arechaga—that agency was only possible by treaty—must be read. He was emphasizing that an agency relationship could only be created with State consent—he says expressed in 'a treaty' because that was the specific focus of the ILC's work—as opposed to the creation of an agency relationship 'by the operation of law'. However, the role of State consent in establishing an agency relationship can be guaranteed by means other than requiring the conclusion of a treaty, and, moreover, consent need not be expressly provided for by a State. A State's consent may be implied from its statements or actions.

The *Iran—US Hostages* case before the International Court provides an example of a case where a State's consent to an agency relationship was implied from its statements. Moreover, this case also emphasizes the necessity for State consent in order to establish an agency relationship, since the International Court resisted basing its finding of Iranian responsibility for the clearly illegal and heinous acts relating to the occupation of the US Embassy in Iran on an agency argument without evidence of Iranian Government consent to the establishment of such a relationship.[16] As the Court stated:

58. No suggestion has been made that the militants, when they executed their attack on the Embassy, had any form of official status as recognized 'agents' or organs of the

---

[14] *YBILC*, 1964, vol.1, 732nd meeting, p.57 (para.45). Emphasis added.

[15] *YBILC*, 1964, vol.1, 733rd meeting, p.60 (para.5).

[16] It is important to bear in mind, however, that attribution and agency are distinct concepts: on this distinction, see *infra* nn.20–22 and corresponding text.

Iranian State. Their conduct in mounting the attack, overrunning the Embassy and seizing its inmates as hostages cannot, therefore, be regarded as imputable to that State on that basis. Their conduct might be considered as itself directly imputable to the Iranian State *only if it were established that, in fact, on the occasion in question the militants acted on behalf of the State, having been charged by some competent organ of the Iranian State to carry out a specific operation.* The information before the Court does not, however, suffice to establish with the requisite certainty the existence at that time of such a link between the militants and any competent organ of the State.[17]

However, the Court did go on to find the existence of the requisite consent for the establishment of an agency relationship from the subsequent statements by the Iranian Government that adopted the unlawful acts in question. The Court held:

74. The policy thus announced by the Ayatollah Khomeini, of maintaining the occupation of the Embassy and the detention of its inmates as hostages for the purpose of exerting pressure on the United States Government was complied with by other Iranian authorities and endorsed by them repeatedly in statements made in various contexts. The result of that policy was fundamentally to transform the legal nature of the situation created by the occupation of the Embassy and the detention of its diplomatic and consular staff as hostages. The approval given to these facts by the Ayatollah Khomeini and other organs of the Iranian State, and the decision to perpetuate them, translated continuing occupation of the Embassy and detention of the hostages into acts of that State. The militants, authors of the invasion and jailers of the hostages, had now become *agents of the Iranian State for whose acts the State itself was internationally responsible.*[18]

In other words, the Court posited that the necessary consent of the Iranian State for the establishment of an agency relationship with the militants was provided by the 'approval given to these facts by the Ayatollah Khomeini and other organs of the Iranian State, and the decision to perpetuate them'.[19]

2. Implied consent: the role of State control

The remaining issue that deserves consideration in terms of establishing an agency relationship is whether a State's consent can be implied from its exercise of control over the acts of an entity such that the latter may be considered an agent of the State. Control is not being put forward here as a necessary condition for the establishment of an agency relationship, but rather as sufficient for the establishment of a State's implied consent in a particular case. Control also plays, of course, a defining role in determining whose acts

---

[17] *United States Diplomatic and Consular Staff in Tehran* case, *ICJ Reports*, 1980, p.3 at p.29. Emphasis added. [18] *Ibid*, p.35. Emphasis added.
[19] *Iran—US Hostages* case, *ICJ Reports*, 1980, p.3 at p.35 (para.74).

are attributable to a State under international law.[20] However it is important not to conflate these separate concepts of attribution and agency. An agent can act more broadly on behalf of a principal to change the latter's rights and duties; whereas attribution is only concerned with the more limited issue of deciding whose acts can a State be held responsible for under international law.

A distinction between the concept of attribution and the broader concept of agency was hinted at early on in the work of James Crawford, the final ILC Special Rapporteur on State Responsibility, when he acknowledged that agency in international law may not necessarily follow from control (the sole determinant of attribution). In his First Report on State Responsibility, James Crawford stated concerning Draft Article 5 of the ILC Draft Articles: ' "agents" for this purpose are persons or entities in fact acting on behalf of the State by reason of some mandate or direction given by a State organ, or (*possibly*) who are to be regarded as acting on behalf of the State by reason of the control exercised over them by such an organ.'[21] In the event, the word 'agent' was not used in the final ILC Articles on State Responsibility, Article 8 of which provides:

The conduct of a person or group of persons shall be considered an act of a State under international law if the person or group of persons is in fact acting on the instructions of, or under the direction or control of, that State in carrying out the conduct.[22]

As such, Article 8 provides that *de facto* control is the sole determinant of attribution, but the sole objective of this provision is to resolve the issue of attribution for the purposes of establishing a State's responsibility and not to resolve the broader issue of determining when an entity acts as an agent for a State. However, it is recognized that Article 8 does admit of a different interpretation, one that conflates the concepts of agency and attribution with the consequence that control appears sufficient to establish an agency relationship. Even if, however, this different interpretation is preferred, when one examines the degree of *de facto* control that is required by Article 8 then it becomes clear that even in this scenario the role of consent as a condition for the establishment of an agency relationship is guaranteed.

The International Court of Justice in the *Nicaragua* case provided the test of 'effective control' in order to determine the degree of control that is required for attribution of the acts of individuals (*in casu*, the contra rebels)

---

[20] It is clear from Article 8 of the ILC Articles that control is sufficient to establish attribution for the purposes of State responsibility: see *infra* n.22 and corresponding text *et seq*. For the historical antecedent to this approach in international law, see R. Ago, *YBILC*, 1979, vol.1., p.7; and C. Eagleton, *The Responsibility of States in International Law* (1928), p.43.

[21] J. Crawford, First Report on State Responsibility, A/CN.4/490/Add.5, 22 July 1998, p.6 (para.166). Emphasis added.

[22] J. Crawford, *The International Law Commission's Articles on State Responsibility: Introduction, Text and Commentaries* (2002), pp.110–113.

to a State (the USA). The Court stated in its famous passage:

> Despite the heavy subsidies and other support provided to them by the United States, there is no clear evidence of the United States having actually exercised such a degree of control in all fields as to justify treating the *contras* as acting on its behalf... All the forms of United States participation mentioned above, and even the general control by the respondent State over a force with a high degree of dependency on it, would not in themselves mean, without further evidence, that the United States directed or enforced the perpetration of the acts contrary to human rights and humanitarian law alleged by the applicant State. Such acts could well be committed by members of the *contras* without the control of the United States. For this conduct to give rise to legal responsibility of the United States, it would in principle have to be proved that that State had *effective control* of the military or paramilitary operations in the course of which the alleged violations were committed.[23]

The International Law Commission elucidated further on the Court's 'effective control' test in the Commentary to Article 8 when it stated:

> Thus while the United States was held responsible for its own support for the *contras*, only in certain individual instances were the acts of the *contras* themselves held attributable to it, *based upon actual participation of and directions given by that State*.[24]

Accordingly, what the 'effective control' test requires for attribution to a State of a particular act is that specific instructions concerning the commission of the particular act have been issued by the State to the individual or group in question. Put differently, by requiring a specific instruction from a State, the 'effective control' test in effect requires that a State has impliedly consented to an individual or group being able to act on its behalf. As such, the condition of State consent for an agency relationship continues to be guaranteed even if the concepts of agency and attribution are conflated.

However, the 'effective control' test has been the subject of criticism by the Appeals Chamber of the International Criminal Tribunal for the former Yugoslavia (ICTY) in the *Tadic* case.[25] The test of 'effective control' was in fact adopted and applied by a Trial Chamber of the ICTY in the *Tadic* case,[26] but the Appeals Chamber went on to overrule the decision when it formulated a different test to determine the degree of control necessary for the acts of

---

[23] *Case concerning Military and Paramilitary Activities in and against Nicaragua (Nicaragua v. United States of America), ICJ Reports* (1986), p.14 at pp.62, 64–65. Emphasis added.

[24] Crawford, *supra* n.22, p.111. Emphasis added.

[25] These two cases were, however, considering the issue of attribution for different purposes, *Nicaragua* for State responsibility and *Tadic* for the application of rules of international humanitarian law: see Crawford, *supra* n.22, p.112.

[26] *Prosecutor v. Dusko Tadic, Judgment*, Trial Chamber, IT-94-1-T, 7 May 1997, para.588. Cf., however, the dissenting opinion on this point by Judge McDonald: *Separate and Dissenting Opinion of Judge McDonald regarding the applicability of Article 2 of the Statute*, 7 May 1997, IT-94-1-T.

military or paramilitary groups to be attributed to the State. The Appeals Chamber stated:

The requirement of international law for the attribution to States of acts performed by private individuals is that the State exercises control over the individuals. The *degree of control* may, however, vary according to the factual circumstances of each case. The Appeals Chamber fails to see why in each and every circumstance international law should require a high threshold for the test of control.[27]

The Appeals Chamber continued:

. . . that international rules do not always require the same degree of control over armed groups or private individuals for the purpose of determining whether an individual not having the status of a State official under internal legislation can be regarded as a *de facto* organ of the State. The extent of the requisite State control varies. Where the question at issue is whether a *single* private individual or a *group that is not militarily organised* has acted as a *de facto* State organ when performing a specific act, it is necessary to ascertain whether specific instructions concerning the commission of that particular act had been issued by that State to the individual or group in question; alternatively, it must be established whether the unlawful act had been publicly endorsed or approved *ex post facto* by the State at issue. By contrast, control by a State over subordinate *armed forces or militias or paramilitary units* may be of an overall character (and must comprise more than the mere provision of financial assistance or military equipment or training). This requirement, however, does not go so far as to include the issuing of specific orders by the State, or its direction of each individual operation. . . . The control required by international law may be deemed to exist when a State (or, in the context of an armed conflict, the Party to the conflict) *has a role in organising, coordinating or planning the military actions* of the military group, in addition to financing, training and equipping or providing operational support to that group. Acts performed by the group or members thereof may be regarded as acts of *de facto* State organs regardless of any specific instruction by the controlling State concerning the commission of each of those acts.[28]

The Appeals Chamber thus replaced the 'effective control' test with an 'overall control' test for the purposes of determining the attribution of acts of armed forces or militia units to a State, since it did not see why international law should in general stipulate a high threshold for the control test. However, it is precisely at this point that the condition of consent for the establishment of an agency relationship plays an important role in this scenario where the concepts of agency and attribution are being conflated. The role of consent in establishing an agency relationship provides an answer to the question posed by the Appeals Chamber as to why international law should require a high threshold for the test of control. An answer here may be that specific instructions or directions by a State, as part of the high threshold test of 'effective control', are necessary since they provide evidence of a State's consent to an

---

[27] *Prosecutor v Tadic*, Appeals Chamber, IT-94-1-A, 15 July 1999, para.117.
[28] *Ibid*, para.137.

entity being able to act as its agent, and that this consent cannot be lightly presumed by the existence of a general or 'overall' degree of control—that is, in the absence of specific instructions or directions from a State.

To conclude on this point, the importance that international law places on States being able to consent to their obligations has the consequence that consent is a prerequisite for the establishment of an agency relationship in international law. There is, however, no specific form that is required for the expression of this consent: a State's consent may be implied from its actions or statements. In the case where a State's consent is implied from the control that it exerts over an international organization, the degree of control that has to be proved is the *Nicaragua* case test of 'effective control' and not the *Tadic* case test of 'overall control'.

3. Consent and the revocability of agency relationships

The consensual basis of an agency relationship has the important consequence that it will, in general, be revocable by the principal at any time. This element of agency in international law is the same as it appears in domestic law.[29] This similarity is not surprising since the rationale for unilateral revocability in both international and domestic law is the same. As Gregory puts it: 'agency is a consensual relationship and a principal, therefore, cannot be compelled to retain another as his agent.'[30] This rationale is arguably applicable with a greater degree of cogency to the case of agency under international law. The importance that international law places on States being able to express freely their consent to the acceptance of obligations means that where these obligations are being entered into on their behalf by an agent, then a State should have the right to terminate this agency relationship in order to ensure that the assumption of its obligations represents at all times the true expression of its will.

This right of termination of an agency relationship exists independently of the underlying treaty or other agreement that provided for the establishment of the agency relationship.[31] In the context of international law this means

---

[29] In domestic law a principal will in general be able to revoke at any time with immediate effect its agent's authority to act on its behalf. For this position in England and the US, see, eg., Reynolds, *supra* n.10, pp.551, 567, Fridman, *supra* n.10, p.389, and Gregory, *supra* n.10, pp.97–98; in the case of France, see J. Guyénot, *The French Law of Agency and Distributorship Agreements* (1976), p.67; and in Germany, see F. Staubach, *The German Law of Agency and Distributorship Agreements*, (1977), p.24. Cf., however, the *sui generis* case of an irrevocable agency: Fridman, *supra* n.10, p.389–391; Reynolds, *supra* n.10, pp.554–562; and Gregory, *supra* n.10, pp.110–112.

This is subject to the important caveat, even in the domestic sphere, that the termination may not affect the position of a third party in its dealings with the agent who has had no notice of such termination (see Reynolds, *supra* n.10, p.551.)   [30] Gregory, *supra* n.10, p.97.

[31] As Reynolds states in the context of domestic law: 'The general rule ... is that the *authority* of an agent ... whether or not expressed to be irrevocable, is revocable, without prejudice to the fact that such revocation may be wrongful as between principal and agent.' (Reynolds, *supra* n.10, pp.567–568.) See also, eg., Gregory, *supra* n.10, p.97.

that a State has the competence to decide at any time whether an agent should be able to continue to act on its behalf regardless of the existence of any agreement that may exist between the principal and agent. As Sereni states:

[A way] in which agency may be terminated is the *revocation by the principal* or the *renunciation by the agent.* It is correct to assume that in international law the principal has power to revoke, and the agent to renounce the authority, although doing so is a violation of an agreement between the parties expressly denying the right to revoke or to renounce. The only effect of a provision in a treaty that the authority cannot be terminated by either party is to create liability for its wrongful termination.[32]

As such, where there is, for example, an agency relationship between a group of States and an international organization that is exercising conferred powers on their behalf, then the conferrals are revocable by the States with immediate effect, even in the case where the treaty providing for the conferrals of powers stipulates that the conferrals are irrevocable. In the case of the latter, a unilateral revocation would provide a basis for allegation of breach of treaty by the organization, but this is a separate issue from the right of termination of the agency relationship.[33]

III. THE ESTABLISHMENT OF AGENCY RELATIONSHIPS
BETWEEN STATES AND INTERNATIONAL ORGANIZATIONS

The establishment of an agency relationship in international law depends, as explained above, on the principal and agent being separate entities; and the relationship between them being consensual. The germane question for our present discussion is the extent to which these conditions can be satisfied in the relationship that exists between an organization and a State or States that have conferred powers on the organization. In considering this question, it is important to distinguish, analytically, between two categories of States that may potentially have an agency relationship with an international organization: member States and non-member States. In both cases there is a presumption against the establishment of an agency relationship between a State and an

---

[32] Sereni, *supra* n.10, p.660. Original emphasis. On revocability being an important part of international agency, see also Bartos in the International Law Commission debates: *YBILC*, vol.1, 1964, 732nd mtg., p.57 (para.42).

[33] In any case this right of unilateral termination is arguably envisaged by Article 56(1)(b) of the 1969 Vienna Convention on the Law of Treaties which provides in effect (for present purposes) that a State can terminate a treaty that does not expressly provide for termination where the right of termination 'may be implied by the nature of the treaty'. The argument runs— in the case of a treaty establishing an agency relationship—that the consent based nature of the relationship which the treaty establishes means that the treaty should be revocable at the discretion of the State or States concerned (the principal). This right would still, however, be subject to Article 56(2) of the 1969 Vienna Convention which provides that 'A party shall give not less than twelve months' notice of its intention to denounce or withdraw from a treaty under paragraph 1'.

organization for the reasons set out below, but in the case of member States the presumption may in practice be stronger.

1. Member States

There is a general presumption against the establishment of an agency relationship between an international organization and its member States.[34] The main reason for the existence of this presumption in such cases is that one of the conditions for establishment of an agency relationship—consent—is not fulfilled on a prima facie basis. Often the very reason for setting up an international organization is precisely to act on a basis independent from member States, a position often evidenced by the separate legal personality of an organization from its members.[35] This does not mean that an international organization can never be an agent for its member States when exercising conferred powers under the terms of its constituent treaty. It is just that there is a presumption against this being the case.

When member States ratify a constituent treaty that confers powers on an organization they are consenting thereby to the organization exercising the power in question, but they are not usually consenting to the organization exercising the power on their behalf (as an agent) such that it can change their legal rights and obligations. More specifically, an international organization with separate legal personality acts on its *own* behalf and not on behalf of its member States when exercising powers under its constituent treaty, and as such there is a general presumption against considering members as having consented to the establishment of an agency relationship simply by virtue of their membership in the organization. It was this approach that was adopted by the English courts in the litigation following the financial collapse of the International Tin Council (ITC), an international organization headquartered in the UK with separate international legal personality from its Member States.

In the ITC cases, one of the arguments made in favour of ITC Member States being liable for the ITC's financial liabilities was that the organization had entered into transactions with third parties as an agent acting on behalf of the Member States who were an undisclosed principal.[36] A useful distinction

---

[34] For statements in support of this presumption, see the following: the decision of the English Court of Appeal in *Maclaine Watson v Department of Trade and Industry*, Court of Appeal, 80 *ILR*, p.39 at p.114; the opinion of Lord Oliver (with whom the other Lords agreed) in *J.H. Rayner Ltd v Department of Trade and Industry*, [1989] 3 W.L.R., p.969 at pp.1016–1017; the opinion of Justice Millet in *Maclaine Watson & Co. v International Tin Council*, [1988] Ch., p.1; J. Crawford in 'Report by Rosalyn Higgins', 66-I *AIDI* (1995), p.334; and K. Zemanek in 'Report by Rosalyn Higgins', *ibid*, p.327.   [35] See Klabbers, *supra* n.7, pp.56–57.
[36] *J.H. Rayner (Mincing Lane) Ltd. v Department of Trade and Industry* [1987] BCLC, p.667, *Maclaine Watson & Co. v International Tin Council* [1988] Ch., p.1, and *Maclaine Watson v Department of Trade and Industry*, Court of Appeal, 80 *ILR*, p.39.

was drawn in the cases between 'constitutional' (or built-in) agency which would arguably derive directly from the ITC's constituent treaty [the 6th International Tin Agreement (ITA6), the treaty most recently constituting the International Tin Council] and 'factual' (or ad hoc) agency for which express authority given by the Members to the Council would have to be established.

The 'constitutional' (built-in) agency argument was dismissed by the English courts on the basis that the ITA6 was a membership agreement, not one forming an agency relationship: the ITA6 established the rights of Members as Members of the ITC, not as principals to the transactions of the ITC. As, for example, Justice Millet in *Maclaine Watson v International Tin Council* stated: 'the treaty [I.T.A.6] is not a contract of partnership or agency but of membership. The relationships it creates are not those of partners or of principal and agent but of an organisation and its members.'[37] This approach was upheld by the English Court of Appeal.[38] Put differently, the courts had found that Member States could not be considered as having implicitly consented to the establishment of an agency relationship when ratifying ITA6.

The English courts also considered whether participation by ITC Member States in the decision-making processes of the ITC Council, as provided for by ITA6, could be equated to control of the organ for the purposes of establishing an agency relationship. The English Court of Appeal—in the separate action brought by the ITC's creditors directly against the UK Department of Trade and Industry (*Maclaine Watson v Department of Trade and Industry*)[39]—rejected the argument that the control being exercised by Member States over the ITC through the ITC Council was sufficient to establish an agency relationship between the ITC and its Members. In so doing, the Court of Appeal in *Maclaine Watson v Department of Trade and Industry* applied the earlier House of Lords decision in *Salomon v Salomon* which had rejected the notion that the existence of control was sufficient per se to allow the piercing of the corporate veil so that a corporation could be considered as an agent for the controlling shareholders.[40] The Court of Appeal stated in the *Maclaine Watson* case concerning the *Salomon* case:

The crucial point on which the House of Lords overruled the Court of Appeal in that landmark case was precisely the rejection of the doctrine that agency between a corporation and its members in relation to the corporation's contracts can be inferred from the control exercisable by the members over the corporation or from the fact that the sole objective of the corporation's contracts was to benefit the members.[41]

[37] *Maclaine Watson v International Tin Council, Chancery Division*, [1988] Ch., p.1 at p.23.
[38] *Maclaine Watson v International Tin Council, Court of Appeal*, [1989] Ch., p.253 at p.257.
[39] *Maclaine Watson v Department of Trade and Industry*, Court of Appeal, 80 *ILR*, p.39.
[40] The Court of Appeal stated: 'The correct analysis of I.T.A.6 is in line with the decision of the House of Lords in *Salomon v. A. Salomon & Co. Ltd.* [1897] A.C. 22 and not with any contract of agency between the members as principals and the council as the members' agent.' (*Maclaine Watson v. Department of Trade and Industry*, Court of Appeal, 80 *ILR*, p.39 at p.114.)
[41] *Ibid*, p.113.

This approach by the Court of Appeal was affirmed on appeal by the House of Lords which stated:

Once given the creation of a separate legal personality by the Order in Council [that established the ITC as a UK corporation], there appears to me to be no escape from the principle established by this House in *Salomon v. A. Salomon and Co. Ltd.* [1897] A.C. 22, where the suggestion that Salomon and Co. Ltd. carried on business as agent for the corporators was firmly and decisively rejected. Mr. Sumption has sought to distinguish the case on the ground that the I.T.C. was brought into existence to carry out the purposes of its members and not for its own purposes and that it is 'composed' of its members and operates under their immediate direction. An analysis was made of... the I.T.A.6 in order to support the suggestion that, unlike a board of directors, the council owes no duties to the I.T.C. but acts entirely for its own benefit. From this it was argued that the I.T.C., as a body, was simply the agent of the members. It is, perhaps, enough for me to say that... I can find no relevant distinction here between the governance of a limited company and the governance of the I.T.C. That they are differently constituted is irrelevant. As Kerr L.J. [1989] Ch. 72, 189, pointed out in the course of his judgment [in the Court of Appeal], whether a corporation acts directly on the instructions of its members, who constitute the directorate, or indirectly because of the members' control in general meeting, makes no difference in principle. The existence of a board of directors in Salomon's case played no part in the decision. An examination of the constitution of the I.T.C., even if permissible, does not support the suggestion of 'constitutional agency'.[42]

The House of Lords thus dismissed the argument that the control being exercised by ITC Member States acting collectively through the decision-making processes of the ITC Council was sufficient to establish a relationship of 'constitutional agency', that is agency established by the ITC's constituent treaty (ITA6). This decision has two broader implications.[43]

First, it provides further support to the approach set out above that the implication of consent to an agency relationship by virtue of control being exercised by a purported principal over a purported agent will not be lightly presumed.[44]

Second, it means that the nature of the control that is necessary to establish an agency relationship between an organization—possessing its own legal personality—and its member States must be control that is being exercised by member States over an organization which is outside the confines of the decision-making processes of the organization.

To summarize, there is a general presumption against member States of an organization having established an agency relationship with the organization

---

[42] *J.H. Rayner v Department of Trade and Industry and Others and Related Appeals*, [1990] 2 *A.C.*, p.418 at p.515, per Lord Oliver.

[43] The general importance for international law of these domestic court pronouncements in the ITC cases has been widely accepted: see, for example, Responsibility of International Organizations, ILC Report of its 54th Session (2002), A/57/10, Chapter VIII, p.237 (para.487).

[44] See *supra* Section II(2).

simply by virtue of their ratification of a constituent treaty and participation
in its decision-making organs. This presumption may, however, be rebutted
where a case of ad hoc agency can be established.

Recalling our earlier discussion on the conditions for an agency relationship, the establishment of a case of ad hoc agency between an organization
and member States will require evidence in a particular case that an organization has accepted the ad hoc conferrals of powers to be exercised on an
agency basis,[45] and that member States have consented—either expressly or
impliedly—to the organization acting on their behalf on an individual or
collective basis.[46] There is an important distinction that needs to be made at
this point in our analysis between the case where member States have expressly
consented to an organization acting on their behalf from the case where consent has arguably been implied. This distinction is of practical importance,
since where members have consented in express terms then there is no
requirement to prove the existence of effective control over the acts of an
organization in order to establish an agency relationship between the members
and the organization. Where, however, there is no such express consent by
States and consent has arguably been implied from a relationship of control
then the member States in question must have exercised control over the
organization in a way that is not envisaged by the organization's constituent
treaty. Further, the degree of control necessary to provide evidence of an
agency relationship will need to be 'effective control'. These distinctions can
be illuminated by considering the two different consent scenarios in the case,
for example, of the possible establishment of an agency relationship between
the North Atlantic Treaty Organization (NATO) and its Member States.

Consider if, for example, a group of NATO Member States expressly stated
that NATO was acting on their behalf in a particular case and that NATO had
expressly accepted these conferrals of powers, then notwithstanding NATO's
separate legal personality[47] the dual requirement for consent would clearly
be fulfilled. The express consent would operate in such a case to rebut the
general presumption that an international organization with separate legal
personality does not act on behalf of its Member States on an individual or
collective basis.

Where, however, there is no express consent by Member States, but
consent is arguably implied, then the test for the degree of control that will
be necessary to establish an agency relationship is, as explained above, the
International Court's more stringent 'effective control' test and not the ICTY's
'overall control' test.[48] This has the important practical consequence that in
such cases it will be necessary to prove an actual instruction or direction by

---

[45] We recall from Chapter 2 that in order for ad hoc conferrals of powers on organizations
to have legal effect they must have been accepted by the organization (see *supra* nn.5–11 and
corresponding text in Chapter 2).   [46] See *supra* Sections II(1)–(2).
[47] Cf. *infra* n.54.   [48] See *supra* Section II(2).

Member States—not envisaged by the constituent treaty—that is subsequently followed by the organization.[49] The likelihood of such an occurrence may not in practice be as remote as may at first seem the case, especially since NATO military commanders continue to serve as part of the armed forces of their Member States concurrent with their NATO command positions.[50]

The question of a possible agency relationship between NATO and its Member States was raised by the Federal Republic of Yugoslavia (FRY) before the International Court in the case brought against NATO Members. The FRY brought this case in response to the NATO bombing of its territory that was carried out in an attempt to stop the widespread human rights violations that were said to be occurring in the FRY province of Kosovo. One of the arguments made by the FRY in the provisional measures phase of the case was that '[t]he command structure of NATO constitutes an instrumentality of the respondent States, acting as their agent'[51] and thus that 'the respondent States are jointly and severally responsible for the actions of the NATO military command structure'.[52] This issue was not argued at length before the International

[49] Where this element of control can be proved there will be obvious issues of *vires* for the organization, but this does not detract from the agency relationship that would be established if the existence of such an instruction or direction was proved. This is of course subject to NATO having accepted these conferrals of powers: see *supra* nn.5–11 and corresponding text in Chapter 2.

[50] It is precisely this type of dual function that gave rise to a possible example of an agency relationship between the UN peace-keeping operation in Somalia (UNOSOM II) and a UN Member State, Italy, that was participating in UNOSOM II. It has been explained in detail elsewhere that UNOSOM II was given by the UN Security Council a military enforcement mandate by Council resolutions 814 and 837. (D. Sarooshi, *The United Nations and the Development of Collective Security* (1999), pp.81–82.) This was subject, however, to the condition that UNOSOM II operate under the command and control of the Secretary-General's Special Representative and the UN Force Commander. (*Ibid.*) Despite this requirement, it seems the Italian contingent that was part of UNOSOM II obtained and followed orders from Rome which were clearly outside the UN chain-of-command. (For a description of such cases, see: S/1994/653, pp.28–29, 45; and J. Hirsh and R. Oakley, *Somalia and Operation Restore Hope: Reflections on Peacemaking and Peacekeeping* (1995), p.119.) In such a case—to the extent that evidence of these orders can be established—it could be argued that UNOSOM II was acting as an agent of Italy and as such that any responsibility arising from these acts are to be attributed to Italy and not the UN. This is arguably more akin to a case of agency rather than simply considering the Italian contingent as being, for the purposes of the action, part of the Italian armed forces per se, because the sole legal basis for the contingent being in Somalia and carrying out an enforcement mandate is the fact that it was part of UNOSOM II. The fact that the contingent may have obeyed orders issued directly from Rome—orders that were clearly outside the UN chain-of-command—does not alter the legal position that the Italian contingent was still part of UNOSOM II. What our previous analysis does illustrate though is that in order for this relationship to be characterised as one of agency, UNOSOM II would have to have consented to the agency relationship. On the more general issue of member State-organization responsibility for peace-keeping operations, see the 'Final Report of the ILA Committee on the Accountability of International Organizations' (2004), p.24, Final Report available at http://www.ila-hq.org/ html/layout_committee.htm.

[51] Oral argument in the case *Yugoslavia v Canada*, CR/99/14, 10 May 1999, p.33 (from ICJ web-site: http://www.icj-cij.org).

[52] *Ibid*, p.38. For a description of the NATO chain-of-command, see the NATO web-site: http://www.nato.int/structur/structure.htm.

Court at this interim measures phase of the case since it is a matter going more to the merits. Nonetheless, Canada did briefly respond in oral argument—although not directly addressing the issue of agency—when it stated before the Court:

Joint and several liability for acts of an international organization, or for the acts of other States acting within such an organization, cannot be established unless the relevant treaty provides for such liability. Article 5 of the 1994 NATO Convention, cited in the first round, provides no such indication of an assumption of joint and several liability, and neither do the provisions of the Handbook respecting the integrated military structure of the organization. The separate liability of Australia in *Nauru* was of course based on the specific terms of the trust instruments in issue in that case, not on general principles on international organizations. The work of the International Law Commission on State Responsibility provides no more support for the joint and several concept. I note as well that these concepts were canvassed in the Tin Council litigation in the United Kingdom, and the outcome would not support the Applicant in the present case.[53]

[53] Oral argument on behalf of Canada in the case *Yugoslavia v Canada*, CR/99/27, 12 May 1999, p.7 (from ICJ web-site: http://www.icj-cij.org). Cf. also the following Oral Pleadings by France in the later Preliminary Objections phase of the case:

'49. Monsieur le président, la France n'entend nullement minorer et encore moins nier le rôle qu'elle a tenu dans l'action collective qui a été entreprise à l'époque pour prévenir une catastrophe humanitaire au Kosovo et mettre un terme aux atrocités qui s'y sont déroulées. Mais, ainsi que l'indique la République fédérale de Yougoslavie elle-même dans son mémoire, "The general rule on attribution of an act to a State is that a State is responsible for an act committed under guidance and control of its organ as well as for an act endorsed by its organ."

50. En l'occurrence, la France n'a pas agi de manière individuelle et autonome. L'ensemble des actes auxquels elle a pris part à ces fins ont été accomplis sous la direction et le contrôle d'organisations internationales—et, au premier chef, de l'OTAN. C'est l'OTAN qui a conçu, décidé et réalisé l'opération militaire qui s'est déroulée sur le territoire yougoslave au printemps 1999. C'est également l'OTAN qui a créé la KFOR et en assure le commandement et le contrôle unifiés, conformément à la résolution 1244 (1999) du Conseil de sécurité, qui, faut-il le rappeler, a autorisé le déploiement de cette force "sous l'égide de l'Organisation des Nations Unies".

51. Consciente de cette difficulté, la République fédérale de Yougoslavie affirme que l'OTAN agit en réalité sous la direction et le contrôle militaires et politiques de ses Etats membres. Cette curieuse conception de la transparence de l'organisation fait évidemment fi de la personnalité juridique internationale qui doit lui être reconnue, conformément aux critères dégagés par votre Cour dans l'avis consultatif relatif à la *Réparation des dommages subis au service des Nations Unies*. ...

52. Ce n'est donc pas à la France, ni aux autres Etats membres de l'OTAN ou à ceux qui participent à la KFOR, que pourraient être attribués les faits allégués, si tant est—ce que je ne crois aucunement—que ces faits soient constitutifs de violations d'obligations internationales. Dès lors, il n'existe pas, dans la présente instance, de différend entre la Serbie et Monténégro et la France dont la Cour puisse connaître.' (Oral Submission made on behalf of France in the *Legality of Use of Force (Serbia and Montenegro v NATO Member States)* case, 20 April 2004, CR/2004/ 12, paras.49–52.) Cf. also the Oral Submissions made on behalf of Portugal in the *Legality of Use of Force (Serbia and Montenegro v NATO Member States)* case, 19 April 2004, CR/2004/9, paras.4.1–4.8; and *ibid*, 22 April 2004, CR/2004/18, paras.4.3, 4.5–4.6. On this case, see also R. Higgins, 'The Responsibility of States Members for the Defaults of International Organizations: Continuing the Dialogue' in S. Schlemmer-Schulte and K. Tung, eds., *Liber Amicorum Ibrahim F.I. Shihata: International Finance and Development Law* (2001), p.442 at p.447.

Based on our detailed analysis above, there are several propositions that emerge relating to this issue of agency in the case. First, there is a clear presumption against the establishment of an agency relationship between NATO and its Member States, assuming that NATO does indeed possess separate legal personality from its Members.[54] Second, in order to rebut this presumption the FRY must prove that both Canada and NATO consented to the establishment of an agency relationship, or, alternatively, that Canada exercised 'effective control' over NATO forces which was outside the confines of Canada's participation in the NATO Council and that NATO consented to this arrangement. Accordingly, in the case of the alternative scenario, the FRY will need to provide evidence of an actual instruction or direction by Canada that is subsequently followed by NATO forces. These elements will likely prove difficult to establish in practice,[55] and as such the presumption against agency will in all probability be maintained if the Court does rule on the issue.

2. Non-member States

The establishment of an agency relationship between an organization and a State does not in theory depend on whether the State in question is a member or not. As established above, there is no 'constitutional' (or built-in) agency that derives from the legal link established between a member State and an organization by its constituent treaty, and as such the position of member State and non-member State would seem identical. However, the ad hoc conferral by a non-member State of powers on an organization by treaty may in practice provide much clearer evidence of express consent to an agency relationship than in the case of a member State where such a separate treaty will be less likely to exist.[56] This has the important consequence that it may in practice be more difficult to establish an agency relationship—in particular to fulfil the consent requirement—in the case of the relationship between one or

---

[54] This, however, may be a contentious issue that will require the International Court, if the cases reach the merits, to determine whether NATO does in fact possess a separate legal personality from its Member States such that the presumption against agency operates. Suffice to note that a number of commentators have regarded NATO as a collective self-defence pact rather than as a regional organization with a separate legal personality. See H. Kelsen, *The Law of the United Nations*, (1951), p.328; B. Simma, ed., *The Charter of the United Nations* (2002, 2nd edn), pp.819, 892, and T. Gazzini, 'NATO Coercive Military Activities in the Yugoslav Crisis (1992–1999)', 12 *EJIL* (2001), p.391 at p.425.

[55] For example, Gazzini, in his descriptive review of NATO military activities in the Yugoslav crisis, states that: 'Throughout the crisis, the NAC [North Atlantic Council] exercised political control—up to August 1995 jointly with the Security Council—and strategic direction over the operations, while the troops were under exclusive NATO command and control. Thus, no military activity was undertaken by NATO forces without a formal decision by the NAC.' (T. Gazzini, 'NATO Coercive Military Activities in the Yugoslav Crisis (1992–1999)', 12 *EJIL* (2001), p.391 at p.415.)

[56] Cf., however, the case of the Peace Treaty between Italy and the UK, US, France, and the Former USSR, which provided for the conferrals of powers on the UN General Assembly: see *supra* n.4 in Chapter 2.

more member States and an organization than in the case where one or more non-member States have conferred powers on an organization. An example of this difficulty being provided by the NATO case set out above.[57]

3. Consequences of the establishment of agency relationships

Where an agency relationship can be established between an international organization and a State, this will have three main consequences. The first is that it makes clear whose legal relations are changed as a consequence of the exercise of conferred powers. Second, it determines the issue of who is responsible for breaches of international law that may occur as a result of the organization's exercise of conferred powers. Finally, it resolves the issue in whose interest should powers be exercised: the State's or the organization's.

(i) An agent can change certain legal relations of its principal

One of the most important consequences of an agency relationship is that an agent when exercising conferred powers can change the principal's legal relations with third parties. But the acts of an agent do not per se change the legal relations between the agent and a third party.[58] As such, where an agency relationship can be established between an organization and one or more States have conferred powers on an organization, then the acts of the organization in the exercise of conferred powers changes only the legal relations of the States in question and not those of the organization. This question of whose legal relations are changed as a consequence of the exercise by an agent of conferred powers is, however, distinct from the question of responsibility for breaches of international law that may occur as a result of the agent's (*in casu*, the organization's) exercise of conferred powers.

(ii) The responsibility of a principal for the acts of its agent

An important consequence of an agency relationship is that the principal is responsible for its agent's acts that are within the scope of conferred powers.[59] Accordingly, where an organization acts[60] as an agent for certain States then

---

[57] See *supra* n.55 and corresponding text.

[58] See Chinkin, *supra* n.3, p.65; and Sereni, *supra* n.10, p.655. This is subject in international law to the third party knowing the identity of the agent: see *supra* n.9 and corresponding text.
For the similar position in domestic law, see Gregory, *supra* n.10, pp.35, 113; in German law see Staubach, *supra* n.29, p.11; and in French law see Guyénot, *supra* n.29, p.181.

[59] As Sereni states: 'The acts performed by the agent within the limits of its authority bind the principal as if they had been personally performed by the latter. When acting within its power, the agent assumes no personal responsibility towards either the principal or the third parties.' (Sereni, *supra* n.10, p.655.) As a general matter, where acts are committed outside the scope of the agent's conferred powers then the principal is not liable for these acts: see Sereni, *ibid.* For the similar position in the domestic law context, see, for example, Reynolds, *supra* n.10, p.1.

[60] On the separate, complex, issue of whose acts can be attributed to an international organization, see Klabbers, *supra* n.7, pp.306–309.

the States concerned are responsible for any unlawful acts committed by the organization in the exercise of conferred powers.[61] This consequence in the case of agency flows, more specifically, from the fact that a State will have consented—either expressly or implicitly—to an organization acting on its behalf.

Moreover, the requirement of consent of an international organization to an agency relationship establishes a general presumption that an organization retains a joint responsibility for any unlawful acts committed.[62] This approach is supported by the fact that, in the case of an agency relationship, an international organization possesses a separate legal personality, and, accordingly, in the absence of an express provision in its constituent treaty to the contrary, the international organization always possesses constitutional control over its actions—even in the case where a State is exercising *de facto* control over the organization—such that the organization could seek to prevent the commission of the unlawful act by issuing an order to override the instruction or other control being exercised by the State. In such a case the failure by the organization to exercise its constitutional control can be said to be an omission that engages a joint responsibility of the organization. Where, however, an organization has in good faith sought to exercise its constitutional control to prevent the commission of an unlawful act but the control by a State over the organization has in any case caused the commission of the act, the argument that an organization possesses a joint, but secondary, responsibility gains greater cogency. This type of situation may even be considered as a type of circumstance precluding wrongfulness on the part of the international organization.[63]

(iii) The fiduciary duty of the agent to act in the interests of its principal

The existence of an agency relationship imposes an obligation on the agent to act in the interests of its principal.[64] As James Crawford has stated in the context of an agency relationship between two States:

The exercise of governmental competence on a basis of agency. It is clear that the exercise of governmental competence by another international person or persons on

---

[61] See C. Amerasinghe in 'Report by Rosalyn Higgins', 66-I *AIDI* (1995), p.353.

[62] The general principle here has been stated by Giorgio Gaja, the ILC Special Rapporteur on the responsibility of international organizations: 'It can certainly be said, as a general principle, that every internationally wrongful act on the part of an international organization entails the international responsibility of that organization.' (G. Gaja, First Report on Responsibility of International Organizations, A/CN.4/532, ILC 56th Session, p.19 (para.35).)

[63] On the differing circumstances precluding wrongfulness in the case of State responsibility, see Chapter V of the ILC Articles on State Responsibility and commentary thereto, contained in Crawford, *supra* n.22, pp.160–190. Cf. V. Lowe, 'Precluding Wrongfulness or Responsibility: A Plea for Excuses', 10 *EJIL* (1999), p.405.

[64] See Sereni, *supra* n.10, p.644. See also in US law, Gregory, *supra* n.10, p.13, and Seavey, *supra* n.10, p.863; in English law see Reynolds, *supra* n.10, p.149 *et seq*, and Fridman, *supra* n.10, p.157 (see also B. Ho, *Hong Kong Agency Law* (1991), p.3); in German law see Staubach, *supra* n.29, p.7; and in French law see Guyénot, *supra* n.29, p.171.

behalf of and by delegation from a State is not inconsistent with formal independence. The foreign affairs and defence powers are quite often so delegated; as are certain economic or technical facilities. *The important element is always that the competence is exercised not independently but in right of the State concerned.*[65]

This fiduciary element of an agency relationship means that where an organization acts as an agent for a State then the organization must exercise conferred powers in the interests of the conferring State. Such a situation may well, however, raise an issue of *vires* for the organization, since it may have its own organizational interest specified by its constituent treaty in pursuance of which it is always bound to act. This *vires* issue may well provide a basis for a member State to claim that the organization is not acting in conformity with an obligation under its constituent treaty to act in the organizational interest. In practice, however, the subjective—and it must be said malleable— nature of an 'organization's interest' is such that it may be difficult to establish that its content is substantially different from that of a conferring State in a particular case.

An identifiable—and practical—consequence of the fiduciary nature of an agency relationship between one or more States and an organization relates to the competence of the organization to sub-confer its powers. Sereni makes the argument cogently in the context of international law when he states:

No principle or rule of international law forbids that the agent be granted the power of appointing a sub-agent for the purpose of the agency. However, the authority of the agent does not necessarily include the power of sub-delegation. This power exists only if it has been granted by the principal.... In international law even more than in any system of national law, the relationship of principal and agent is a fiduciary one. *Since every international transaction includes some element of discretion, the principal ordinarily relies upon the personal qualities of the agent.* It is, then, to be presumed that the subject appointed to perform some functions cannot sub-delegate another subject to fulfill them on behalf of the principal, unless expressly authorized. This presumption applies even when international agency is established in the interest of the principal.[66]

This position is certainly different from that in our next category of 'delegation' where the delegate—*in casu*, the organization—does arguably possess a limited general competence to sub-delegate conferred powers without an express authorization to do so being necessary.[67]

To conclude more generally on our discussion of agency, there are two conditions for the establishment of an agency relationship in international law: first, that the principal and agent are separate legal entities, and, second, that both the principal and agent consent—either expressly of impliedly—to

---

[65] J. Crawford, *The Creation of States in International Law* (1979), p.54. Emphasis added.

[66] Sereni, *supra* n.10, p.653. Emphasis added.

[67] This issue has already been considered at length, see D. Sarooshi, *The United Nations and the Development of Collective Security* (1999), Chapter 1.

the relationship. However, in our case where one or more States confer powers on an organization there is a presumption against the establishment of an agency relationship since the condition of consent is not fulfilled on a prima facie basis. It is only a presumption against agency and not a rule since there are cases where an international organization may possibly act as an agent for a State or group of States. Where such cases of agency can be established then it has the following consequences: the organization in the exercise of conferred powers can change the legal relations of the State in question but does not change its own legal relations; both the State and the organization will in general terms be jointly liable for any unlawful acts committed by the organization; and, finally, the organization is under a fiduciary duty to act in the interests of the State concerned, even though this may raise an issue of *vires* for the organization under its constituent treaty.

5

Delegations of Powers to International Organizations

The category of delegations of powers to an organization is at a point on our spectrum which represents a greater degree of conferrals by States than in the case of agency but which is more limited than in the case of transfers. As such, delegations lie somewhere between transfers and the starting point on our spectrum of an agency position. There are several definitional elements of delegations which illustrate its differing degree of conferral from these other two categories.

The main difference between an agency position and delegations is that in the case of the latter the State does not have the competence to exert direct control over the way in which conferred powers are being exercised by the organization. In this respect, delegations of powers are identical in our typology to the case of transfers.

There are two definitional differences in our typology between delegations and transfers. The first is that delegations of powers are revocable by a State; while in the case of transfers the conferrals will generally be irrevocable.[1] Second, in the case of delegations the State retains for itself the right to exercise the powers concurrent with, and independent of, the organization's exercise of powers; while in the case of transfers the organization has an exclusive competence to exercise the conferred powers. After considering these two elements of delegations, we then turn to examine the consequences that flow from this type of conferrals for the State-organization relationship.

I. THE REVOCABLE NATURE OF DELEGATIONS OF POWERS

It is necessary to start our discussion of revocability with an important caveat: if a State is determined in practice to revoke its conferrals of powers then of course the law is a weak bulwark.[2] We recall from Chapter 3 that this potential difficulty with revocability as an instrument of measurement of the degree of conferrals means that greater emphasis is placed on the second and third characteristics of conferrals when determining our typology of conferrals.[3] This leads to a category of conferrals where, even though they are revocable,

[1] Cf. the exceptional category of cases discussed *infra* nn.3–4 and corresponding text.
[2] For consideration of the policy reasons which militate in general terms against withdrawal by States from a constituent treaty that confers powers on international organizations, see Section II(3) in Chapter 7.   [3] See Section II(1) in Chapter 3.

they are to be characterized as transfers and not as delegations since they strongly exhibit the second and third characteristics of transfers of powers. This category is considered in more detail below in Chapter 6.[4]

However, the issue of revocability does nonetheless provide some measure of the extent to which a conferring State considers that it has given away its powers to an organization. It is very unlikely that a State will ignore entirely the law in the equation of factors that go to make up its decision to revoke its conferral of powers on an organization—which often in practice requires the State to withdraw from the organization—and as such the more difficult it is for the State to reclaim by law its powers then arguably the greater the degree of conferral that a State has initially made to the organization.

The first definitional element of a delegation is that the State has the competence under the instrument of conferral to revoke the conferral of powers at its own discretion. The legal basis of this competence to revoke powers in the case of a delegation is different from that in the case of agency: in the case of agency the competence flows from the nature of the legal relationship;[5] while in the case of delegations it does not flow from the nature of the relationship between States and the organization but must be expressly or implicitly provided for in the instrument of conferrals.

In the case where a treaty expressly provides for revocation of a conferral by, for example, stipulating clearly that a member State has the right to withdraw from the treaty, then revocation would be clearly lawful pursuant to Article 54 of the 1969 Vienna Convention on the Law of Treaties.[6] The constituent treaties of many international organizations do expressly give members a right to withdraw unilaterally, and, to the extent these treaties contain conferrals of powers, they can generally be considered as cases of delegations.[7] The usual limitation on this right is that a notice period is required only after the expiry of which will the withdrawal have legal effect.[8] The shortest such

---

[4] See *infra* nn.14–18 and corresponding text in Chapter 6.

[5] See Section II(3) in Chapter 4.

[6] Article 54 of the Vienna Convention provides, in part, that a State may withdraw from a treaty if there is express provision allowing for withdrawal.

[7] See, for example, the provisions of the constituent treaties of the following international organizations: Food and Agricultural Organization, Article 19; African Union, Article 31.1; Universal Postal Union, Article 12; World Meteorological Organization, Article 30(a); International Labour Organization, Article 1.5; European Bank for Reconstruction and Development, Article 37.2; International Telecommunications Union, Article 57.2; Economic Community of West African States, Article 64; International Civil Aviation Organization, Article 95; International Maritime Organization, Article 73(a); North Atlantic Treaty Organization, Article 13; and Organisation for Economic Co-operation and Development, Article 17 (as cited in H. Schermers and N. Blokker, *International Institutional Law* (2003, 4th edn), p.92 (nn.177–178).)

[8] Consider, for example, the constituent treaties of the following international organizations: Food and Agricultural Organization, Article 19 (12 months); International Civil Aviation Organization, Article 95 (12 months); International Telecommunications Union, Article 57(2) (12 months); International Maritime Organization, Article 73(a) (12 months); Universal Postal Union, Article 12 (12 months); and North Atlantic Treaty Organization, Article 13 (12 months)

notice period is 90 days—contained in the constituent treaties of several of the commodity organizations[9]—while in the cases, for example, of the International Labour Organization and the Organization of American States it is two years.[10] The relatively short duration of these notice periods is such that member States can be considered as having the right to revoke unilaterally their powers and thus these conferrals can be said to fall clearly within the category of delegations. Where, however, the specified notice period is more than say five years, then there is an issue whether these conferrals should be considered as transfers of powers and not delegations, since the duration is such that for all practical purposes it can be considered as being in effect irrevocable. For the purposes of our typology the acceptance by a State in a treaty conferring powers of a five-year notice period for withdrawal does arguably indicate that a State has accepted that it has given away powers to an organization to a much greater degree than in the case where, for example, there was only a one-year notice requirement for withdrawal.

The characterization of conferrals of powers as delegations is even more problematic in the case where there is no express provision allowing for unilateral withdrawal by a State from the treaty. In such cases the issue of lawful unilateral withdrawal—for present purposes the lawful revocability of conferrals of powers—is governed by Article 56(1) of the 1969 Vienna Convention on the Law of Treaties which provides:

A treaty which contains no provision regarding its termination and which does not provide for denunciation or withdrawal is not subject to denunciation or withdrawal unless: (a) it is established that the parties intended to admit the possibility of denunciation or withdrawal; or (b) a right of denunciation or withdrawal may be implied by the nature of the treaty.[11]

Where, accordingly, there is no express withdrawal clause in the treaty conferring powers, then the issue of revocability will depend on the intention of the States parties or, alternatively, on whether the nature of constituent treaties is such that unilateral withdrawal is allowed.[12]

(as cited in Schermers and Blokker, *supra* n.7, p.83 (n.159).) Cf., however, Article XVIII (D) of the Statute of the International Atomic Energy Agency which provides that a Member can 'withdraw from the Agency by notice in writing to that effect given to the depositary Government referred to in paragraph C of article XXI, which shall promptly inform the Board of Governors and all members.'

[9] See the provisions of the constituent treaty of the four commodity organizations contained in Schermers and Blokker, *supra* n.7, p.93 (n.179).

[10] See Schermers and Blokker, *ibid*, n.178.

[11] See also I. Brownlie, *Principles of Public International Law* (2003, 6th edn), p.592, and citations contained therein at n.82; and, for analysis of the International Court's jurisprudence on this presumption, see H. Thirlway, 'The Law and Procedure of the International Court of Justice 1960–1989, Part 4', 63 *BYBIL* (1992), p.1 at pp.63–71.

[12] See more generally on the issue of withdrawal of a member State from an international organization: M. Akehurst, 'Withdrawal from International Organizations', 32 *Current Legal Problems* (1979), p.143; Schermers and Blokker, *supra* n.7, pp.82–94; N. Feinberg, 'Unilateral Withdrawal from an International Organization', 39 *BYBIL* (1963), p.189; J. Klabbers, *An*

The intention of the States parties will have to be ascertained in a particular case using, as Amerasinghe has stated, 'all the tools of interpretation... to determine the real "intention" behind the constitution.'[13] It is not necessary for our present discussion to examine in detail the tools of interpretation that are used to interpret a constituent treaty.[14] If, however, the intention of States parties can be proved in a case so that the presumption in the *chapeau* of Article 56 can be rebutted—so a State does possess the right to withdraw unilaterally from a treaty that confers powers on an organization—then the conferrals of powers should be characterized, according to our typology, as delegations and not as transfers due to their revocability. In the case of a treaty where no definite intention allowing for withdrawal can be established, then the only other possible basis for lawful withdrawal is where the nature of the treaty provides such a right.

The issue of the nature of a treaty being such that it provides a right of unilateral withdrawal was the focus of considerable attention by several of the International Law Commission's (ILC's) Special Rapporteurs on the Law of Treaties.[15] In his Second Report, Sir Humphrey Waldock proposed a Draft Article 17(3) which listed a number of treaties that were, due to their nature, to be terminable on notice. Concerning withdrawal from a constituent treaty, the proposed Draft Article 17(3)(b) provided:

> In the case of a treaty which is the constituent instrument of an international organization, unless the usage of the organization otherwise prescribes, a party shall have the right to withdraw from the treaty and from the organization by giving such notice as the competent organ of the organization, in accordance with its applicable voting procedure, shall decide to be appropriate.[16]

There was, however, disagreement between ILC members over the inclusion of the proposed Article 17 into the ILC Draft Articles[17] and as a result the

Introduction to International Institutional Law (2002), pp.93–94; K. Widdows, 'The Unilateral Denunciation of Treaties Containing No Denunciation Clause', 53 *BYBIL* (1982), p.83; B. Conforti, *The Law and Practice of the United Nations* (2000, 2nd edn), pp.42–43; H. Kelsen, *The Law of the United Nations* (1950), pp.122–135; N. White, *The Law of International Organisations* (1996), pp.62–63; and P. Sands and P. Klein, *Bowett's Law of International Institutions* (2001, 5th edn), pp.546–549.

[13] C.F. Amerasinghe, *Principles of the Institutional Law of International Organizations* (1996), p.121.

[14] On this, see for example: I. Brownlie, *Principles of Public International Law* (2003, 6th edn), pp.657–658; G. Saarbrücken, 'The Interpretation of the Charter' in B. Simma, ed., *The Charter of the United Nations* (2002, 2nd edn), p.25; H. Thirlway, 'The Law and Procedure of the International Court of Justice 1960–1989, Part Eight', 67 *BYBIL* (1996), p.1 at pp.20–31; and C.F. Amerasinghe, *Principles of the Institutional Law of International Organizations* (1996), pp.23–65.

[15] See, in particular, Sir Gerald Fitzmaurice's Second Report, A/CN.4/107, *Yearbook of the International Law Commission*, 1957, vol.2, p.16 *et seq*; and Sir Humphrey Waldock's Second Report, A/CN.4/156, *Yearbook of the International Law Commission*, 1963, vol.2, p.36 at p.63 *et seq*.

[16] Sir Humphrey Waldock's Second Report, A/CN.4/156, *Yearbook of the International Law Commission*, 1963, vol.2, p.36 at p.64.   [17] See Widdows, *supra* n.12, pp.89–90.

final Draft Articles dropped any express reference to the right of States
to be able to withdraw unilaterally from, inter alia, a constituent treaty.[18]
Accordingly, the possible inclusion of constituent treaties within the scope
of Article 56(1)(b) falls to be resolved by reference to the limited State and
organizational practice. The practice on this issue has been considered in some
detail by a number of authoritative commentators and the weight of evidence
clearly seems to indicate that the nature of constituent treaties is such that it
does not allow for unilateral withdrawal by a State.[19] Put differently, there is
nothing special about the nature of constituent treaties that justifies unilateral
withdrawal by a member State in the absence of a withdrawal clause. This
means that constituent treaties without a withdrawal clause are in the same
position as treaties that confer powers on an organization on an ad hoc basis
without an express withdrawal clause: both are subject to the presumption
against unilateral withdrawal contained in the *chapeau* of Article 56 of the
Vienna Convention. This presumption against unilateral revocability means
that there is a presumption in favour of conferrals in such treaties being characterized as transfers of powers and not as delegations.[20] Where, however,
conferrals of powers are revocable then it does satisfy the first definitional
element of delegations. The practical consequence of this revocability is that
it gives a State more options in the case of delegations—as compared to the
case of transfers—when it wishes to take measures against an organization to
change the way a conferred power is being exercised. These measures are
considered in more detail below in Chapter 7.

II. THE STATE'S COMPETENCE TO EXERCISE DELEGATED POWERS CONCURRENTLY WITH THAT OF THE ORGANIZATION

The second definitional element in our category of delegations is that the
State retains the right to exercise conferred powers concurrently with that of

[18] Draft Article 39 of the ILC provided: 'A treaty which contains no provision regarding its termination and which does not provide for denunciation or withdrawal is not subject to denunciation or withdrawal unless it otherwise appears that the parties intended to admit the possibility of denunciation or withdrawal.' (*Yearbook of the International Law Commission*, 1966, vol.I, Part 1, p.122.) This text of course being changed at the Vienna Conference to its final formulation in Article 56 of the 1969 Vienna Convention on the Law of Treaties.
[19] Akehurst, *supra* n.12, p.149; Feinberg, *supra* n.12, p.218; and Widdows, *supra* n.12, p.102.
[20] Cf., however, cases such as the Charter of the United Nations and the Constitution of the World Health Organization where there is no express provision allowing for withdrawal by a State from membership, but where there is evidence that the parties intended to allow for the possibility of withdrawal in exceptional cases thus arguably rebutting the presumption in accordance with Article 56(1)(a) of the 1969 Vienna Convention on the Law of Treaties. In the case of the UN there is an interpretative declaration that was adopted by States parties which although disapproving of withdrawal does allow for the possibility 'because of exceptional circumstances': for the text of this declaration, see Schermers and Blokker, *supra* n.7, p.96. A similar declaration was made by States parties to the constituent treaty of the WHO: for the text of this declaration, see Schermers and Blokker, *ibid.*

the organization.[21] As a general matter, the conferral of powers on an organization does not *ipso facto* mean that a State has limited its own competence to exercise the conferred powers. To the contrary, if a State has not limited its competence to exercise conferred powers, then, applying the *Lotus* case principle,[22] the State can exercise powers on a unilateral basis even while the conferral to the organization remains in force. An example of this is provided by the conferrals by UN Member States of treaty-making powers on the UN:[23] Member States did not restrict their rights to conclude treaties outside the confines of the Organization, and, accordingly, authoritative commentators such as Parry contend that UN Member States still retain their powers to conclude treaties independent of the UN and even in the same areas as the Organization.[24]

There is, however, an important exception to this general approach in the case where a State has consented to be bound—either in its internal legal system or on the international plane—by obligations that flow from the organization's exercise of conferred powers. In such cases the State can be said to have implicitly accepted that it is bound not to do anything outside the framework of the organization that might impinge on the organization's exercise of powers and as such it can be said to have agreed to limit its right to exercise powers in favour of the organization. Put differently, the organization is the sole place for the lawful exercise of conferred powers. This type of case involves transfers of powers and not delegations since the State no longer has the competence to exercise the conferred powers on a unilateral basis.[25]

States have in any case been wary of granting organizations the competence to make decisions that bind them, and have as a result been creative when formulating the way in which powers are to be conferred on international organizations. For example, the World Health Organization, the Universal Postal Union, and the International Civil Aviation Organization are given powers such that an organ of the organization can adopt binding regulations by majority decision, but in such cases the Member States have an express right to contract out of, or make reservations to, the application of a specific regulation to them, usually before it enters into force.[26] In terms of our typology, such conferrals

---

[21] This can be contrasted with the case of a transfer of power where the organization is the sole place for the lawful exercise of the power. See Section II in Chapter 6.

[22] As the Permanent Court of International Justice held in its famous passage in the *Lotus* case: 'Restrictions upon the independence of States cannot therefore be presumed.' (*PCIJ Reports*, Series A, No.10, p.4 at p.18).

[23] The UN has both express powers to conclude treaties and an implied power. For detailed consideration of both these types of powers, see C. Parry, 'The Treaty-Making Power of the United Nations', 26 *BYBIL* (1949), p.108.   [24] Parry, *ibid*, pp.121, 129, 142–145.

[25] See Section II in Chapter 6.

[26] See, for example, A. Chayes and A. Chayes, *The New Sovereignty: Compliance with International Regulatory Agreements* (1995), pp.226–227; F. Kirgis, 'Aviation' in O. Schachter and C. Joyner, eds., *United Nations Legal Order*, vol.2, (1995), p.825 at pp.826–827, 831–832; and T. Buergenthal, *Law-Making in the International Civil Aviation Organization* (1969).

are delegations and not transfers, since it is not the exercise of powers per se that automatically binds the member States, but the State's subsequent acceptance of the decision on the international plane that confers binding force on the organ's exercise of powers. In such cases it is clear that member States could decide to contract out of the potential obligation and then be free to pursue its own approach to the particular issue outside of the confines of the organization.[27]

The case of the UN Human Rights Committee (HRC) is arguably a case of delegations by States of powers. The HRC—technically a UN treaty organ, established by the 1966 International Covenant on Civil and Political Rights ('ICCPR')[28]—has been given the competence to hear reports that must be submitted by States parties (pursuant to Article 40) on their implementation of ICCPR obligations as well as the competence to hear individual complaints brought by persons claiming a violation of their rights against those States that have ratified the First Optional Protocol to the ICCPR.[29] But in both types of cases any decisions by the HRC are not binding on States parties.[30] This represents a good example of a situation where States will allow the contestation of sovereign values (*in casu*, human rights) within the context of an international body, but will not allow the outcome of this process to be binding.

However, even where States intend only to delegate and not transfer powers to an organization the ability to maintain this distinction in practice once the conferral has taken place will often prove difficult. This will particularly be the case where the organization has been given the competence to render binding obligations for the conferring States in one or more areas but not in others: in other words, where States have both transferred and delegated powers to an organization.[31] The practice of international organizations in such cases has often been to expand the scope of their 'transferred' powers and thereby encroach into areas that were originally intended to have involved an exercise by the organization only of 'delegated' powers. It is in this way that conferrals of powers on an organization will often be moved by an organization from the category of delegations into that of transfers. A good example here is the case of the European Community where subsequent judicial decisions by the

---

[27] Cf., however, Kirgis who contends in the case of ICAO that Member States cannot opt out of certain ICAO rules, in particular those relating to navigation over the high seas and other ocean areas where freedom of overflight prevails: F. Kirgis, 'Aviation' in O. Schachter and C. Joyner, eds., *United Nations Legal Order*, vol.2, (1995), p.825 at p.854.

[28] D. Sarooshi, 'The Legal Framework Governing United Nations Subsidiary Organs', 67 *BYIL* (1996), p.413 at p.433 (n.84).

[29] This is subject to the pre-conditions set out in the First Optional Protocol: for the text of the First Protocol, see I. Brownlie and G. Goodwin-Gill, *Basic Documents on Human Rights* (2002, 4th edn), Document 29, p.199.

[30] D. McGoldrick, *The Human Rights Committee* (1991), p.151; and L. Helfer and A-M. Slaughter, 'Toward a Theory of Effective Supranational Adjudication', 107 *Yale Law Journal* (1997–1998), p.273 at p.351.   [31] See Section I in Chapter 3.

European Court of Justice and acquiescence by EC Members to these decisions have led to a 'mutation' in the nature of certain powers[32] as well as their type of conferral.[33] These mutations are not problematic where they take place with the unanimous consent, tacit or express, of the States that have conferred the powers. The difficulty arises, however, where there is opposition by an individual member State or dissenting group of member States to the decision of an organ of the organization that purports to change the nature of the conferrals of powers. The question that arises in such a case is whether a dissenting State could purport to withdraw from the treaty providing for conferrals of powers on the basis that the mutation of a delegation into a transfer represents a fundamental change of circumstances (*rebus sic stantibus*) within the scope of Article 62(1)(b) of the 1969 Vienna Convention on the Law of Treaties.[34]

The International Court of Justice in the *Fisheries Jurisdiction* case has authoritatively stated in relation to Article 62(1)(b) that:

in order that a change of circumstances may give rise to a ground for invoking the termination of a treaty it is also necessary that it should have resulted in a radical transformation of the extent of the obligations still to be performed. The change must have increased the burden of the obligations to be executed to the extent of rendering the performance something essentially different from that originally undertaken.[35]

---

[32] In the early ECJ case of *Costa v ENEL*, Advocate-General Lagrange stated in the case: 'Community regulations, even the most important ones, are not legislative measures nor even, as is sometimes said, "quasi-legislative measures" but rather measures emanating from an *executive power* (Council or Commission) which can only act within the framework of the powers delegated to it by the Treaty and within the jurisdictional control of the Court of Justice.' (Opinion of Advocate-General Lagrange in *Costa v ENEL, ECR* 1964, p.600 at pp.604–605.) However, 14 years later in the case of *Amministrazione delle Finanze dello Stato v Simmenthal S.p.A*, the European Court of Justice clearly spoke in terms of the exercise by the Community of 'its legislative power'. (*Amministrazione delle Finanze dello Stato v Simmenthal S.p.A, ECR* 1978, p.629 at p.643.) This 'legislative power' of the Community is now well-accepted by EC Member States. See, for example, the decision of the House of Lords in the case of *Factortame Ltd and others v Secretary of State for Transport (No. 2)*, [1991] 1 *All ER*, p.70 at pp.106–107 (per Lord Bridge).

[33] Consider, for example, the evolution of the EC's exclusive competence, *vis-à-vis* its Member States, to conclude treaties in certain areas: see, for example, J. Weiler, *The Constitution of Europe* (1999), p.53 *et seq*; and C. Shachor-Landau, 'The International Legal Personality of the EEC and its Treaty-Making Power', 20 *Israel Law Review* (1985), p.341 at pp.359–360.

[34] Article 62(1)(b) provides the following: 'A fundamental change of circumstances which has occurred with regard to those existing at the time of conclusion of a treaty, and which was not foreseen by the parties, may not be invoked as a ground for terminating or withdrawing from the treaty unless: . . . (b) the effect of the change is radically to transform the extent of obligations still to be performed under the treaty.' The Court in the *Fisheries Jurisdiction* case held that: 'Article 62 of the Vienna Convention on the Law of Treaties, . . . may in many respects be considered as a codification of existing customary law on the subject of the termination of a treaty relationship on account of change of circumstances'. (*Fisheries Jurisdiction* case, *ICJ Reports*, 1973, p.3 at p.63.) On the application of Article 62 to the UN Charter—ie concerning the relations between the UN and its Member States—see E. Zoller, 'The "Corporate Will" of the United Nations and the Rights of the Minority', 81 *AJIL* (1987), p.610 at pp.626–629.

[35] *Fisheries Jurisdiction* case, *I.C.J. Reports*, 1973, p.3 at p.21.

Based on this view, the change by an organization of a delegation of powers into a transfer can be characterised as a 'fundamental change of circumstance' under Article 62(1)(b), since, in the case of a transfer, States are now bound by decisions of the organization in the exercise of the conferred powers while in the previous case of a delegation the State was not so bound and could even have exercised the powers in a way that was contrary to the organization's exercise of powers. It is this radical transformation of the nature of the obligation in such cases that will in general terms[36] provide a dissenting State with a legal basis to withdraw from the treaty conferring powers.[37]

Let us now turn to examine the consequences of conferrals being characterized as delegations for the relationship between delegating States and the organization.

III. CONSEQUENCES OF DELEGATIONS OF POWERS FOR THE STATE-ORGANIZATION RELATIONSHIP

There are two main consequences that flow from the characterization of particular conferrals of powers as being delegations. The first relates to fiduciary issues between delegating States and an organization; while the second relates to issues of responsibility of the member States and the organization.

1. Fiduciary issues

The rather obvious consequence of States not being bound by the organization's exercise of delegated powers is that States are free to accept obligations flowing from their individual exercise of powers. The only entity whose legal relations are changed as a result of the exercise of delegated powers is the organization's. To put this differently, the organization exercises delegated powers to achieve its organizational interest and does not act on behalf of delegating States in the exercise of delegated powers. The organization does not owe any fiduciary duties to its member States. This is in stark contrast to the case of an agency relationship between States and an organization, set out in Chapter 4,[38] and also to the case of transfers of powers, considered in Chapter 6,

---

[36] There are however additional legal conditions that must be fulfilled before a State can rely successfully on a fundamental change of circumstances to withdraw from a treaty. As the International Court in the *Gabcíkovo-Nagymaros Project (Hungary v Slovakia)* case stated: 'A fundamental change of circumstances must have been unforeseen; the existence of the circumstances at the time of the Treaty's conclusion must have constituted an essential basis of the consent of the parties to be bound by the Treaty.' (*Gabcíkovo-Nagymaros Project (Hungary v Slovakia)* case, *ICJ Reports*, 1997, p.7 at p.65.)

[37] Such a competence has already been expressly recognized in the case of formal amendment in the constituent treaties of a number of international organizations such as, for example, Article XVIII(D) of the IAEA Statute (available from IAEA web-site at http://www.iaea.org/) and implicitly in the *travaux préparatoires* of the UN Charter (for the text of this *travaux*, see Schermers and Blokker, *supra* n.7, p.96). [38] See Section III(3)(iii) in Chapter 4.

where it is arguably the State that owes the fiduciary duty towards the organization.[39]

2. Issues of responsibility

In the case where an international organization commits an internationally wrongful act it seems clear that this entails the international responsibility of the organization.[40] The remaining question is whether such an act can be attributed to a State that has delegated powers to an organization thereby establishing a State's primary responsibility under international law. In the case of agency relationships, considered above in Chapter 4, the issue of responsibility was clear: the control exercised by States over an organization meant that its acts were attributable to States.[41] In cases of delegations, however, such control does not exist and, applying by analogy the International Law Commission's (ILC's) Articles on State Responsibility, there would seem to be no other possible bases for attribution of an organization's wrongful acts to delegating States. But this only relates to the issue of State responsibility for an organization's acts. There are three other circumstances where a State can be held responsible in connection with an internationally wrongful act by an organization that exercises delegated powers. In all three cases the responsibility of the State does not flow from its relationship with the organization to which it has delegated powers, but from its own acts or omissions.

We recall that in the case of delegations a State is not bound by the organization's exercise of delegated powers. Where, accordingly, a State chooses to participate in, or implement domestically, an internationally wrongful act committed by an international organization exercising delegated powers then the State will be held responsible on a primary basis for its own commission of an internationally wrongful act pursuant to Article 1 of the ILC's Articles on State Responsibility.[42] The State cannot seek to escape responsibility for its own acts in such cases by hiding behind the non-binding decision of an organization in the case of delegations of powers. The second case where a State's responsibility can be engaged in relation to the exercise by an organization of delegated powers is where a State aids or assists the organization in the commission of an internationally wrongful act. This responsibility flows from the application, *mutatis mutandis*, of Article 16 of the ILC's Articles on State Responsibility, which provides that:

A State which aids or assists another State in the commission of an internationally wrongful act by the latter is internationally responsible for doing so if: (a) that State

---

[39] See Section III(1) in Chapter 6.
[40] See G. Gaja, First Report on Responsibility of International Organizations, A/CN.4/532, ILC 56th Session, p.19 (para.35).   [41] See Section III(3)(ii) in Chapter 4.
[42] Article 1 provides that 'Every internationally wrongful act of a State entails the international responsibility of that State.' (J. Crawford, *The International Law Commission's Articles on State Responsibility: Introduction, Text and Commentaries* (2002), p.77.)

does so with knowledge of the circumstances of the internationally wrongful act; and (b) the act would be internationally wrongful if committed by that State.[43]

If these conditions in (a) and (b) are met in a case, then a State would be held responsible for its act of rendering aid or assistance to an organization in its commission of an internationally wrongful act. The non-binding nature of the decisions of an organization exercising delegated powers means that any such aid or assistance given by a State to an organization is entirely voluntary and as such is caught by Article 16.[44]

The discussion above has focused on the issue of the primary responsibility of States, but this does not exclude the possibility of a secondary responsibility of States that may arise from an organization's exercise of delegated powers. This secondary responsibility is arguably engaged where States actively pursue or support within the international organization the decision that causes the commission of the internationally wrongful act. It is even arguable that States should take action within the organization—for example, voting against a decision—to try and ensure that the organization does not commit an internationally wrongful act, and that the failure to do so may engage a secondary responsibility of the State for the act of the organization.[45] This rule of secondary responsibility is necessary, arguably, in order to ensure the systemic integrity of international law.[46] Otherwise it would be a simple matter for States to avoid their obligations under international law by establishing an international organization to which they delegate powers and then to disclaim all responsibility for the way in which those powers are exercised within the organization.

---

[43] Contained in Crawford, *ibid*, p.148.

[44] On the importance of the voluntary nature of acts for application of Article 16, see Crawford, *ibid*. On Article 16 more generally, see V. Lowe, 'Responsibility for the Conduct of Other States', *Japanese Journal of International Law* (2002), p.1.

[45] Cf. Jan Klabbers who suggests a different, though related, basis of liability when he states: 'if the member-states fail to exercise proper control over the acts of the organization, then they may be held responsible for negligence.' (Klabbers, *supra* n.12, p.302.)

[46] In support of this type of approach, the US Supreme Court in *First National City Bank v Banco Para El Comercio Exterior De Cuba* found that governments cannot 'avoid the requirements of international law simply by creating juridical entities [and thereby delegating certain powers to them] whenever the need arises.' (*First National City Bank v Banco Para El Comercio Exterior De Cuba*, 462 *U.S.*, p.611 at p.633.) See also, in support, I. Brownlie, 'State Responsibility: The Problem of Delegation' in K. Ginther, G. Hafner, W. Lang, H. Neuhold and L. Sucharipa-Behrmann, eds., *Völkerrecht zwischen normativem anspruch und politischer Realität* (1994), p.299 at pp.300–301.

6

Transfers of Powers to International Organizations

An important element of the thesis being advanced in this work is that the greater the degree of conferrals by States of powers on international organizations the more demand there is from domestic arms of governments to be able to engage in the processes of contestation of sovereign powers within organizations in order to maintain, to the extent these arms of government deem necessary, *their* conceptions of sovereignty's constituent values.[1] This is well illustrated by a number of instances of transfers of powers to organizations— including, notably, the cases of European Communities ('EC') and the World Trade Organization ('WTO')—which are considered below.[2]

This demand leads, however, to difficulty since, as we shall see, the greater the degree of conferrals by States of sovereign powers on organizations the less are member States able to exercise direct control over organizations in the exercise of these powers. We recall from Chapter 3 that important features of transfers of powers are that they are generally irrevocable, States cannot exercise direct control over the organization, and States consent to be bound by the decisions of an organization. The reason why the term transfer has been chosen to describe this present category of conferrals is that the constitutions of a number of States provide in express terms for their governments being able to 'transfer' sovereign powers to international organizations,[3] and the type

---

[1] See *supra* nn.11–15 and corresponding text in Chapter 3.

[2] This chapter focuses in more detail on the transfers of powers to the WTO, since this reflects the reality that the majority of transfers are in practice 'partial transfers' as in the case of the WTO and not 'full transfers' as in the case of the EC. On the differences between these two categories of transfers of powers, see *infra* Section II.

[3] Consider, for example, the position in the following States: Article 24 of the German Constitution provides that '(1) The Federation may by legislation transfer sovereign powers to intergovernmental institutions. (2) For the maintenance of peace, the Federation may join a system of mutual collective security; in doing so it will consent to such limitations upon its rights of sovereignty as will bring about and secure a peaceful and lasting order in Europe and among the nations of the world.'; Article 92 of the Constitution of the Netherlands provides, 'Legislative, executive and judicial powers may be conferred on international institutions by or pursuant to a treaty, subject, where necessary, to the provisions of Article 91, paragraph 3 [the requirement that treaties which conflict with the Constitution must be approved by a two-thirds majority vote in the Parliament].' For the antecedent provision of this article see: J. Van Panhuys, 'The Netherlands Constitution and International Law', 58 *AJIL* (1964), p.88 at pp.98–99; Article 11 of the Italian Constitution provides for a transfer of sovereign powers to international organizations. The Italian Constitutional Court has interpreted this provision in the case of *Frontini v Ministro delle Finanze* to find that the transfer of law-making powers to the EC was consistent with the authorization under Article 11 to transfer sovereign powers to international organizations, since the Treaty provides sufficient guarantees of due process and because the

of conferrals envisaged by such transfers corresponds well to the definitional elements of the term as it is used in our analysis.

Let us now turn to examine in more detail the characteristics of the category of transfers of powers before turning to consider examples of transfers and the important implications they have had for the contestation of sovereignty's constituent values both within international organizations and on the domestic plane.

I. THE IRREVOCABLE NATURE OF TRANSFERS OF POWERS

The irrevocability of transfers of powers allows them, in general,[4] to be clearly distinguished from cases of delegations of powers which are revocable by the State at any time. In the case where a treaty confers powers but does not specify whether a State can withdraw from the treaty on a unilateral basis, there is a rebuttable presumption, as already explained in Chapter 5, which says that these conferrals are irrevocable and can thus be characterized as transfers.[5] In the case, for example, of the EC where there is no express provision for withdrawal contained in the EC Treaty, this has certainly been the approach

Italian State participates in the formulation of Community acts. (Judgment No.183 of Dec.27, 1973, 39 Rac. uff. 503 (1973), 1973 Giur. cost. 2401. See also A. La Pergola and P. Del Duca, 'Community Law, International Law and the Italian Constitution', 79 *AJIL* (1985), p.598 at p.610); In the case of France, the decision of the *Conseil Constitutionnel* found that the 'transfer of powers' in the Maastricht Treaty was compatible with the French Constitution. (Case 92–308 (1992), *Journal Officiel de la République Française (J.O.R.F.)* 5354. For comment, see P. Oliver, 'The French Constitution and the Treaty of Maastricht', 43 *ICLQ* (1994), p.1 at pp.11–12; and A. Pellet, 'A French Constitutional Perspective on Treaty Implementation' in T. Franck, ed., *Delegating State Powers: The Effect of Treaty Regimes on Democracy and Sovereignty* (2000), p.281). See also, for example, the provisions of the following constitutions which authorize the transfer of sovereign powers to international organizations: Article 25 *Bis* of the Belgian Constitution of 7 February 1831 (as amended in 1988); Article 93 of the Spanish Constitution of 29 December 1978; Section 20 of the Danish Constitution of 5 June 1953 (on this provision see P. Germer, 'European influences on the national administrative laws from the point of view of the Member States: Danish Report' in J. Schwarze, ed., *Administrative Law under European Influence: on the convergence of the administrative laws of the EU Member States* (1996), p.377 at pp.403–404); Article 28 of the Greek Constitution of 7 June 1975; Articles 9(2), 23(a)–(f) in the case of the Austrian Federal Constitution 2000 (on these provisions see C. Grabenwarter, 'The Austrian Federal Constitution and Peace between States', 51 *ZöR* (1996), p.61 at pp.76–81; and I. Seidl-Hohenveldern, 'Constitutional Problems involved in Austria's Accession to the EU', 32 *CMLR* (1995), p.727); and for a useful summary in the cases of Bulgaria, Hungary, Czech Republic, Poland, Russia, and Romania, see E. Salzberger and S. Voigt, 'Economic Analysis of Constitutional Law: On Constitutional Processes and the Delegation of Power, with Special Emphasis on Israel and Central and Eastern Europe', 3 *Theoretical Inq. L* (2002), p.207 at pp.253–257. Moreover, the UK Government has stated in a public document: '. . . EC organs such as the European Commission have governmental powers that derive from a limitation of sovereignty and transfer of powers by member States.' ('State responsibility: comments and observations received from governments', A/CN.4/488, 25 March 1998, p.40.)

[4] Cf. the important exceptional category of conferrals of powers which although being revocable can still be characterized as transfers: see *supra* nn.8–9 and corresponding text in Chapter 3.

[5] See *supra* nn.19–20 and corresponding text in Chapter 5.

adopted by the European Court of Justice ('ECJ') in a long line of cases where it has consistently held that conferrals by Member States of powers on the EC are irrevocable.[6] In, for example, its landmark decision in *Costa v ENEL*, the ECJ stated:

By creating a Community of unlimited duration, having its own institutions, its own personality, its own legal capacity and capacity of representation on the international plane and, more particularly, real powers stemming from a limitation of sovereignty or a transfer of powers from the States to the Community, the Member States have limited their sovereign rights, albeit within limited fields, and have thus created a body of law which binds both their nationals and themselves. . . . The transfer by the States from their domestic legal system to the Community legal system of the rights and obligations arising under the Treaty carries with it a permanent limitation of their sovereign rights, against which a subsequent unilateral act incompatible with the concept of the Community cannot prevail.[7]

But this formal legal position does not necessarily give an accurate picture of what States[8]—or their arms of government—consider is, or should be, the actual position on this issue.[9] It was the Constitutional Court of the Federal Republic of Germany (the Bundesverfassungsgericht: 'BVG') that insisted in

---

[6] For commentators who contend that EC Member States cannot withdraw unilaterally from the Treaty, see, for example, J.H.H. Weiler, 'Alternatives to withdrawal from an international organization: the case of the European Economic Community', 20 *Israel Law Review* (1985), p.282 at pp.284–287; M. Akehurst, 'Withdrawal from International Organizations', 32 *Current Legal Problems* (1979), p.143 at pp.150–152; J. Usher, *European Community Law and National Law—The Irreversible Transfer* (1981); and I. Macleod, I. Hendry, and S. Hyett, *The External Relations of the European Communities* (1996), p.40.

[7] *Costa v ENEL*, ECR 1964, p.585 at pp.593–594. See also on this point: *Commission of the European Communities v The French Republic*, 48 *ILR* p.217 at p.222; and *Commission of the European Communities v Italian Republic*, ECR 1972, p.527 at p.532.

[8] Cf., of course, the decision by Greenland (not formally a member, but a Danish dependent territory) to leave the EC following a referendum in 1982. See F. Weiss, 'Greenland's withdrawal from the European Communities', 10 *European Law Review* (1985), p.173; and R. Friel, 'Providing a Constitutional Framework for Withdrawal from the EU: Article 59 of the Draft European Constitution', 53(2) *ICLQ* (2004), p.407 at p.409 *et seq*.

[9] Consider, for example, the debates within the UK and France concerning their membership in the EC. The UK Government in a report presented to Parliament in 1975 took the view that 'Parliament by the European Communities Act 1972 authorised the application in this country of directly applicable Community law and to that extent has delegated its powers. Parliament has however the undoubted power to repeal that Act, on which our ability to fulfil our Treaty obligations still depends. Thus our membership of the Community in the future depends on the continuing assent of Parliament.' (*Membership of the European Community: Report on Renegotiation, Presented to Parliament by the Prime Minister by Command of Her Majesty, March 1975*, Cmnd. 6003, p.39. See also the statement by Lord Mackay: *H.L. Hansard*, Vol.573, cols.1450–1451, 3 July 1996.) A similar approach was taken to the continued membership of France in the EC by the French Minister of Justice when trying to guide the Constitutional *loi* Bill concerning French ratification of the Treaty on European Union through the French National Assembly. (National Assembly, *Rapport au nom de la commission des lois constitutionnelles, de la législation et de l'administration générale de la Republique sur le projet de loi constitutionnelles* (No.2623) *ajoutant à la Constitution un titre*: 'De l'Union européenne', No.2676, registered 4 May 1992, p.42.)

its decision in the *Maastricht* case[10] that Member States do have the right to withdraw unilaterally from the Community. The Court stated:

The Federal Republic of Germany...remains, even after the entry into force of the Union Treaty, a member of a union of States whose Community authority derives from the Member States and can have binding effect on German sovereign territory only by virtue of the German implementing order. Germany is one of the 'masters of the Treaties', who have based their commitment to be bound by the Union Treaty, which is concluded 'for an unlimited period' (Article Q of the EUT), on their intention to remain in long-term membership, but who could equally, in the final analysis, revoke that membership by adopting an act with the opposite effect. The validity and application of European law in Germany depend on the implementing order contained in the Law Approving the Treaty. Germany thus retains the quality of a sovereign State in its own right and the status of sovereign equality with other States within the meaning of Article 2(1) of the Charter of the United Nations. . . .[11]

This represents nothing less than a direct challenge to the ECJ's decision in *Costa v ENEL*.[12] And yet the BVG's decision resonated with other Member States, thus having far-reaching consequences. Most importantly, in its current draft form the Treaty establishing a Constitution for Europe now actually provides in Article 59(1) that '1. Any Member State may decide to withdraw from the European Union in accordance with its own constitutional requirements.'[13]

The example of the European Union only serves to underline the point made in Chapter 3 that the revocability of conferrals of powers is not always a precise measure of the extent to which States consider that they have given away their powers to an organization. We recall from Chapter 3 that there is an exceptional category of conferrals of powers which although being revocable should be characterized as transfers since the conferring States have no direct control over the organization's exercise of powers (our second indicia of the extent to which States have given away powers to an organization)[14] and,

[10] *Maastricht* case, 89 *BverfGE* 155, paras.439 as translated and contained in A. Oppenheimer, ed., *The Relationship between European Community Law and National Law: The Cases* (1994), p.526. On this case, see J. Frowein, 'Das *Maastricht*—Urteil und die Grenzen der Verfassungsgerichtsbarkeit' ('The *Maastricht* Judgment and the Limits of Constitutional Jurisdiction'), 54 *ZaöRV* (1994), p.1; D. König, 'Das Urteil des Bundesverfassungsgerichts zum Vertrag von Maastricht—ein Stolperstein auf dem Weg in die europäische Integration?' ('The Judgment of the Bundesverfassungsgerichts (Federal Constitutional Court) on the Maastricht Treaty—An Obstacle On the Way to European Integration?'), 54 *ZaöRV* (1994), p.17; J.H.H. Weiler, 'Demos, Telos and the German *Maastricht* Decision', Harvard Jean Monnet Working Paper No.6/95, http://www.law.harvard.edu/programs/JeanMonnet/papers/95/9506ind. html; G. Nolte, 'Constitutional Implications of German Participation in Treaty Regimes' in T. Franck, ed., *Delegating State Powers: The Effect of Treaty Regimes on Democracy and Sovereignty* (2000), p.261 at p.268; and H. Hahn, 'La Cour Constitutionnelle Federale D'Allemagne et le Traite de Maastricht', 98 *Revue Générale de Droit International Public* (1994), p.107.

[11] *Maastricht* case, 89 *BverfGE* 155, paras.439 as translated and contained in A. Oppenheimer, ed., *The Relationship between European Community Law and National Law: The Cases* (1994), p.526 at pp.557–558.   [12] See *supra* n.7 and corresponding text.

[13] *Draft Treaty establishing a Constitution for Europe*, as submitted to the President of the European Council in Rome on 18 July 2003, CONV 850/03.

[14] See *supra* nn.8–9 and corresponding text in Chapter 3.

moreover, the organization possesses the sole right to exercise conferred powers (our third indicia).[15] A good example of this exception is provided in the case of transfers by States of powers to the dispute settlement organs of the WTO. Article XV of the Marrakesh Agreement, which established the WTO as an international organization, provides that a Member State can withdraw unilaterally from the WTO.[16] However, it is clear that the type of conferrals of powers envisaged by the WTO Dispute Settlement Understanding (which established the WTO dispute settlement system)[17] is such that decisions of the WTO Dispute Settlement Body (and the Panel and Appellate Body reports they adopt) are binding on WTO Member States in the particular dispute at hand and that Member States have no direct control over these decisions.[18] It is these two characteristics of the conferrals in the case of the WTO dispute settlement system which militate strongly in favour of these conferrals being characterized as transfers on our spectrum and not as delegations.

II. A STATE'S CONSENT TO BE BOUND BY OBLIGATIONS THAT FLOW FROM AN ORGANIZATION'S EXERCISE OF CONFERRED POWERS: 'PARTIAL TRANSFERS' AND 'FULL TRANSFERS' OF POWERS

The State that transfers powers to an international organization does not confer its powers *in toto* on the organization. It retains the powers as part of its sovereignty, but has agreed to limit its right to exercise these powers in favour of an exclusive right of the organization to exercise the conferred powers. Put differently, the organization is the sole place for the lawful exercise of transferred powers. But it is particularly difficult to measure the precise degree to which States have given away their powers in the case of transfers. It is for this reason that there is a need to distinguish between 'partial transfers' and 'full transfers'. The difference between these two sub-categories depends on the extent to which States can be said to have consented to be bound by obligations that flow from an organization's exercise of conferred powers.

---

[15] See Section II(2) in Chapter 3.

[16] Article XV provides that 'Any Member may withdraw from this Agreement. Such withdrawal shall apply both to this Agreement and the Multilateral Trade Agreements and shall take effect upon the expiration of six months from the date on which written notice of withdrawal is received by the Director-General of the WTO.' (Contained in WTO, *The Legal Texts: The Results of the Uruguay Round of Multilateral Trade Negotiations* (1999), p.4 at p.13.)

[17] For the text of the Dispute Settlement Understanding, see WTO, *The Legal Texts: The Results of the Uruguay Round of Multilateral Trade Negotiations* (1999), p.354.

[18] On the binding nature of WTO Panel and Appellate Body Reports in a particular case, see the following articles of the WTO Dispute Settlement Understanding: Articles 21(1), 22(1), 22(8), and 26(1)(b) (Dispute Settlement Understanding, Annex 2 to the WTO Agreement, *ibid*, pp.368, 370, 372, 374). See also the authoritative article by J. Jackson, 'The WTO Dispute Settlement Understanding—Misunderstandings on the Nature of Legal Obligation', 91 *AJIL* (1997), p.60.

In the case of 'partial transfers', a State agrees to be bound by obligations that flow from the organization's exercise of powers on the international plane. An example of a partial transfer is provided by the case of the WTO dispute settlement system where States have consented to be bound on the international plane by decisions of the WTO panels and Appellate Body in a case.[19]

In the case of 'full transfers', however, the State has also agreed to give direct effect within its domestic legal order to the obligations that flow from the organization's exercise of powers such that they can be relied on by persons within the State without the need for separate domestic legislation.[20] The best, and most obvious, instance of a 'full transfer' is the case of the EC where, for example, EC Council Regulations have direct effect within the legal systems of Member States[21] and will, in the view of the ECJ, prevail over all domestic law sources.[22]

The important issue that arises in both sub-categories of transfers is what role, if any, do individual States that have conferred powers and their various organs of government play in the exercise of powers by the organization. The formal legal position may appear to be clear and can be summarized as follows.

The State that has transferred powers cannot purport unilaterally either to seek to adopt its own authoritative interpretation of the scope of the powers it has transferred to the organization or to judge with binding authority whether the organization was acting *ultra vires* when exercising transferred powers. The technical reason for this is that where States have by treaty accepted the obligation to be bound by the organization's exercised of conferred powers then it is for the organization and not a single State to render an authoritative interpretation of the scope and use of the transferred power and any obligations that flow therefrom. The very purpose of such a treaty is to remove the locus of decision-making concerning the exercise of a power from the State and to place it in the hands of the organization. In some cases the position is made even clearer by the treaty when it designates a particular organ as having the competence to render an

---

[19] On the binding nature of WTO Panel and Appellate Body Reports in a particular case, see the following articles of the WTO Dispute Settlement Understanding: Articles 21(1), 22(1), 22(8), and 26(1)(b) (Dispute Settlement Understanding, Annex 2 to the WTO Agreement, *ibid*, pp.368, 370, 372, 374). See also the authoritative article by J. Jackson, 'The WTO Dispute Settlement Understanding—Misunderstandings on the Nature of Legal Obligation', 91 *AJIL* (1997), p.60.

[20] There has in fact been a long-standing practice of States conferring powers of binding decision on an international organization, even where that decision directly binds individuals within a State. For a good description of the early practice, see P. Jessup, *A Modern Law of Nations* (1968), pp.18–19.

[21] See, for example, *Van Gend en Loos v Nederlandse administratie der belastingen*, [1963] *ECR*, p.1 at p.12.

[22] See, for example, *Costa v ENEL*, [1964] *ECR*, p.585 at p.594; and *Amministrazione delle Finanze dello Stato v Simmenthal S.p.A*, *ECR* 1978, p.629 at p.643.

authoritative interpretation of the provisions of the constituent treaty and the content of obligations of member States. In the case, for example, of the EC Treaty it is the ECJ that has been given such a power of authoritative interpretation.[23] This position does not of course prohibit the States that have transferred powers deciding collectively to amend the terms of the treaty by formal amendment or other authoritative decision in order to change the scope or use of the transferred power to reflect an interpretation different from that being held previously by the organization. However, *stricto sensu*, until this can be achieved it is the interpretation of the organization that will prevail.

But it is precisely this type of formalistic legal analysis which gives international lawyers a reputation for being out of touch with the important implications of the exercise by international organizations of sovereign powers.

In practice the effective implementation within a State of an organization's decision will require, even in the case of fully transferred powers, the implicit consent of all three arms of government. The legislature and judiciary in particular will have to accept and apply—or, more accurately in some cases, not block—the decisions of the organization that fall within their respective spheres of competence. This consent to 'full transfers' is not a one-off. It will be tested—and reaffirmed—each time that an organ of government disagrees with a particular decision by the organization but decides nonetheless to go along with the decision. This provides a hitherto unrecognized source of legitimacy for international organizations exercising transferred powers, but it also of course allows the arms of domestic government to control the manner and extent of application of the organization's decisions within their domestic legal systems.

At a more fundamental level, what is at stake in the case of transferred powers is not simply the formulation and application of some technical rule or standard by an international organization but the exercise of sovereign powers of government which in order to be *sovereign in nature* must be exercised, we recall from Chapter 1, according to sovereign values that are an integral part of their exercise whether on the domestic or international plane.[24] We also recall from Chapter 1 that these sovereign values play an important part in the process of a society deciding who it considers itself to be—and inextricably linked to this issue—how it should be governed. It should thus come as no surprise that the domestic arms of government will contest the exercise by international organizations of conferred sovereign powers, especially where they consider that powers are being exercised in a manner that compromises their sovereign values. An easily identifiable place where these sovereign values of States are manifested is in their constitutions.

---

[23] See, for example, *Foto-Frost v Hauptzollamt Lübeck-Ost*, 1987 *ECR*, p.4199 at pp.4230–4232.   [24] See Section I(4) in Chapter 1.

Joseph Weiler eloquently makes the point when he states:

Our national constitutions are perceived by us as doing more than simply structuring the respective powers of government and the relationships between public authority and individuals or between the state and other agents. Our constitutions are said to encapsulate fundamental values of the polity and this, in turn, is said to be a reflection of our collective identity as a people, as a nation, as a state, as a Community, as a Union. When we are proud and attached to our constitutions we are so for these very reasons. They are about restricting power, not enlarging it; they protect fundamental rights of the individual; and they define a collective identity which does not make us feel queasy the way some forms of ethnic identity might. Thus, in the endless and tiresome debates about the European Union constitutional order, national courts have become in the last decade far more aggressive in their constitutional self-understanding.... National courts are no longer at the vanguard of the 'new European legal order', bringing the rule of law to transnational relations, and empowering, through EC law, individuals *vis-à-vis* Member State authority. Instead they stand at the gate and defend national constitutions against illicit encroachment from Brussels. They have received a sympathetic hearing, since they are perceived as protecting fundamental human rights as well as protecting national identity.[25]

This is exactly the kind of contestation of sovereign values that was discussed in Chapter 1 and is nowhere better exemplified than in the contestation, alluded to by Joseph Weiler, by national constitutional courts of sovereign powers that have been transferred to the EC.

1. The contestation of sovereign values by domestic courts: the case of the 'full transfer' of powers to the EC

The constitutional court that has led the way in questioning the locus of authoritative decision-making by the EC in the exercise of transferred powers is the BVG.[26] In its *Maastricht* decision[27] the BVG held that *it* has the competence to determine the scope of the powers that Germany has transferred to the EC, and to determine, in effect, whether the EC is acting within the limits of the scope of these powers in a particular case. The BVG stated:

If, for instance, European institutions or authorities were to apply or extend the Union Treaty in some way which was no longer covered by the Treaty in the form which constituted the basis of the German law approving it, the resulting legal acts would not be binding on German sovereign territory. The German organs of State would be prevented, on constitutional grounds, from applying those legal acts in Germany.

---

[25] J.H.H. Weiler, 'Federalism Without Constitutionalism: Europe's *Sonderweg*' in K. Nicoladis and R. Howse, eds, *The Federal Vision: Legitimacy and Levels of Governance in the United States and the European Union* (2001), p.54 at pp.62–63.

[26] For a comprehensive account and analysis of previous BVG decisions in a similar, although not so strident, vein, see P. Craig and G. de Burca, *EU Law* (2003, 3rd edn), Chapter 8.

[27] *Maastricht* case, 89 *BverfGE* 155 as translated and contained in A. Oppenheimer, ed., *The Relationship between European Community Law and National Law: The Cases* (1994), p.526.

Accordingly, the Federal Constitutional Court examines whether legal acts of the European institutions and bodies keep within or exceed the limits of the sovereign rights granted to them.[28]

In other words, the BVG is seeking to retain for itself the right to reject the application of those acts of the Community which it decides are *ultra vires* the powers transferred by Germany to the Community.[29] The Court goes even further when it said that it will act, if necessary, to ensure the protection of basic human rights in a case where *it* decides they are being compromised by EC action.[30] In the Court's own words:

> The Federal Constitutional Court guarantees, by virtue of its jurisdiction... that persons resident in Germany are assured in general of effective protection of basic rights, even in relation to the sovereign power of the Communities, and that this protection is essentially to be regarded as substantively equivalent to the protection of basic rights laid down as inalienable by the Basic Law, especially as the Court guarantees in general the substance of the basic rights. The Federal Constitutional Court thus also safeguards that substance vis-à-vis the sovereign power of the Community.[31]

This approach by the German constitutional court can be contrasted with that of France, Italy, Belgium, the United Kingdom, and the Netherlands where respective constitutional courts have not yet dealt directly with the issue of who has the ultimate power to decide how far EU competences extend. In the case, for example, of France, a possible reason why such a case has not yet been decided may well be due to the Constitutional Council not having to decide issues of competence as part of the French state system compared to the BVG's role within the German federal structure.[32] But it may also be a reflection of a greater degree of subordination of the judiciary to political power in France than is the case in Germany.[33]

---

[28] *Maastricht* case, 89 *BverfGE* 155, paras.438–439 as translated and contained in A. Oppenheimer, ed., *The Relationship between European Community Law and National Law: The Cases* (1994), p.526 at p.556.

[29] On this continuing approach by German courts, see: N. Reich, 'Judge-made "Europe à la carte": Some Remarks on Recent Conflicts between European and German Constitutional Law Provoked by the Banana Litigation', 7 *EJIL* (1996), p.103.

[30] The BVG had arguably intimated such an approach in its earlier *Eurocontrol I* decision: see G. Nolte, 'Constitutional Implications of German Participation in Treaty Regimes' in T. Franck, ed., *Delegating State Powers: The Effect of Treaty Regimes on Democracy and Sovereignty* (2000), p.261 at pp.270–271.

[31] *Maastricht* case, 89 *BverfGE* 155, paras.434–435 as translated and contained in A. Oppenheimer, ed., *The Relationship between European Community Law and National Law: The Cases* (1994), p.526 at pp.545–546.

[32] On the constitutional position in France and for potential future changes in this position, see A. Pellet, 'A French Constitutional Perspective on Treaty Implementation' in T. Franck, ed., *Delegating State Powers: The Effect of Treaty Regimes on Democracy and Sovereignty* (2000), p.279.

[33] See J. Plötner, 'Report on France' in A-M. Slaughter, A. Sweet, J.H.H. Weiler, eds., *The European Court and National Courts—Doctrine and Jurisprudence: Legal Change in Its Social Context* (1998), p.41 at p.53. See more generally the work by Alec Stone, *The Birth of Judicial Politics in France: the Constitutional Council in Comparative Perspective* (1992).

The BVG has not, however, been the only constitutional court of an EC Member State to pronounce in this way. The Supreme Court of Denmark adopted a virtually identical approach in a decision of 6 April 1998 that arose following the second Danish referendum on ratification of the Maastricht Treaty.[34] In a case which challenged Denmark's Act of Accession to the EC Treaty, the Supreme Court dismissed the application of the plaintiffs when it held that the ratification and incorporation into Danish law of the Maastricht Treaty was consistent with the 1953 Danish Constitution. However, the Court went on to find that Section 20 of the Danish Constitution which provides for conferrals of powers on international organizations 'does not permit that an international organization is entrusted with the issuance of acts of law or the making of decisions that are contrary to provisions in the Constitution, including its rights of freedom. Indeed, the authorities of the Realm have themselves no such power.'[35] The Court went on to hold that although the Act of Accession implies that the power to review the validity and legality of EC acts is vested in the ECJ, the Danish Courts still have, however, the right to review Community decisions for their consistency with Denmark's Act of Accession to the EC Treaty. The Supreme Court held that Danish courts,

cannot be deprived of their right to try questions as to whether an EC act of law exceeds the limits for the transfer of sovereignty made by the Act of Accession. Therefore, Danish courts must rule that an EC act is inapplicable in Denmark if the extraordinary situation should arise that with the required certainty it can be established that an EC act which has been upheld by the EC Court of Justice is based on an application of the Treaty which lies beyond the transfer of sovereignty according to the Act of Accession. Similar interpretations apply with regard to community-law rules and legal principles which are based on the practice of the EC Court of Justice.[36]

In order to resolve this apparent stand-off between these domestic constitutional courts and the EC, the best way forward for the Union is to develop its own sovereign values that attach to the exercise of transferred sovereign powers. It is no coincidence that the proclamation of the comprehensive Charter of Fundamental Rights of the Union—which contains civil and political rights as well as social, economic, and cultural rights[37]—occurred only

[34] In the first referendum a slim majority of the Danish population voted against ratification of the Maastricht Treaty. In the second referendum the Danish population gave their opinion that the government should ratify the Treaty. However, the required domestic ratification procedure only requires a five-sixths majority of parliament (the Folketing) in order to ratify such an international agreement and as such the holding of both these referenda was solely for domestic political reasons. (S. Harck and H. Olsen, 'International Decisions: Decision Concerning the Maastricht Treaty', 93 *AJIL* (1999), p.209.)

[35] 1998 *UfR* at H 869, para.9.2, as cited in Harck and Olsen, *ibid*, p.211 (n.12).

[36] 1998 *UfR* at H 871, para.9.6, as cited in Harck and Olsen, *ibid*, p.212 (n.19).

[37] See the Charter of Fundamental Rights of the European Union, 7 December 2000, 2000 O.J. (C364), reprinted in 40 *ILM* (2001), p.266. For a useful discussion of the Charter of Fundamental Rights and in particular of the opposing positions which led to it not being adopted at Nice as a binding set of norms, see: X. Yataganas, 'The Treaty of Nice: The Sharing of Power

after the BVG and Danish Supreme Court decisions and provides in the first paragraph of its preamble the following: 'The peoples of Europe, in creating an ever closer union among them, are resolved to share a peaceful future based on common values.'[38] Moreover, this Charter of Fundamental Rights of the Union has most recently been incorporated into Part II of the Draft Treaty Establishing a Constitution for Europe. Having appeared to consider that mere incorporation of the Charter is sufficient to appease domestic constitutional courts, the Draft Constitution in Article 10(1) provides for clear primacy of EU law over national law[39] and, moreover, in Article 10(2) stipulates that 'Member States shall take all appropriate measures, general or particular, to ensure fulfilment of the obligations flowing from the Constitution or resulting from the Union Institutions' acts.' While this may be the final position in formal terms if the Constitution is adopted as presently formulated, the history of sovereignty and its contestation teaches us that this Charter of Fundamental Rights will not be the end of the matter but only the starting point.[40] The following statement by Martti Koskenniemi is particularly apposite here:

Everyone knows that politics are not 'really' about translating natural rights into positive law; that at issue are struggle and compromise, power and ideology, and not

and the Institutional Balance in the European Union—A Continental Perspective', 1/01 *Jean Monnet Working Paper* (2001), available at http://www.jeanmonnetprogram.org/papers/01/010101.html.

[38] *Ibid.* For a cogent critique of this Charter and for a comprehensive analysis of the deficiencies in the EU's existing approach to human rights in practice, see P. Alston and J.H.H. Weiler, 'An "Ever Closer Union" in Need of a Human Rights Policy: The European Union and Human Rights' in P. Alston, ed., *The EU and Human Rights* (1999), p.3. For a number of important reform proposals to address these deficiencies, see Alston and Weiler, *ibid*, and P. Leino, 'All Dressed Up and Nowhere to Go: The Debate on the EU Charter of Fundamental Rights', 11 *Finnish Yearbook of International Law* (2000), p.37; and for more general discussion of the EU's approach to human rights, see, from amongst a voluminous literature, P. Craig, 'Constitutions, Constitutionalism, and the European Union', 7 *European Law Journal* (2001), p.125 at p.141 *et seq*, M. Kumm and V. Ferreres Comella, 'The Future of Constitutional Conflict in the European Union: Constitutional Supremacy after the Constitutional Treaty', 5(4) *Jean Monnet Working Paper* (2004), available at http://www.jeanmonnetprogram.org/papers/04/040501-15.html, Leino, *ibid*, G. de Búrca, 'Fundamental Human Rights and the Reach of EC Law', 13 *Oxford Journal of Legal Studies* (1993), p.283, N. Neuwahl and A. Rosas, eds., *The European Union and Human Rights* (1995), A. Clapham, *Human Rights and the European Community: A Critical Overview* (1991), vol.1, and K. Lenaerts, 'Fundamental Rights to be Included in a Community Catalogue', 16 *European Law Review* (1991), p.367.

[39] 'Article 10: Union law 1. The Constitution, and law adopted by the Union's Institutions in exercising competences conferred on it, shall have primacy over the law of the Member States.' (*Draft Treaty establishing a Constitution for Europe*, as submitted to the President of the European Council in Rome on 18 July 2003, CONV 850/03).

[40] Cf. M. Kumm and V. Ferreres Comella, 'The Future of Constitutional Conflict in the European Union: Constitutional Supremacy after the Constitutional Treaty', 5(4) *Jean Monnet Working Paper* (2004), available at http://www.jeanmonnetprogram.org/papers/04/040501-15.html, Sections II, III(2), & IV.

derivations from transparent and automatically knowable normative demands. Nor can the critiques of formalism and realism be undone. Everyone knows that administration and adjudication have to do with discretion, and that, however much such discretion is dressed in the technical language of rights and 'balancing', the outcomes reflect broad cultural and political preferences that have nothing inalienable about them.[41]

In furtherance of their broad cultural and political preferences, the domestic arms of governments—including, *in casu*, domestic constitutional courts—will continue to contest sovereign values (including, for example, the content of human rights) that attach to the exercise of governmental powers by the EU. Viewed in the perspective of our first chapter outlining the essentially contestable nature of the concept of sovereignty, these contestations can only be a positive practice since it ensures that the sovereign values adopted and subsequently developed by the organization will reflect, in addition to that of the executive arms of governments of EU Member States, the approaches and practices of the highest courts of member States and, ideally, their parliaments.

2. The contestation of sovereign values by domestic legislatures: the case of the 'partial transfer' by the US of powers to the WTO

The role that can be played by a domestic legislature in contesting the exercise by international organizations of transferred powers may be said to depend on such factors as the degree to which the legislature is controlled by the government, the extent to which the legislature is circumscribed by constitutional limitations from engaging in such contestation, or indeed the extent to which the legislature has delegated its powers to the government. The extent to which these factors prevail within a State will of course vary widely, but in order to illustrate how they can operate in a concrete case this section considers in some detail the role played by the US Congress in contesting one of its sovereign values within first the General Agreement on Tariffs and Trade 1947 ('GATT') and then the WTO.

(i) The US Congress and transfers of powers to international organizations

Within the US Congress, the notion that the US may transfer in full its powers to international organizations is highly controversial. Within the US legal system this issue is largely framed as whether or not the decisions and rulings of an international organization are 'self-executing'—that is, do they require some form of implementation by Congress before they can be relied on by individuals before US courts. The US Congress has vigorously propounded

---

[41] M. Koskenniemi, 'The Effects of Rights on Political Culture' in P. Alston, ed., *The EU and Human Rights* (1999), p.99 at p.115.

its approach that decisions of organizations are not self-executing,[42] and, importantly, they have been supported in this by the US courts.[43] Congress has made clear where necessary that it considers conferrals of powers to international organizations as involving, in our terms, only 'partial transfers' of powers rather than 'full transfers'.[44] It has done this even in a case, such as the Chemical Weapons Convention, where it would seem that the treaty mandates 'full transfers' and not 'partial transfers' of powers.[45] This general approach is clearly designed to retain for Congress the right to contest the decision of an organization *within the US legal order* by using, if it deems necessary, values different from those used by the organization in exercising the transferred powers. This does not of course mean that Congress will employ the rather crude method of overt non-compliance with an organization's decision, although this is of course always an option. There are the more subtle techniques of incorporating US values in the domestic implementing legislation;[46] and the method of interpreting the organization's decision as narrowly as possible in order to mitigate its domestic consequences, a technique whose use is not of course restricted to the US Congress.[47]

---

[42] See C. Bradley, 'International Delegations, the Structural Constitution, and Non-Self-Execution', 55 *Stanford Law Review* (2003), p.1557 at pp.1594–1595.

[43] For consideration of the case-law, see, for example, C. Bradley, 'International Delegations, the Structural Constitution, and Non-Self-Execution', 55 *Stanford Law Review* (2003), p.1557 at p.1591.
This is part of the broader debate relating to the issue of the self-execution of treaties within US law: for an opponent of such an approach, see J. Yoo, 'Globalism and the Constitution: Treaties, Non-Self-Execution, and the Original Understanding', 99 *Columbia Law Review* (1999), p.1955; but cf. L. Henkin, *Foreign Affairs and the Constitution* (1996, 2nd edn), pp.201–202; and C.M. Vazquez, 'Laughing at Treaties', 99 *Columbia Law Review* (1999), p.2154 at p.2173 *et seq.*

[44] See, for example, the case of the WTO dispute settlement system considered in Section II(2) below.

[45] The Convention on the Prohibition of the Development, Production, Stockpiling and Use of Chemical Weapons and on their Destruction (the 'Chemical Weapons Convention', 3 January 1993, reprinted in 32 *ILM* (1993), p.800) establishes the Organization for the Prohibition of Chemical Weapons ('OPCW') as an international organization and confers on its Technical Secretariat a number of broad-ranging powers which include, for example, powers to decide on and conduct searches of public *and privately* owned property within the territory of Member States (Chemical Weapons Convention, Annex on Implementation and Verification, Part II, *ibid*); but cf. the US Chemical Weapons Convention Implementation Act which seeks to ensure the observance of basic US conceptions of rights when in s 6725 it makes an OPCW inspection conditional in the first instance on obtaining the consent of the private owner or operator of the premises to be inspected and in the case where this consent is refused then the US Government is to seek a search warrant from a US magistrate judge (Chemical Weapons Convention Implementation Act, 22 USC s 6725.)

[46] A good example of this is provided by the US Chemical Weapons Implementation Act: see *supra* n.45.

[47] Cf., for example, the problems with EC implementation of the decisions by WTO Panels and the Appellate Body in the *European Communities—Regime For The Importation, Sale And Distribution Of Bananas* cases, see M. Salas and J. Jackson, 'Procedural Overview of the WTO EC- Bananas Dispute, 3(1) *JIEL* (2000), p.145 and J. Jackson and P. Grané, 'The Saga Continues: An Update on the Banana Dispute and Its Procedural Offspring', 4(3) *JIEL* (2001), p.581.

Even, however, a legislature as powerful as the US Congress cannot insulate its domestic legal system entirely from the effects of the exercise by an organization of transferred powers.[48] This is well-illustrated by the case of the 'partial transfer' by the US of powers to the WTO.

(ii) The 'partial transfer' by the US of powers to the WTO

In Chapter 1 the claim was made, and discussed at length, that the very existence of international organizations, such as the WTO, performs an important ontological function since these organizations provide a forum, transcendental to the State, where conceptions of sovereignty—and more specifically the content of sovereign values—can be contested on the international plane. In the case of the WTO this has been taken further by the provision of a dispute settlement system where WTO panels and the Appellate Body have in practice been given the authority to determine the values that underlie and inform the WTO and its Agreements in the context of resolving particular disputes between Members. Consider, for example, the application by the panels and Appellate Body in cases before them of 'principles' that they have gleaned from the WTO Agreements. These principles in substantive terms represent nothing more than the promotion of certain values—existing within the WTO Agreements—by the WTO judiciary. Consider by way of mention the principle of free trade ('trade liberalization') which represents in substance a clear policy choice preferring the operation of a free market and in particular the autonomy of corporations and traders within that market to the opposing position of extensive regulation that impedes the operations of these corporations and traders.[49] Consider also the two non-discrimination principles of Most Favoured Nation and National Treatment which are in substance a reflection of the application of the value of equality—that governments should ensure that like cases are treated equally.[50] It is thus no surprise that, within the WTO jurisprudence on these two non-discrimination principles,

---

[48] Moreover, as John Jackson has noted: 'Even without those effects [self-executing or otherwise being directly applicable within a domestic legal system], a treaty can have important domestic legal effects, such as influencing how domestic courts interpret domestic legislation. Beyond that, a treaty norm even without domestic legal effect can have weight in some domestic policy debates where some advocates will stress that positions contrary to their views would raise serious international or treaty concerns.' (J. Jackson, 'The Great 1994 Sovereignty Debate: United States Acceptance and Implementation of the Uruguay Round Results', 36 *Columbia Journal of Transnational Law* (1998), p.157 at p.172.)

[49] For extensive consideration of the value of 'corporate economic autonomy', see Section II(2)(ii)(a).

[50] The value of equality is not embraced, however, in a systemic way by the WTO in the sense, for example, that the WTO does not try to ensure that all States become more equal by embracing a theory of distributional equality: for such a theory, see R. Dworkin, *Sovereign Virtue: The Theory and Practice of Equality* (2000), p.12 *et seq.*

the most controversial issue has been the test to determine 'likeness':[51] for this is the touchstone for determining the application of the value of equality in a particular case.[52]

However, decisions by the WTO panels and Appellate Body remain at a political level subject to contestation by Member States within the WTO[53] and also, importantly, subject to contestation within Member States. A good example of the latter is provided by the approach of the US Congress to the WTO dispute settlement system: only the US Congress can decide how it will, if at all, change US law to comply with a specific panel or Appellate Body decision in a case.[54] This approach in turn illustrates an aspect of the value of 'economic autonomy' that the US, through a process of contestation, is seeking both (i) to project internationally through the WTO, and (ii) to ensure in its own relationships with the WTO and its Member States. By 'economic autonomy' is meant the capacity of an entity to make independent decisions about its own economic future. This value of economic autonomy arguably has two aspects that influence US governmental action in relation to the international trading system: corporate economic autonomy and nation-State economic autonomy.

(a) Economic autonomy as a value of US sovereignty

There is considerable controversy over the extent to which corporate economic autonomy should be guaranteed in a modern economy. There is broad acceptance of a general macro-economic position that espouses the importance of the free market in achieving competitiveness and, so the argument

---

[51] For MFN, see J. Jackson, W. Davey, and A. Sykes, *Legal Problems of International Economic Relations: Cases, Materials and Text* (1995), pp.444–451 and M. Matsushita, T. Schoenbaum, and P. Mavroidis, *The World Trade Organization: Law, Practice, and Policy* (2003), pp.150–151; and for National Treatment, see Matsushita, Schoenbaum, and Mavroidis, *ibid*, pp.158–162.

[52] The application of this value of equality within the two non-discrimination principles is itself subject, however, to considerable constraint. There are significant exceptions that exist: suffice to mention the significant exception for customs unions and free trade areas as provided for by Article XXIV of GATT 1994: for detailed consideration of this exception, see the WTO case: *Turkey—Restrictions on Imports of Textile and Clothing Products*, Panel Report, WT/DS34/R, 31 May 1999 and Appellate Body Report, WT/DS34/AB/R, 22 October 1999.

[53] Consider, for example, the *de facto* change in approach by the Appellate Body in the *Asbestos* case over the *amicus curiae* issue as compared to its previous approach in the *Shrimp-Turtle* case. This change was largely in response to significant dissent voiced by developing country Member States in the WTO General Council: see more generally P. Mavroidis, '*Amicus Curiae* Briefs Before The WTO: Much Ado About Nothing', 2(1) *Jean Monnet Working Paper* (2001), available at: http://www.jeanmonnetprogram.org/papers/01/010201.rtf. This opposition by developing country Members to *amicus curiae* briefs has continued more recently in response to US and EC proposals to reform the DSU and provide a framework for the submission of such briefs before WTO panels and the Appellate Body: see D. Sarooshi, 'Reform of the WTO Dispute Settlement Understanding' in I. Mbirimi, B. Chilala, and R. Grynberg, eds., *From Doha to Cancun: Delivering a Development Round* (2003), p.105.

[54] See *infra* nn.122–123 and corresponding text.

runs, generating maximum productivity and economic growth within an economy. Within this general approach, however, there can be said to exist a spectrum of more specific approaches. At one end of the spectrum is a complete laissez faire approach that dictates little or no government intervention in the market in order to ensure that the government does not answer the basic economic questions—such as what is to be produced, how is it to be produced, how much is to be produced, and for whom is it to be produced. At the other end of our spectrum is an approach that places considerable emphasis on preventing market externalities (such as corporate scandals and pensions scheme difficulties) and as such mandates the importance of the market—and for our purposes corporations—operating within a significant institutional, or at least regulatory, framework. Where a country like the US can be said to lie on this spectrum at a particular point in time will of course depend largely on the approach of a particular Executive and Congress.[55] As a general matter, however, the US can be said to have embraced to a considerable degree corporate economic autonomy as a value with the consequence that successive US governments have sought to maintain low levels of taxation and minimal levels of regulation of corporate actors.[56] This approach is, moreover, clearly evidenced by the US expressly rejecting the use of an industrial policy within its economy in order to minimize the level of governmental intervention within the US market.[57]

The acceptance and implementation in practice by the US of this value of corporate economic autonomy[58] has important implications for the multilateral trading system. Where other States do not, according to the US, guarantee in practice this value at least to a certain degree within their economies then the US has taken measures—often on a unilateral basis—to ensure that US firms are not being prejudiced by the lack of a US industrial policy while other

[55] See, for an example, *infra* nn.94–97.
[56] See, for example, C. Molyneux, *Domestic Structures and International Trade: The Unfair Trade Instruments of the United States and European Union* (2001), p.42.
[57] See Molyneux, *ibid*, pp.49–50.
[58] This does not mean, however, that the Executive and Congress have not intervened on a large number of occasions within the US market to protect domestic producers. For example, Congress bowed to increasing pressure in the 1970s from special interest groups to afford protection to domestic industries, especially the steel and auto industries, which sought protection from imports and support for their export markets. In the case, for example, of US steel producers, they sought and received government protection initially in the form of Voluntary Export Restraint Agreements ('VERs') concluded with first Japanese and European industries, and then Swedish and EC producers. These VERs had the effect of limiting imports of specialty steel into the US. More recently, however, President Bush introduced in 2002 a number of safeguard measures to afford protection to the US steel industry, see *infra* n.90.

From amongst the voluminous literature on US government protection of its steel producers, see, for example, D. Beane, *The United States and GATT: A Relational Study* (2000), p.213; P. Mundo, *National Politics in a Global Economy: The Domestic Sources of US Trade Policy* (1999), pp.233–239; and H. Prechel, 'Steel and the State: Industry Politics and Business Policy Formation, 1940–1989', 55 *American Sociological Review* (1990), p.648 at p.656.

States do pursue such a policy conferring thereby an 'unfair' benefit on their firms. It is precisely in order to ensure US competitiveness in global markets that the US has sought to project through the multilateral trading system its approach of government non-intervention in the market (based on the value of corporate economic autonomy) as a fundamental principle on which the system is to be based. This projection of corporate economic autonomy is particularly well-illustrated by the US approach to the issue of government subsidization in first the GATT and more recently in the WTO; an issue considered below in more detail.[59]

Turning now to our second aspect of economic autonomy, that of the nation-State, the claim being made here is that *one of the ways* of understanding why the US strives to maintain to a considerable degree this type of autonomy is precisely to ensure that it can project internationally its value of corporate economic autonomy. In this way the values of corporate economic autonomy and nation-State economic autonomy are inextricably linked. It is this understanding which provides insight into the contradictory practice of the US in contesting this value of economic autonomy of the nation-State within first the GATT and more recently within the WTO. The US has sought to retain a very considerable degree of autonomy in making decisions on trade both in terms of its international trading position but especially in relation to its own domestic trade law and practice;[60] while on the other hand the US has sought to use first the GATT and now the WTO to require other States to change their international trading arrangements and more specifically their domestic trading regimes. The US Congress and, to a lesser extent, the Executive have always been open about pursuing protectionist policies on an ad hoc basis within the US legal order in order to respond to what are perceived to be unfair trading advantages gained by foreign producers as a consequence of foreign government action in, for example, the case of subsidies or lack of effective foreign government action in, for example, the case of predatory pricing by foreign firms.[61] This US resort to ad hoc protectionism is not any worse than other States,[62] but the point is that it is not any better. Put differently, the US has not led by example in the projection internationally of the value of corporate economic autonomy (a value which other States do not so openly espouse), but by persuasion and in some cases economic coercion. But in a country such as the US where special interest groups have access and

---

[59] See Section II(2)(ii)(c) below.

[60] See, for example, T. Stewart, ed., *The GATT Uruguay Round: A Negotiating History (1986–1994)*, Vol.I, pp.860–862.

[61] As Molyneux states: 'Between 1980 and 1999, the United States initiated 315 countervailing duty procedures and 784 anti-dumping investigations. Its trade protectionist policy was further strengthened by the use of Section 301 as an export protectionist instrument. The [European] Community would also follow the same policy.... From 1980 to 1999 the Commission initiated more than seven hundred and fifteen anti-dumping and countervailing duty cases.' (Molyneux, *supra* n.56, pp.31–32.)   [62] Cf. the case of the EC in using 'unfair trade' instruments: *ibid*.

considerable influence over legislators,[63] some may argue that as a matter of design such an outcome may be inevitable. This brings us to a discussion of the contestation of economic sovereignty within the US, the contours of which are important when seeking to understand US contestation of the value of economic autonomy within first the GATT and now the WTO.

(b) The contestation of economic sovereignty within the US: the Congress-Executive relationship and trade policy control

There is in practice an uneasy power-sharing arrangement between the President and Congress in the control and conduct of trade policy on both the national and international planes. The reason for this is that while Congress has under Article I of the Constitution absolute and plenary powers to regulate foreign trade within the US, these powers are, however, balanced by Article II of the Constitution which confers on the President the power to conduct foreign relations including the foreign commerce of the United States.

The beginning of the last century saw Congress as the main arm of government exercising trade policy powers, but there was then a marked shift in power towards the Executive that occurred after the disastrous Congressional experience with its 1930 Smoot-Hawley legislation which raised significantly overall US tariff levels in response to special interest representations.[64] This action led to other States raising their tariff barriers with the consequence that world trade stagnated.[65] This experience saw Congress delegate to the Executive—by the 1934 Reciprocal Trade Agreements Act (RTAA)—the power to manage and set trade policy, primarily tariff-levels.[66] The RTAA was used to good effect by the Executive and between 1934 and 1945 the US entered into 32 bilateral trade agreements

---

[63] Baldwin and Magee, for example, conclude that campaign contributions influenced US legislators' votes on the NAFTA and Uruguay Round bills. They state: 'The major conclusion of this study is that political contributions to legislators by organized labor and business groups significantly affected the voting outcome on two (NAFTA and GATT) of the three trade bills analyzed. We estimate that labor contributions or access to legislators gained through these contributions resulted in 67 extra votes against NAFTA and 57 extra votes against the GATT Uruguay Round bill. Contributions from business groups resulted in 41 extra votes in favor of NAFTA and 35 extra votes for the GATT bill.... We estimate the price for labor groups to sway one vote against NAFTA and GATT to be about $352,000 and $313,000 respectively.... We interpret these various results as evidence that legislators are responding on trade legislation to the economic and social concerns of their constituencies as well as to the wishes of their major contributors.' (R. Baldwin and C. Magee, 'Is trade policy for sale? Congressional voting on recent trade bills', 105 *Public Choice* (2000), p.79 at p.99.)

[64] See P. Low, *Trading Free: The GATT and US Trade Policy* (1993), pp.53–54.

[65] As Destler states: 'for the United States, imports dropped from $4.40 billion in 1929 to $1.45 billion in 1933, and exports plunged even more: from $5.16 billion to $1.65 billion'. (I. Destler, *American Trade Politics* (1992, 2nd edn), p.11.)

[66] See J. Jackson, 'The General Agreement on Tariffs and Trade in United States domestic law' in J. Jackson, *The Jurisprudence of GATT and the WTO* (2000), p.195 at p.199.

with 27 countries, granting tariff concessions on 64% of dutiable imports and reducing tariff rates to an average of 44%.[67] Congress in the early years of the RTAA did not insist on approving these trade agreements, but it did make the grant of negotiating authority to the Executive temporary: the RTAA needed to be renewed by legislation every three years, the need for this renewal process continuing until the 1960s.[68] This new power and prestige given to the Executive came at a very considerable cost: the President now bore responsibility for trade policy. This has allowed Congress to shift politically sensitive trade policy demands onto the President, and this has been accompanied by Congress continually seeking to direct and constrain the Executive in the way that it exercises trade policy powers.

The 1962 Trade Expansion Act marked the first significant attempt by Congress to control the Executive in the exercise of trade policy powers. Many members of Congress viewed the State Department as insufficiently engaged or concerned with domestic economic interests in order to negotiate trade issues on behalf of the US, and so Congress created the position of Special Representative for Trade Negotiations (the predecessor to the Office of the Special Representative for Trade Negotiations which was later transformed into the US Trade Representative) to be the chief US representative in international trade negotiations.[69] Moreover, the 1962 Act required that two representatives drawn from both the House of Representatives and the Senate be accredited as members of US trade delegations in an attempt to ensure greater Congressional control and participation in trade negotiations.[70]

---

[67] Beane, *supra* n.58, pp.177–178.

[68] In the late 1940s and throughout the 1950s, Congress kept the Executive on a tight leash only renewing the RTAA on a one- or two-year basis (1948, 1951, 1953, 1954, 1955, 1958, and 1962). (Beane, *supra* n.58, p.187.) This, unsurprisingly, constrained the Executive's ability to negotiate in the GATT rounds on tariff reductions during this period. (*Ibid.*) Nonetheless, the renewed RTAA was the basis for the President to negotiate on behalf of the US in the first four GATT trade rounds. It was only in 1962 that Congress adopted the Trade Expansion Act which for the first time specifically authorized 'GATT' negotiations. It was also the first time that Congress gave express official recognition to the GATT and accepted its role in the trading regime.

[69] Trade Expansion Act of 1962, Pub. L. No. 87-794, 76 Stat. 872 (1962), s 241. The STR provided a focal point for conflict between the Executive and Congress over trade, and subsequent Presidents tried to reduce the powers and budget of the STR. (Molyneux, *supra* n.56, 79.) Congress responded in the 1974 Trade Act by recreating the STR as the Office of the Special Representative for Trade Negotiations and by making it a statutorily based unit in the Executive Office of the President thereby ensuring that it could not be abolished without the support of the legislature. (S141 of the Trade Act of 1974, P.L. 93-618, as amended (repealing S241 of the Trade Expansion Act of 1962, P.L. 87-794).)

[70] Trade Expansion Act of 1962, Pub. L. No. 87-794, 76 Stat. 872 (1962), s 243. Moreover, the President was required to seek advice from the Tariff Commission (re-named by s 2231 of the 1974 Trade Act as the International Trade Commission) on the effects of proposed tariff reductions or duty-free treatment, and also to hold public hearings. (Trade Expansion Act of 1962, Pub. L. No. 87-794, 76 Stat. 872 (1962), ss 221–224.) This provision was carried over, with modifications, into ss 131–134 of the Trade Act of 1974 and s 1111 of the Omnibus Trade and Competitiveness Act of 1988.

A significant point of conflict emerged in the Congress-Executive relationship when during the Kennedy Round the Executive negotiated and accepted an International Antidumping Code which involved, *inter alia*, modification of the US method of determining customs valuation.[71] Congress considered that the Executive had, in accepting this Code, exceeded its negotiating authority, and in 1968 enacted a Statute providing that nothing contained in the International Antidumping Code shall be construed to restrict the discretion of the US International Trade Commission in performing its duties and functions under the Antidumping Act of 1921, and, moreover, that in performing their duties and functions under the Act, the Secretary of the Treasury and the Commission shall (i) resolve any conflict between the Code and the Act in favour of the Act, and (ii) take into account the provisions of the Code only insofar as they are consistent with the Act.[72] It was not until 1979 with the end of the Tokyo Round that the US Congress accepted a slightly changed international agreement on anti-dumping. The refusal by Congress to ratify the International Antidumping Code was a severe blow to the Executive's perceived ability, among its trading partners, to negotiate an agreement and then deliver upon the agreement's provisions. This led to reluctance by US trading partners to negotiate with the Executive, and this in turn led President Nixon to seek from Congress a legislative framework that would grant the Executive more specific negotiating authority.

What emerged from this request by President Nixon was the 'fast-track' approval process which requires the Executive to consult with Congress and the private sector on any non-tariff arrangements the President planned to negotiate, but which in turn provides for a set of expedited legislative procedures that Congress will follow in deciding whether to accept, without amendment, bills that implement the results of a trade negotiation. This fast-track approval process, first established by Section 151 of the 1974 Trade Act, provides that fast-track authority can apply to the following: (i) implementing legislation that approves trade agreements, (ii) any statement of administrative action proposed to implement those agreements, and (iii) any necessary or appropriate changes in law (including amendments and repeals).[73]

---

[71] See generally F. Snyder, 'The Origins of the "Nonmarket Economy": Ideas, Pluralism, and Power in EC Anti-dumping Law about China', *7 European Law Journal* (2001), p.369 at pp.387–392; and J. Barcelo, 'Antidumping Laws as Barriers to Trade—The United States and the International Antidumping Code', *57 Cornell Law Review* (1972), p.491 at pp.532–558.

[72] Public Law 90-634, Title II, § 201, 82 Stat 1347, Oct. 24, 1968. For a case where US courts upheld the provisions of this legislation over those of the International Antidumping Code, see *Timken Co. v Simon* (1976) 176 U.S. App DC 219, 539 F.2d 221.

[73] This is subject to the President notifying Congress of an intention to enter into the agreement 90 days prior to signing the agreement, and thereafter transmitting to Congress the final agreement and draft implementing legislation. (D. Leebron, 'Implementation of the Uruguay Round Results in the United States' in J. Jackson and A. Sykes, eds., *Implementing the Uruguay Round* (1997), p.175 at p.190.) Upon submission of the implementing bill, both Houses of Congress are to refer it immediately to their appropriate committees which have a forty-five day

The possession by the Executive of fast-track authority obviously gives it more credibility when negotiating trade agreements on behalf of the US and it also expressly authorizes the President to enter into agreements relating to non-tariff barriers.[74] However, the 1974 Act also gave Congress a greater opportunity to influence and control the Executive during negotiations by requiring that the President consult with Congress[75] and private sector advisory committees throughout any trade negotiations,[76] and that any agreement be implemented within the US by Congressional legislation.[77] This is clear evidence of a Congressional intent to retain US economic autonomy but also to ensure its separation of power vis-à-vis the Executive in the sense of always retaining final control over the content of US legislation.[78] These elements have been retained by Congress despite the evolution of fast-track authority into what is now called Trade Promotion Authority. For example, an implementing bill submitted formally by the President to Congress pursuant to Trade Promotion Authority is actually drafted by Congressional committees and the USTR, and only once a single bill emerges can it then at that relatively final stage be subject to changes by the President before being submitted to Congress under the Trade Promotion Authority (formerly known as fast-track) procedure.

maximum time-limit to report on the bill after which there is a further fifteen day period before the vote in both Houses takes place. There are no amendments permitted to the bill either in committee or on the floor of the Houses, and debate is limited strictly to 20 hours. (*Ibid*, p.191.) As such, within 60 days of submission by the President the implementing bill will be either adopted or rejected by Congress.

[74] The Tokyo Round results of 1979 were the first agreements to be implemented by use of the fast-track process. See Leebron, *ibid*, p.190; and J. Jackson, 'United States law and implementation of the Tokyo Round negotiation' in J. Jackson, J. Louis, and M. Matsushita, eds., *Implementing the Tokyo Round: national constitutions and international economic rules* (1984), p.139.

[75] Moreover, Congress provided in the 1988 Act that the fast-track procedure may be nullified if the Executive branch fails to consult adequately with the Congress. (Section 1103 (c) (1) (E), 19 USC s 2903 (1995).) The Executive's authority was constrained by Congress in the Omnibus Trade and Competitiveness Act of 1988 which linked fast-track authority to the achievement by the Executive of sixteen negotiating objectives set out in the Act. On these objectives, see Leebron, *supra* n.73, p.194 (n.83).

[76] The most important committee, the Advisory Committee for Trade Policy and Negotiations ['ACTPN'], was established by the 1974 Act and is today composed of up to forty-five individuals representing 'non-federal governments, labour, industry, agriculture, small business, service industries, retailers, non-governmental environmental and conservation organizations, and consumer interests.' (Section 135, 1974 Trade Act, 19 USC s 2155 (b) (1), added by s 128, URAA. The reference to environmental and conservation groups was added by the URAA, and the reference to non-federal governments was added by the 1988 Act: Leebron, *supra* n.73, p.197 (n.93).) The ACTPN fully endorsed, with the exception of the labor representative, the Uruguay Round Agreements: see Leebron, *ibid*, p.197.

[77] Sections 102(e), 131–135 of the 1974 Trade Act.

[78] Moreover, fast-track authority was only granted initially for three years and required renewal every two years: Leebron, *supra* n.73, p.195. As such, each of the three Presidents who were in office during the Uruguay Round negotiations had to seek fast-track authority (Reagan, 1988; Bush, 1991; and Clinton, 1993) for the continuance of US participation in the Round. After the adoption of the Uruguay Round Agreements Act by Congress, the Executive's Trade

   This control by Congress over the implementation of trade agreements has seen it try to ensure that US law can respond to foreign government action or inaction that is perceived to be in violation of its value of corporate economic autonomy. A good example of this is provided by an aspect of the US approach to subsidies adopted in the Uruguay Round Agreements Act (URAA). Previous GATT cases had decided that an 'arm's length' sale of a former State-owned company (for example, a steel manufacturer) was sufficient to terminate the benefits of any subsidies that had been bestowed on it prior to the sale.[79] This was heavily contested by the US steel industry during the Uruguay Round, but the final WTO Agreement on Subsidies and Countervailing Measures did not require any change in this rule and indeed the initial draft of the US implementing legislation submitted by the Executive contained no provision dealing with such changes of ownership.[80] However, as Leebron notes:

An amendment was introduced as part of a package of Congressional staff recommendations that appeared to give the Commerce Department greater leeway to find that such subsidies continued after sale and could therefore be countervailed. Supported by the steel industry, the new provision was adopted as part of the implementing legislation.[81]

   This approach, encapsulated in the URAA,[82] led the US to continue to impose countervailing duties against certain imports of UK steel[83] which inevitably resulted in a WTO case, the *US—Hot Rolled Lead* case.[84]
   In this case, the alleged subsidies that were countervailed related principally to equity infusions granted by the UK Government to the former State-owned company, British Steel Corporation (BSC), between 1977 and 1986. For the purposes of our present discussion it is sufficient to note that in 1986 BSC merged with a private company, subsequently established a subsidiary, and then in 1988 was fully privatized by the selling of shares in the former State-owned companies (BSC and the subsidiary) on the stock market.[85] Countervailing

---

Promotion Authority (what was formerly called 'fast-track' authority) lapsed and was not renewed by Congress. It took a strong push by the Executive, including the USTR, to regain this authorization from Congress: see USTR Report of 30 April 2001, p.4, available at: http://www.ustr.gov/enforcement/super301.pdf. Congress finally granted Trade Promotion Authority to the Executive by passage of the Trade Act of 2002 which entered into force on 6 August 2002. The 2002 Act grants trade negotiating authority to the Executive until 1 June 2005 with the possibility of a two-year extension.

   [79] Leebron, *ibid*, p.203.   [80] *Ibid*.   [81] *Ibid*, pp.203–204.
   [82] See s 251 (a), URAA, amending s 771 (5), Tariff Act 1930, codified at 19 USC s 1677.
   [83] In the case of countervailing duties imposed against US imports of Mexican steel and the resultant WTO case, see *infra* n.89.
   [84] *US—Imposition of Countervailing Duties on Certain Hot-Rolled Lead and Bismuth Carbon Steel Products Originating in the United Kingdom* case (the '*Hot Rolled Lead* case'), Panel Report, WT/DS138/R, 23 December 1999; and *Hot Rolled Lead* case, Appellate Body Report, WT/DS138/AB/R, 10 May 2000.
   [85] For a detailed description of the path to privatization of the British Steel Corporation, see the *US Hot Rolled Lead* case, Panel Report, WT/DS138/R, 23 December 1999.

duties had originally been imposed by the US Department of Commerce (USDOC) on imports of leaded bars in 1993 on the basis that the pre-1986 subsidies had 'travelled' through to the privatized companies. This was despite the USDOC finding that the sale of these shares was at arm's length, for fair market value, and consistent with commercial considerations. Since then there had been a number of USDOC annual reviews of the countervailing duties applied to imports of leaded bars originating in the UK. The EC challenged in particular the countervailing duties maintained following reviews of leaded bar imports in the years 1994 through to 1996. The USDOC had in these instances decided to maintain the countervailing duties since it continued to find that a certain proportion of the financial contributions granted to BSC pre-1986 by the UK Government had 'passed through' to, and continued to benefit, the privatized companies.

The US made clear in the case its strident and general opposition to government intervention in the market to support domestic production when it argued that the meaning of one of the important definitional elements of a 'subsidy' in the SCM Agreement—whether the purported 'subsidy' had conferred a 'benefit'[86]—should be construed in very broad terms. More specifically, the US argued that the relevant 'benefit' is an advantage to a company's productive operations rather than an advantage given to specific legal or natural persons, and as such a subsidy can be presumed to follow the productive operations that were subsidized without needing to have regard to changes in ownership. *In casu*, the US went on to argue that the USDOC was not required to find the existence of a 'benefit' specifically in the case of the new, privatized, companies since their operations are 'essentially the same as' the operations of the former State-owned BSC, that is, they are all engaged in the same productive operations.

This approach was decisively dismissed by both the Panel[87] and Appellate Body[88] when they held that: (i) the recipient of a 'benefit' in Article 1.1(b) of the SCM Agreement must be a 'natural or legal person', and as such the USDOC review should have examined whether a 'benefit' accrued to the newly privatized companies following the changes in ownership rather than simply continuing the prior imposed countervailing duties; and (ii) the payment by the successor companies of fair market value for BSC and its subsidiary meant that they had not received a 'benefit' from the government's earlier 'financial contributions', and as such the countervailing duties imposed by the US Government were in violation of Article 10 of the SCM Agreement.

---

[86] Interestingly, the antecedent to the SCM concept that a subsidy must confer a benefit is provided by US law and in particular the decision of the US Court of International Trade (USCIT) in *Carlisle Tire and Rubber Co. v. United States*, 564 F. Supp., p.834 at pp.837–838.

[87] *US Hot Rolled Lead* case, Panel Report, WT/DS138/R, 23 December 1999, paras.6.69–6.70, 6.81–6.82, 6.86.

[88] *US Hot Rolled Lead* case, Appellate Body Report, WT/DS138/AB/R, 10 May 2000, pp.58, 74.

It seems clear that the US rationale for the imposition of countervailing duties in this case flows from its opposition to the original UK Government subsidization of its steel industry, the initial non-observance of the value of corporate economic autonomy. As such, the subsequent sale of the steel company for fair market value, after the government intervention had already taken place to establish the steel company as a viable entity, did not affect the value judgment by the US of the original government intervention in the market nor indeed its view that such interventions should be discouraged by penalizing the successor (privatized) corporations.[89] This attempt by the US to contest the application of its value of corporate economic autonomy before a WTO panel and Appellate Body provides a particularly stark contrast to recent protectionist measures enacted by the US Government to shore up its ailing steel industry.[90] This contrast is highlighted further when consideration is had of the extent to which the US has sought to project internationally its value of corporate economic autonomy, especially in relation to government subsidies.[91]

Consider, for example, the following US statement contained in a communication to the WTO entitled 'Subsidies Disciplines Requiring Clarification and Improvement':

... there is widespread and longstanding agreement that government subsidies distort the efficient allocation and utilization of resources, thereby undermining the best

---

[89] See also the case brought by Mexico against the US (*US-Countervailing Duties on Steel Plate from Mexico*, request for the establishment of a Panel, WT/DS280/2, 8 August 2003) where it challenges a 1998 USDOC decision to apply its 'change-in-ownership' methodology. USDOC imposed countervailing duties on a Mexican producer of carbon steel plate on the basis that the producer was the same entity before and after its privatization and as such the subsidies granted to the previously subsidized company continued to confer a benefit upon the company after privatization.

[90] See, for example, the 10 safeguard measures introduced by President Bush on 5 March 2002 ('Presidential Proclamation 7529', 67 *Federal Register* 10553, 7 March, 2002) and applied by the US on 20 March 2002 which established increases in duty and a tariff-rate quota pursuant to s 203 of the Trade Act on imports of certain steel products. This controversial measure was challenged by a number of States before a WTO Panel which ruled in their favour by holding that in the main the US measures were inconsistent with a number of the provisions of the WTO Safeguards Agreement and Article XIX of GATT 1994: see *Unites States—Definitive Safeguard Measures on Imports of Certain Steel Products*, Panel Reports, WT/DS248/R, WT/DS249/R, WT/DS251/R, WT/DS252/R, WT/DS253/R, WT/DS254/R, WT/DS258/R, WT/DS259/R, 11 July 2003; and *United States—Definitive Safeguard Measures on Imports of Certain Steel Products*, Appellate Body Report, WT/DS248/AB/R, WT/DS249/AB/R, WT/DS251/AB/R, WT/DS252/AB/R, WT/DS253/AB/R, WT/DS254/AB/R, WT/DS258/AB/R, WT/DS259/AB/R, 10 November 2003. Subsequently, the President on 8 December 2003 terminated these import restrictions on steel by a Presidential proclamation that made no mention of the WTO ruling, but rather emphasized instead that the safeguard measure had now met most of its objectives: see 'Presidential Proclamation 7741', 68 *Federal Register* 68483; and 'President's Statement on Steel Proclamation', 4 December 2003, available at http://www.whitehouse.gov/news/releases/2003/12/20031204-5.html.
This protectionist approach by the US government towards domestic steel production is not without precedent: see *supra* n.58.

[91] For a concise history of US trade disputes with a number of States over subsidies, see Stewart, *supra* n.60, pp.826–833.

foundation of economic growth and development. The subsidy-induced production distortions that occur domestically frequently spill-over internationally, distorting the efficient flow of trade and diminishing the economic development and growth potential of all participants in the world economy. One of the fundamental economic principles upon which the trading system is based is that trade flows should be determined by comparative advantage and market forces, not government intervention. In recognition of this principle, Members have over time committed to increasingly stringent and mutually beneficial rules on the provision of subsidies.[92]

The same communication contains a clear statement of the US ideological commitment to the value of corporate economic autonomy and, moreover, the extent to which the US would like to see this value applied by other States:

[We have previously noted] the importance of addressing those national government distortive subsidies 'that are so entrenched or disguised within countries' political and economic systems that it will take some time to identify and implement the appropriate multilateral disciplines necessary to root all of them out'. Many of these distortive practices take the form of indirect subsidies to specific companies or industries in which governments act through government-owned, government-controlled or government-directed private entities to provide financial support to companies, which would either not be available from the private sector or would not be available on the same terms.... Under the existing terms of the Subsidies Agreement, the government provision of equity capital to a specific company or industry does not confer a benefit unless the investment decision can be regarded as inconsistent with the usual investment practice of private investors. While this standard needs clarification, the more fundamental issue is: should governments be investing in private sector companies and, if so, under what circumstances?... If the equity markets determine that a company will not generate a market return, the actions of any government which determines otherwise should be subject to strengthened disciplines.[93]

This approach to the value of corporate economic autonomy is not, however, free from considerable contestation even within the US, and it will necessarily change with different US administrations who place differing emphases on corporate economic autonomy as a basic value that should be maintained. This is well-illustrated by the Clinton Administration which had a very different approach to that of the earlier Bush Administration on the issue of government subsidization of research and development (R&D) work being carried out by corporations. The (first) Bush Administration had consistently opposed all non-actionable subsidies, including R&D subsidies, and clearly sought to encourage other States to accept its value of corporate

---

[92] 'Subsidies Disciplines Requiring Clarification and Improvement', Negotiating Group on Rules, Communication from the United States, TN/RL/W/78, (19 March 2003), p.1. For similar US statements, see US Communication, TN/RL/W/27, 22 October 2002; and 'Special and Differential Treatment and the Subsidies Agreement', TN/RL/W/33, 2 December 2002, p.3.
[93] 'Subsidies Disciplines Requiring Clarification and Improvement', *ibid*, pp.3–4.

economic autonomy during the Uruguay Round negotiations.[94] However, the Clinton Administration reversed this approach once it came into power and actually pressed for increases in the amount that a government could contribute to R&D activities in the Uruguay Round negotiations[95] since it sought to foster industrial competitiveness and economic growth precisely, in part, by using R&D investments.[96] It seems clear that this approach of the Clinton Administration was designed to develop future technologies in which the US would enjoy a comparative advantage. As US Trade Representative Kantor explained in stark terms while giving testimony before the House of Representative Ways and Means Committee,

Subject to specific, limiting criteria, the [SCM] Agreement makes three types of subsidies non-actionable. Government assistance for industrial research and development is non-actionable if the assistance for "industrial research" is limited to 75 percent of eligible research costs and the assistance for "pre-competitive development activity" (through the creation of the first, non-commercial prototype) is limited to 50 percent of eligible costs. This will enable the Clinton Administration to continue to co-operate with industry to develop the technologies of tomorrow without the threat of counter-vailing duty actions, while ensuring that other countries cannot provide development or production subsidies free from such actions. . . . We made substantial changes in the so-called subsidies text in order to make sure that we could have government-private partnerships for fundamental, basic and applied research; in order that we can do things as we did with SEMATECH, which was one of the reasons our semiconductor industry made such a wonderful comeback in the late 1980s and early 1990s and now

[94] Stewart provides a useful summary of one instance of contestation of this value within the Uruguay Round: 'On September 27, 1990 . . . . [T]he United States submitted a new proposal, in which it addressed anew the subject of domestic subsidies, and urged that certain domestic subsidies be prohibited. . . . The United States proposed that Article 1(1) of the Chairman's text should be amended to include a list of specific practices which it believed should be prohib-ited . . . . The EC criticized the proposal for *assuming that domestic subsidies, in themselves, were trade-distortive*, while developing countries, such as India and Brazil, expressed the view that the new proposal was too extreme in curbing domestic subsidies, *which they view as useful instruments of national economic development*. The *US position*, however, reflecting the trade negotiation objectives stated by Congress in the 1988 Trade Act, *remained that domestic subsidies must be restricted.*' (Stewart, *supra* n.60, pp.872–873. Emphasis added.)
[95] This complete reversal of US policy on R&D subsidies in the Uruguay Round negotiations was noted by the Wall Street Journal in the following terms: 'On the issue of research subsidies, the U.S. faced a . . . problem. The Bush administration wanted to wean the world of government subsidies; the current [Clinton] administration wants to use the government to spark research-based industries. The result is that the Clintonites had to argue strenuously to liberalize subsidy limits that the Bush team fought to impose. In the end, the U.S. and EC agreed that governments could pay at least 50% of the cost of applied-research projects—enough to ensure that Mr Clinton's pet projects in automobile and electronics research won't run afoul of GATT.' ('Trade Acceptance: After Years of Talks, GATT Is At Last Ready To Sign Off on A Pact', *Wall Street Journal*, 15 December 1993, at A7, as quoted in T. Stewart (ed.), *The GATT Uruguay Round: A Negotiating History (1986–1994)*, Vol.IV, p.234 (n.48).)
[96] *The GATT Subsidies Code and its Impact on R&D: Hearing before the Subcommittee on Technology, Environment, and Aviation of the House Committee on Science, Space, and Technology*, 103d Cong., 2d Sess. 13–15 (1994) (Statement of John Gibbons, Director of the White House Office of Science and Technology Policy), as quoted in Stewart, *supra* n.95, pp.232–233 (n.44.).

dominates the world market in semiconductors; in order that we can have the government appropriately involved in a way that would put us in a competitive position, if not better than a competitive position in the world as we develop new technologies.[97]

This approach not only represents a marked departure from the previous US approach of seeking to ensure the maintenance of the value of corporate economic autonomy, but also seeks to ensure that the comparative advantage which the US enjoys in the production of a large number of goods is preserved, indeed frozen, by the SCM Agreement which prevents foreign governments trying to improve their comparative advantage through such means, to quote USTR Kantor, as 'development or production subsidies'; while the US government was[98] to be left free 'to continue to co-operate with industry to develop the technologies of tomorrow without the threat of countervailing duty actions'.[99]

Let us now turn, finally, to examine efforts by the US Congress to project internationally the observance of corporate economic autonomy through first the GATT and then the WTO.

(c) The US Congress and efforts to project observance of corporate economic autonomy

The failure by the US Congress to ratify the International Trade Organization (ITO) Charter not only extinguished the embryonic existence of the ITO,[100] but compromised the ability of the US to lead and impose its vision of an international economic order on the community of States through the mechanism of the ITO and even through the GATT.[101] As such, Congress was forced to try

---

[97] As quoted in Stewart, *ibid*, p.235 (n.52).

[98] Article 31 of the SCM Agreement provides that the R&D exemption contained in Article 8 would only apply initially for a provisional period of five years. The continued application of Article 8 was then to be dependent on a decision by the SCM Committee to continue its application. However the SCM Committee failed to reach a consensus on an extension before 31 December 1999, and as such the R&D exemption in Article 8 ceased to have effect. See the Report of the WTO Committee on Subsidies and Countervailing Measures, WTO Doc. G/L/408, 10 November 2000, 12.   [99] See *supra* n.97 and corresponding text.

[100] The legislation to ratify the ITO was being held up in a Congressional sub-committee to the point that the Executive withdrew it from consideration. (Beane, *supra* n.58, p.10.) For a comprehensive account of the deliberations on the ITO and in particular on the US contribution see R. Hudec, *Essays on the Nature of International Trade Law* (1999), p.25 *et seq*; and on the role of US internal political processes in forming the approach of the US Government towards the ITO, see S. Ariel Aaronson, *Trade and the American Dream: A Social History of Postwar Trade Policy* (1996).

[101] Beane, *supra* n.58, 192. This can be contrasted with the position of the US in the very early years of the GATT where it often simply insisted upon something and it was agreed by GATT Contracting Parties. In fact, of the 26 articles in the original US proposal for GATT 1947, 23 of these were basically accepted as written and the three others, despite some opposition and slight modifications, were also accepted. (Beane, *supra* n.58, p.10.) By the time of the fifth GATT Round, the so-called 'Dillon Round' (Geneva, 1961–1962), there were, however, two significant changes that affected the economic power of the US. The first is that the EEC for the first time negotiated as a single entity on behalf of its Member States and as such instantly posed

and ensure observance internationally of its values—including that of corporate economic autonomy—by taking unilateral measures against States who did not comply adequately, in the US view, with the observance of these values within their economies. This US quest for a 'level playing field' in the trading system increasingly came to reflect the prevailing US view that its inability in some areas to compete abroad was in significant part due to the unfair trading practices of other States[102] and, accordingly, that the US Executive and Congress had a key role to play in achieving competitiveness by reducing foreign government intervention within their economies.[103]

It was in particular the 1962 Trade Expansion Act that marked an important shift in US policy towards the taking of unilateral trade actions against other States: Congress granted to the President a limited right to take retaliatory action against foreign governments who had caused harm to US companies. For example, Section 262 directed the President to react against unfair agricultural trade practices of countries exporting to the US. Congress, however, became increasingly unhappy over the reluctance and slowness of the President to take measures under Section 262. There was also increasing frustration within Congress at the inadequacies in the GATT dispute resolution procedures in terms of both their speed and addressing US competitive concerns. Accordingly, Congress pursued unilateral measures with even more vigour in its 1974 Trade Act.

The 1974 Act established a more formal procedure for aiding US companies who had been injured by foreign competition. Individuals could directly petition agencies of the US government for assistance and this was intended to force the Executive to take action. This was coupled with Section 301 of the 1974 Act which gave the Executive a stronger capacity to take unilateral action than the earlier 1962 Act by authorizing retaliatory action against

---

an industrial bloc that offset US power and influence. Second, there were increasing numbers of States attaining independence from colonialism and these developing countries were increasingly acceding to GATT and were beginning to demand more from the US in negotiations. More recently, after the conclusion of the Uruguay Round, the USTR made a surprising admission about US economic power in one of its Section 301 Reports: 'There was a time when U.S. involvement in international trade negotiations was a prerequisite for them to succeed. That is no longer true. Other countries are writing the rules of the international trading system as they negotiate without us. The EU has free trade or customs agreements with 27 countries, and 20 of these agreements have been signed since 1990. The EU is in the process of negotiating 15 more. Last year, the European Union and Mexico—the second-largest market for American exports—entered into a free trade agreement. The EU is also negotiating free-trade agreements with the Mercosur nations and the countries of the Gulf Cooperation Council. Japan is negotiating a free trade agreement with Singapore, and is exploring free trade agreements with Mexico, Korea, and Chile. There are approximately 130 free trade agreements in force globally, but the United States has only two agreements in force: one is with Canada and Mexico (NAFTA), and the other with Israel.' (USTR Report of 30 April 2001, p.4, available on USTR web-site at: http://www.ustr.gov.)

[102] See, for example, J. Finger, 'The meaning of "Unfair" in United States import policy', 1 *Minnesota Journal of Global Trade* (1992), p.35.   [103] Leebron, *supra* n.73, pp.185.

another State's 'unreasonable' and 'unjustifiable' trade practices which affect US commercial interests. There was still, however, Congressional frustration with slow or inadequate Executive action and this led to Congress varying Section 301 in subsequent legislation that sought to require the Executive to make greater use of these retaliatory powers. For example, the 1988 Omnibus Trade and Competitiveness Act transferred Section 301 authority from the President to the USTR[104] (known as 'Super 301') for the following: (i) to determine the trigger of Section 301 action, that is whether foreign trade practices are 'unjustifiable', 'unreasonable', or 'discriminatory'; (ii) to decide whether and what action is appropriate; and (iii) to decide what implementing action should be taken.[105] Congress also made retaliatory action mandatory in response to 'unjustifiable' action. The 1988 Act did, however, afford the USTR a number of exceptional circumstances in which case it would not have to pursue Section 301 action. These circumstances are where: (i) the practice was not GATT inconsistent, (ii) the foreign country was eliminating the act, (iii) the other country offered compensation, (iv) in extraordinary cases the adverse impact on the US economy would outweigh the gains of pursuing action, and (v) the retaliation would cause serious harm to the national security of the United States. With the conclusion of the Uruguay Round Agreements and the establishment in particular of the WTO dispute settlement system, the first of these Section 301 exceptions was amended by US implementing legislation, the Uruguay Round Agreements Act to provide that Section 301 action by the USTR is not required if the WTO Dispute Settlement Body adopts a report finding that the foreign government act, policy or practice at issue 'is not a violation of, or inconsistent with, the rights of the United States, or does not deny, nullify, or impair benefits to the United States under any trade agreement.'[106] However, 'Super 301' was still seen by US trading partners as a basis for aggressive US unilateralism,[107] and the fact that it survived as part of US law despite the Uruguay Round[108] resulted, unsurprisingly, in a challenge under the WTO's dispute settlement system.

[104] S 1301(a) of the 1988 Omnibus Trade and Competitiveness Act (amending s 301 of the 1974 Trade Act).
[105] It was pursuant to these provisions that the USTR began its practice of conducting formal consultations with a State and if necessary initiating GATT dispute settlement procedures on behalf of the US. The USTR was required by the 1988 Act to initiate investigations and get an elimination, reduction, or compensation on negative trade practices within a three-year period from when it was identified. Moreover, the USTR had to submit an annual report to Congress on any progress against such actions or indicate other Section 301 actions needed to resolve the issue.   [106] S 301(a)(2)(A), 19 USC §2411(a)(2)(A)(ii).
[107] See J. Jackson, 'The Great 1994 Sovereignty Debate: United States acceptance and implementation of the Uruguay Round results' in J. Jackson, *The Jurisprudence of GATT and the WTO* (2000), p.367 at p.391.
[108] Congress expressly preserved Section 301 authority when in Section 102 (a) (2) of the URAA it stated that nothing in the Act shall be construed '. . . (B) To limit any authority conferred under any law of the United States, including Section 301 of the Trade Act of 1974, Unless specifically provided for in this Act.'

Let us turn to consider briefly the important *US—Sections 301–310 of the Trade Act of 1974* case.[109]

The EC claimed in the case that:

by adopting, maintaining on its statute book and applying Sections 301–310 of the 1974 Trade Act after the entry into force of the Uruguay Round Agreements, the US has breached the historical deal that was struck in Marrakech between the US and the other Uruguay Round participants.... this deal consists of a trade-off between, on the one hand, the practical certainty of adoption by the Dispute Settlement Body of panel and Appellate Body reports and of authorization for Members to suspend concessions—in the EC's view, an explicit US request—and, on the other hand, the complete and definitive abandoning by the US of its long-standing policy of unilateral action. The EC submits that the second leg of this deal, which is, in its view, the core of the present Panel procedure, has been enshrined in the following WTO provisions: Articles 3, 21, 22 and, most importantly, 23 of the DSU and Article XVI:4 of the WTO Agreement.[110]

The US response to these claims was that its law was WTO consistent since:

Sections 301–310 permit the US to comply with DSU [WTO Dispute Settlement Understanding] rules and procedures in every case: Section 304 permits the USTR to base his or her determinations on adopted panel and Appellate Body findings in every case; and Sections 305 and 306 permit the USTR, in every case, to request and receive DSB authorization to suspend concessions in accordance with Article 22 of the DSU.[111]

The Panel in deciding this case found that the relevant sections of the 1974 Trade Act, ss 304–306, did indeed constitute a prima facie violation of certain DSU provisions,[112] but that a violation could not be confirmed in the case.[113] The Panel based this decision on essentially a US promise, made both in a Statement of Administrative Action (submitted by the President to, and approved by, the Congress) and also before the Panel, that any Section 301 determination that there has been a violation or denial of US rights would be based only on a panel or Appellate Body decision adopted by the DSB.[114] This led the Panel to find Section 304[115]—and, using the same reasoning, ss 305[116] and 306[117]—as not being inconsistent with US obligations under the DSU.

For the internationalist, this express undertaking by the US is a positive step towards multilateralism and compliance with WTO obligations. However a word of caution is required. It would be a mistake to ignore the importance placed by Congress on, for example, its value of corporate economic autonomy and the ability of the US to project internationally this value, especially where its non-observance is perceived to be undermining US competitiveness.

---

[109] *United States—Sections 301–310 of the Trade Act of 1974* case, WT/DS152/R, 22 December 1999.   [110] *Ibid*, para.7.2.
[111] *Ibid*, para.7.9.   [112] *Ibid*, para.7.97.   [113] *Ibid*, para.7.98.
[114] *Ibid*, paras.7.109, 7.112.   [115] *Ibid*, para.7.135.   [116] *Ibid*, paras.7.184–7.185.
[117] *Ibid*, para.7.170.

This is well-illustrated by the debates in Congress on acceptance and implementation of the results of the Uruguay Round. As John Jackson recounts:

The US Congress made it very clear...that it would not tolerate changes in section 301, and the Executive negotiating position followed that mandate. Consequently, except for some minor procedural amendments, section 301 remains intact.... This [statutory provision], however, was perhaps the most important political bellwether of the sovereignty considerations in the Congress during the 1994 debate.[118]

However, the main opposition by certain influential members of Congress to accepting the results of the Uruguay Round was over the perceived 'loss of US sovereignty' that would take place if Congress gave its consent to the WTO Agreements.[119] As Leebron states: 'One theme dominated the debate over the Uruguay Round Agreements in the United States, and this was sovereignty. In this context, "sovereignty" primarily meant autonomy to determine various aspects of US policy.'[120] More specifically, the concern was in relation to the WTO dispute settlement system.[121]

(d) The US Congress and the establishment of the WTO dispute settlement system

The technique that was adopted by Congress to counter these sovereignty concerns was to ensure that the Uruguay Round Agreements were not self-executing or did not otherwise constitute a basis for a cause of action in US law.[122] Moreover, members of Congress were assured that if the DSB decided in a case that US legislation requires amendment to conform to the Uruguay Round Agreements, then the normal legislative process would have to be followed to change the legislation in question. Put differently, Congress retains the right to contest the exercise by the WTO dispute settlement system of transferred powers by retaining the right to implement these decisions within the US legal order. This was a retrogressive step: the 1979 Trade Agreements

[118] J. Jackson, 'The Great 1994 Sovereignty Debate: United States acceptance and implementation of the Uruguay Round results' in J. Jackson, *The Jurisprudence of GATT and the WTO* (2000), p.367 at p.391.

[119] This was, for example, the view of Republican Senate Leader Robert Dole: J. Jackson, 'The Great 1994 Sovereignty Debate: United States Acceptance and Implementation of the Uruguay Round Results', 36 *Columbia Journal of Transnational Law* (1998), p.157; and Mundo, *supra* n.58, p.137.   [120] Leebron, *supra* n.73, pp.176, 210–211.

[121] See J. Jackson, 'The Great 1994 Sovereignty Debate: United States acceptance and implementation of the Uruguay Round results' in J. Jackson, *The Jurisprudence of GATT and the WTO* (2000), p.367 at p.388; and Leebron, *supra* n.73, pp.176, 210–211.

[122] *Ibid*, pp.211–212. There was in any case an express limit placed by Congress on the extent to which the URAA may be interpreted as altering US laws or administrative regulations not expressly specified in the Act. The Act states that it shall not be construed '(A) To amend or modify any law of the United States, including any law relating to—(i) the protection of human, animal, or plant life or health, (ii) the protection of the environment, or (iii) worker safety, or (B) To limit any authority conferred under any law of the United States, including Section 301 of the Trade Act of 1974, Unless specifically provided for in this Act.' (S 102 (a) (2) (A)–(B) of the URAA.)

Act implementing the Tokyo Round notably gave the President the authority to change US legislation to comply with either a GATT dispute settlement ruling or an amendment to any of the covered Agreements.[123]

This approach to WTO dispute settlement decisions was also extended by Congress to include Congressional agencies. If agency regulations or practices are found to violate the WTO agreements, then modification can only take place after an extensive consultation exercise with relevant Congressional committees and private sector interests.[124] This position is in stark contrast to the position of US executive agencies—for example, the US Department of Commerce (USDOC) and its subsidiary body the International Trade Administration (ITA)—under the URAA. The USTR has considerable more discretion in relation to implementation of a WTO dispute settlement finding if it requires changes being made to the regulations or practices of the USDOC or ITA.[125]

Moreover, a deal was struck between President Clinton and Senate Minority Leader Dole (soon to be Majority Leader after the newly elected Congress was sworn in)[126] to ensure safe passage of the URAA but also to assuage Senator Dole's concerns about the perceived loss of US sovereignty by ratification of the WTO Agreements. The compromise measure was to provide the US with a clear exit route out of the WTO should the Organization, in the view of a proposed Commission, negatively affect US interests.[127] In the end this proposed Commission was not established, but there has nonetheless been serious attempts made by the US Congress at least to consider the issue of withdrawal. For example, Congress requested that the General Accounting Office (GAO)[128] undertake a study of the WTO dispute settlement system and its impact on foreign trade practices and on US laws and regulations in order to ascertain whether continued US participation in the WTO was in the national interest. The GAO stated in summation:

Overall, our analysis shows that the United States has gained more than it has lost in the WTO dispute settlement system to date. WTO cases have resulted in a substantial number of changes in foreign trade practices, while their effect on U.S. laws and

---

[123] Leebron, *supra* n.73, p.214.   [124] *Ibid*, p.221.

[125] In the case of the USDOC, see s 129 (b), URAA, 19 USC s 3538 (b), as cited in Leebron, *Ibid*, p.222 (nn.177, 178).

[126] Before the vote on the Uruguay Round implementing bill could take place, there were congressional elections in November 1994 which saw a Republic takeover of Congress. President Clinton persuaded congressional leaders to vote on the UR implementing bill before the new Congress was sworn in, but this was subject to the deal concluded between President Clinton and Senate Leader Dole. See A. Rubin, 'Dole, Clinton Compromise Greases Wheels for GATT', *Congressional Quarterly Weekly Report*, 26 November 1994, Vol.52, No.46, p.3405.

[127] This was known as the 'three-strikes and we're out' clause. If a Commission of US judges who were to review WTO decisions found that the WTO had acted arbitrarily against US interests in three cases, then it could propose a joint congressional resolution instructing the President to withdraw the US from the WTO.

[128] The GAO is an agency of Congress. More information on its activities can be found at: http://www.gao.gov.

regulations has been minimal. In about three-quarters of the 25 cases filed by the United States, other WTO members agreed to change their practices, in some instances offering commercial benefits to the United States. For example, in response to a 1998 WTO ruling on Japanese distilled liquor taxes, Japan accelerated its tariff elimination and reduced discriminatory taxes on competing alcohol imports. The year following the resolution of the case, US exports of whiskey to Japan, one of the largest U.S. markets for distilled spirits, increased by 18 percent, or $10 million. As for the United States, in 5 of the 17 cases in which it was a defendant, two U.S. laws, two U.S. regulations, and one set of U.S. guidelines were changed or subject to change. These changes have been relatively minor to date and the majority of them have had limited or no commercial consequences for the United States. For example, in one case challenging increased U.S. duties on Korean semiconductor imports, the United States took action to comply with [a] WTO ruling while still maintaining the duties.[129]

Largely on the basis of this Report, the US House of Representatives rejected a proposed resolution, by a vote of 363 to 56, that sought to withdraw congressional approval of US membership in the WTO.[130]

Whether the commissioning by Congress of the GAO Report[131] is part of a broader attempt to retain for the US the competence to determine when other States are acting in violation of values such as corporate economic autonomy remains to be seen.[132] What is clear, however, is that where Congress considers that the common values being formulated through the processes of contestation in the WTO do not adequately reflect US values or worse still are perceived to be undermining US competitiveness then this will be the point at which the US commitment to the rule of law in the multilateral trading system—and compromise over its value of nation-State economic autonomy—will really be put to the test.

This analysis leads us to question why then did the US—and in particular the US Congress—actually push for the establishment of a binding dispute settlement system within the WTO? Does this not in general terms run contrary to the US value of nation-State economic autonomy? The US Congress had sought for a long time to resist the establishment of an international organization with binding powers in relation to trade liberalization.[133] Obviously now the US Congress and Executive considered that there were benefits in establishing a binding system of dispute resolution here that justified departure from this value in the case of international economic disputes.[134] Let us turn to examine some of the considerations relating to this issue.

---

[129] Report of the US General Accounting Office, 'World Trade Organization: U.S. Experience to Date in Dispute Settlement System', 14 June 2000, contained in S. Murphy, 'Contemporary practice of the United States relating to international law', 94 *AJIL* (2000), p.677 at p.698 (n.3).   [130] 94 *AJIL* (2000), p.698 (n.4).

[131] See *supra* nn.128–129 and corresponding text.

[132] This may of course involve a violation by the US of its WTO obligations: cf. the *Sections 301–310* case, *supra* n.112 and corresponding text.

[133] See Beane, *supra* n.58, pp.253–254.

[134] The final Congressional vote approving the WTO Agreements and the implementing legislation (the URAA) was by an overwhelming majority (288 to 146 in the House of

(e) Why did the US push for the establishment of the WTO dispute settlement system?

The US still possesses a large degree of economic power and it has been reluctant, as set out above, to compromise on its value of nation-State economic autonomy. It is thus at first glance paradoxical that the US pushed for the establishment of a binding dispute settlement system within the WTO which restricts considerably its freedom of unilateral action.

In order to understand this situation it is instructive to employ the innovative theoretical approach that has been developed by Ran Hirschl when considering why hegemonic elites—such as power holders in legislatures and executives—at the domestic level not only countenance, but more importantly push for, the empowerment of the judiciary, especially since this seems to run contrary, at a prima facie level, to the interests of these power holders whose power will be constrained by the courts.[135] His approach is based on the view that political power holders will usually try and shape an institutional structure that will best serve their interests. It is Hirschl's main thesis that has the most interesting implications for our discussion. He states that,

> judicial empowerment is in many cases the consequence of a conscious strategy undertaken by threatened political and economic elites seeking to preserve their hegemony vis-à-vis the growing influence of "peripheral" groups in crucial majoritarian policy-making arenas. In response to perceived threats by peripheral groups, elites who possess disproportionate access to and influence upon the legal arena often initiate a constitutional entrenchment of rights in order to insulate policymaking from popular political pressure. Power is transferred from majoritarian decision-making arenas to national high courts, where they assume their policy preferences will find greater support.... In other words, judicial empowerment through the constitutional fortification of rights may provide an efficient institutional way for hegemonic sociopolitical forces to preserve their hegemony and to secure their policy preferences even when majoritarian decision-making processes are not operating to their advantage.[136]

This approach contains explanatory power for the insistence by the US Congress and Executive during the Uruguay Round that the resulting WTO Agreements must contain a binding and effective dispute settlement system.[137] It was clear by the time of the Uruguay Round that the US had lost its

Representatives, and 76 to 24 in the Senate), but it did not approach the nearly consensual vote in favour of the implementing legislation of the Tokyo Round agreements. (Leebron, *supra* n.73, p.175 (n.2).)

[135] R. Hirschl, 'The Political Origins of Judicial Empowerment through Constitutionalization: Lessons from Four Constitutional Revolutions', 25 *Law & Social Inquiry* (2000), p.91.

[136] R. Hirschl, 'The Political Origins of Judicial Empowerment through Constitutionalization: Lessons from Four Constitutional Revolutions', 25 *Law & Social Inquiry* (2000), p.91 at pp.91, 95.

[137] On this US insistence, see the EC statement in the *Section 301* case: *supra* n.110 and corresponding text.

hegemonic position in the international economy. It was no longer simply able to dictate the rules. The early days of the GATT where the US virtually wrote the whole treaty, and subsequently other rules, while others simply signed on had long since vanished:[138] the rise in economic power and influence of the EC and Japan had seen to this during the preceding decades. What must also have been clear to the US during the Uruguay Round negotiations was that the establishment of an international organization to oversee the implementation, and provide a focus for future development, of the rules governing world trade would empower developing countries by virtue of their majority in the organization. It is easy to predict that over time this may see the bringing forward of long-harboured claims for distributive justice. Viewed in this context of a potential future loss of power the US decision to push for a binding and effective dispute settlement system was entirely logical and accords with Hirschl's account of judicial empowerment at the domestic level. Since the US had been the main player, and in the early years of the GATT the only real player, in the drawing up of the rules governing trade that are largely encapsulated in the WTO Agreements, the establishment of a judiciary to implement and provide for enforcement of these rules could only be to its benefit. To put this point more conceptually: the encapsulation in the WTO Agreements of the US value of corporate economic autonomy and its strong general preference for the operation of the market was the most significant feature that the US may have been seeking to preserve by pushing for the establishment of a binding WTO dispute settlement system. Having overseen the entrenchment of this value first in the GATT, then in its side codes, and finally in the WTO, the time was ripe for the institution of a binding system of dispute resolution which would ensure the perpetuation of these values through their application in specific cases and also, importantly, by the establishment of a DSU jurisprudence on the matter, which though lacking a formal binding effect in future cases is certainly in practice treated as highly persuasive.

This aspiration, to the extent that it was an objective of US policy, has been more than fully realized in the first 10 years of operation of the DSU. But with the WTO structure how could it have been any different? The Appellate Body is expressly prohibited from rendering an authoritative interpretation of the Agreements thus precluding the facility of changing the text over time or, importantly, changing the values that inform its application of the text, since this is within the exclusive competence of the Ministerial Conference or the General Council under Article IX:2 of the Marrakesh Agreement Establishing the WTO ('WTO Charter'). In practice, both the Ministerial Conference (which in any case meets only once every two years) and the General Council may well find it difficult to meet the high threshold of a three-fourths majority required for such a decision. As such, there is a clear institutional bias against

---

[138] On this early US power, see *supra* n.101.

change of the WTO Agreements through interpretation.[139] This approach is further supported by the US implementing legislation, the URAA, which states that 'it is the objective of the United States to ensure that the Ministerial Conference and the General Council continue the practice of decisionmaking by consensus.'[140] This bias against change places considerable systemic importance on the continual reinforcement by the Appellate Body of the underlying values of the WTO Agreements.[141] It is this feature of the Appellate Body's role that commends the application of Hirschl's thesis to understanding the US support of the WTO dispute settlement system. It was thus no surprise that the GAO Report, discussed above, told Congress that the WTO DSU benefited the US national interest and that, as such, Congress should not decide to try and withdraw the US from the organization.[142]

III. CONSEQUENCES OF TRANSFERS OF POWERS FOR THE STATE-ORGANIZATION RELATIONSHIP

1. Fiduciary issues

An organization's exclusive right to exercise transferred powers provides the basis for the argument that member States should not do anything outside the framework of the organization, at least on the international plane, that might impinge on the organization's exercise of powers. The European Court of Justice (ECJ) has certainly adopted this strict position in a series of cases concerning the exclusive competence of the EC, vis-à-vis its Member States, to conclude treaties[143] in certain areas that bind all Member States.[144] The first of

[139] Moreover, the complicated procedures for formal amendment of the WTO Agreements set out in Article X of the WTO Charter also militate against change. See E. Stein, 'International Integration and Democracy: No Love at First Sight', 95 *AJIL* (2001), p.489 at p.501.

[140] URAA, 19 U.S.C. §3532(a).

[141] There is, however, the use by developing countries of the WTO dispute settlement proceedings; but these only serve to reinforce the application of the values already contained in the WTO Agreements. Cf. though the DSU reform proposals currently being considered by the WTO: D. Sarooshi, 'Reform of the World Trade Organisation Dispute Settlement Understanding: A Critical Juncture for Developing Countries' in I. Mbirimi, B. Chilala, and R. Grynberg, eds., *From Doha to Cancun: Delivering a Development Round* (2003), p.105.

[142] See *supra* n.129 and corresponding text.

[143] This can be contrasted with the case of the delegation of a treaty-making power by States to the United Nations: see *supra* nn.23–24 and corresponding text in Chapter 5.

[144] There is extensive scholarly commentary on this treaty-making power, see for example, M. Akehurst, 'Decisions of the Court of Justice of the European Communities During 1971–1972', 46 *BYBIL* (1972–1973), p.439; J.H.H. Weiler, 'The Transformation of Europe', 100 *Yale LJ* (1991), p.2403, and *The Constitution of Europe* (1999), pp.171–175; F. Berman, 'Community Law and International Law: How Far Does Either Belong to the Other?' in B. Markesinis, ed., *The Clifford Chance Lectures: Bridging the Channel* (1996), Chapter 12 at p.255 *et seq*; and M. Kaniel, *The Exclusive Treaty-Making Power of the European Community up to the Period of the Single European Act* (1996).

these cases, the *ERTA* case, concerned the exclusive competence of the EC to conclude treaties in the sphere of transport, even though the EEC Treaty did not in express terms make such a competence exclusive.[145] The ECJ stated in the *ERTA* case:

... each time the Community, with a view to implementing a common policy envisaged by the Treaty, adopts provisions laying down common rules, whatever form these may take, the Member States no longer have the right, acting individually or even collectively, to undertake obligations with third countries which affect those rules. ... Under Article 3(e), the adoption of a common policy in the sphere of transport is specially mentioned amongst the objectives of the Community. Under Article 5, the Member States are required on the one hand to take all appropriate measures to ensure fulfilment of the obligations arising out of the Treaty or resulting from action taken by the institutions and, on the other hand, to abstain from any measure which might jeopardize the attainment of the objectives of the Treaty. If these two provisions are read in conjunction, it follows that to the extent to which Community rules are promulgated for the attainment of the objectives of the Treaty, the Member States cannot, outside the framework of the Community institutions, assume obligations which might affect those rules or alter their scope.[146]

The extent to which such a fiduciary obligation will exist in the case of transfers will largely depend on the exact terms of a particular transfer. What is clear, however, is that the exclusive competence of the organization to exercise transferred powers gives the organization the interest, and arguably the influence, to see that the binding obligation is complied with by member States. To this extent, any such fiduciary duty that is owed in the case of a transfer of powers may, as in the case of the EC just discussed, be strictly monitored by the international organization.

2. *Issues of responsibility*

We recall from Chapter 5 that where an international organization commits an internationally wrongful act then it is clear that this entails the international responsibility of the organization.[147] However, the more complex matter is whether States can be held responsible on a primary or secondary basis for an internationally wrongful act committed by an organization exercising transferred powers. Let us consider this matter in our separate categories of partial and full transfers of powers.

---

[145] The EC does not, however, possess an exclusive competence to conclude treaties in all areas of its operation. There is a shared competence that the EC and member States possess to conclude treaties in certain areas. See, for example, *Re the Competence of the European Community to Conclude International Agreements concerning Services and the Protection of Intellectual Property, Opinion 1/94*, 105 *ILR* p.75; and *Opinion 2/91, ECR* (1993-I), p.1061 at p.1084.   [146] *ERTA* case, [1971] *ECR*, p.263 at pp.274–275.

[147] See *supra* n.40 and corresponding text in Chapter 5.

(i) Partial transfers of powers

In the case of partial transfers the State is bound on the international plane to comply with decisions of an organization over which the State has no direct control. But the lack of direct control by a State over an internationally wrongful act committed by an organization does not thereby exclude all potential bases of responsibility for the State. Control is only sufficient and not necessary for establishing attribution for the purposes of State responsibility. There is still arguably a potential basis for attributing the internationally wrongful acts of an organization to transferring States by application of Article 5 of the International Law Commission's (ILC's) Articles on State Responsibility. This provision, relating to the conduct of persons or entities exercising elements of governmental authority, states:

> The conduct of a person or entity which is not an organ of the State under article 4 but which is empowered by the law of that State to exercise elements of the governmental authority shall be considered an act of the State under international law, provided the person or entity is acting in that capacity in the particular instance.[148]

It seems clear that such an 'entity' could include an international organization that exercises conferred powers of government. As James Crawford, the final ILC Special Rapporteur on State Responsibility, stated: '[t]here is no doubt that an organ of an international organization may perform governmental functions for or in relation to States....'[149] The ILC Commentary on this provision goes on to state that '[t]he justification for attributing to the State under international law the conduct of "para-statal" entities lies in the fact that the internal law of the State has conferred on the entity in question the exercise of certain elements of the governmental authority.'[150] But the Commentary provides a limitation to the potential scope of application of this provision when it states that '[t]he formulation of article 5 clearly limits it to entities which are empowered by internal law to exercise governmental authority.'[151] It should be made clear that this limitation does not require the exercise of governmental authority necessarily to have binding effect within a State's domestic legal system. Article 5 does clearly apply in such a case of fully transferred powers,[152] but it is also arguably applicable in the case of a partial transfer of powers where a State will have *agreed under its internal law* to be bound by the organization's exercise of powers on the international plane.

In addition to this potential case of attribution there are arguably three other potential bases for States being held responsible for internationally wrongful

---

[148] Contained in J. Crawford, *The International Law Commission's Articles on State Responsibility: Introduction, Text and Commentaries* (2002), p.100.

[149] J. Crawford, First Report on State Responsibility, A/CN.4/490/Add.5, pp.27–28.

[150] J. Crawford, *The International Law Commission's Articles on State Responsibility: Introduction, Text and Commentaries* (2002), p.101.   [151] *Ibid.*

[152] See *infra* Section III(2)(ii).

acts of an organization exercising partially transferred powers. Two of these bases flow from the State's *own* acts or omissions.

The first is where a State's implementation within its domestic legal system of an organization's decision involves it committing an internationally wrongful act. We recall that in the case of partial transfers of powers the organization's decision does not have direct effect within the State's legal system and as such it can choose not to give domestic legal effect to a decision where this would involve the commission of an internationally wrongful act. If the State were, however, to implement the organization's decision and commit an internationally wrongful act then it would clearly be held responsible under international law for this act pursuant to Article 1 of the ILC's Articles on State Responsibility.[153] And yet this is obviously problematic for the State concerned since it is being required in such a case to disobey its clear obligation on the international plane which flows from the organization's exercise of transferred powers. It is for this reason that when States transfer powers to an organization they must try and ensure that the organization's exercise of powers cannot lead to the imposition of obligations on the State that are inconsistent with a prior treaty obligation owed to another State (or indeed to another organization) that is not a party to the treaty that transfers powers.

In practice, however, it may be very difficult for a State to determine in advance whether the transfer of powers to an international organization may lead to such a conflict of treaty obligations. A possible way to avoid such a conflict is for the negotiating States to decide to 'delegate' and not 'transfer' their powers to an organization so that they will not be bound to comply with decisions taken by the organization when exercising conferred powers.[154] Moreover, we recall from Chapter 5 that in the case of delegations the State retains the right to exercise its power independent of the organization and can thus do so in a way that is consistent with its prior treaty obligations. However, providing for delegations will not of course always be desirable or indeed possible (for example, where a State joins an international organization whose constituent treaty already provides for transfers). Nonetheless, even in those cases where negotiating States do wish to transfer in part their powers to an organization there are two possible ways they can seek to deal with the problem of conflicting obligations. First, the negotiating States could employ the model of various UN Specialized Agencies whose organs have a general competence to pass decisions that bind member States subject to members being able to 'opt-out' of a particular decision such that it does not have binding force for the State.[155] This model would allow States the flexibility to

---

[153] For the text of Article 1, see *supra* n.42 in Chapter 5.
[154] On this consequence of delegations of powers as opposed to transfers, see Section II in Chapter 5.   [155] See *supra* nn.26–27 and corresponding text in Chapter 5.

opt-out of specific decisions to ensure that they were in compliance with their other treaty obligations. Second, States should consult with third parties to take their views on the matter. This practical measure may be of legal importance, since it may provide a successful basis for preclusion[156] of an allegation of breach of a treaty made by a third party if it had earlier agreed to the State's transfer of power.

The second case where a State's responsibility can be engaged in relation to the exercise by an organization of partially transferred powers is where a State aids or assists the organization in the commission of an internationally wrongful act. This responsibility flows from the application, *mutatis mutandis*, of Article 16 of the ILC's Articles on State Responsibility. The discussion of Article 16 above in Chapter 5 applies equally—though with one important exception—to the case of partial transfers of powers.[157] The exception in the case of partial transfers is that the acts of the State caught by Article 16 are only those taken within its domestic legal system. We recall from Chapter 5 that an important element of the acts of aid or assistance covered by Article 16 is that they are entirely voluntary[158] and since in the case of partial transfers the State is bound on the international plane by decisions of the organization then the State can only be held primarily responsible for those voluntary acts of aid or assistance rendered to an organization within its domestic legal system where it is not so bound.[159]

There is, nonetheless, a potential secondary responsibility of States that flows from the commission by an organization of an internationally wrongful act in the exercise of partially transferred powers. This secondary responsibility is arguably engaged where States actively pursue or support the particular decision in the international organization that causes the commission of the internationally wrongful act. The basis for such a secondary responsibility has already been considered above in Chapter 5 and there are no reasons why this should not apply equally in the case of an organization exercising partially transferred powers.[160]

(ii) Full transfers of powers

In the case of full transfers the decision of the organization binds the State on the international plane but also has direct effect within a State's legal system.

---

[156] On the operation of preclusion—the international law analogue of rules of estoppel known to common law jurisdictions—see H. Thirlway, 'The Law and Procedure of the International Court of Justice 1960–1989, Part One', 60 *BYBIL* (1989), p.1 at pp.47–49; I. Brownlie, *Principles of Public International Law* (2003, 6th edn), pp.615–616; and D. Bowett, 'Estoppel before International Tribunals and its Relation to Acquiescence', 33 *BYBIL* (1957), p.176.

[157] See *supra* nn.43–44 and corresponding text in Chapter 5.

[158] See *supra* n.44 and corresponding text in Chapter 5.

[159] Cf. the secondary responsibility of States in the case of partial transfers: *infra* n.160 and corresponding text.   [160] See *supra* nn.45–46 and corresponding text in Chapter 5.

In these cases the main basis for the internationally wrongful acts of an organization being attributable to a transferring State is by application of Article 5 of the ILC Articles. Cases of full transfers are clearly instances where States have conferred on an organization 'the exercise of certain elements of governmental authority' and thus, according to Article 5, 'shall be considered an act of the State under international law'. Moreover, the main limitation placed by the ILC Commentary on the scope of application of the Article—that it is limited 'to entities which are empowered by internal law to exercise governmental authority'—is more than adequately fulfilled in the case of full transfers where decisions of the organization go further to have a direct effect within the State's legal system. A good example of the potential application of Article 5 is where an organization exercises transferred powers in such a way that it violates the human rights obligations owed by States. In such cases, a State cannot be heard to plead that its hands were tied by the organization's exercise of transferred powers. The jurisprudence of the European Court of Human Rights ('the Court') is instructive on this point. As the Court stated in the *Waite and Kennedy* case:

The Court is of the opinion that where States establish international organisations in order to pursue or strengthen their cooperation in certain fields of activities, and where they attribute to these organisations certain competences and accord them immunities, there may be implications as to the protection of fundamental rights. It would be incompatible with the purpose and object of the Convention, however, if the Contracting States were thereby absolved from their responsibility under the Convention in relation to the field of activity covered by such attribution. It should be recalled that the Convention is intended to guarantee not theoretical or illusory rights, but rights that are practical and effective.[161]

Moreover, the case of *Matthews v United Kingdom*[162] was concerned, in part, with the question whether the United Kingdom could be held responsible on an individual basis for an alleged act of the EC that was said to be in violation of the European Convention on Human Rights ['the Convention']. The act in question was a decision of the European Council[163] that laid down provisions concerning the election of the members of the European Parliament which in effect excluded those persons who were living

---

[161] *Richard Waite and Terry Kennedy v Germany*, Application no. 26083/94, 18 February 1999, para.67. For a similar approach by the European Court of Human Rights, see *Beer and Regan v Germany*, Application no. 28934/95, European Court of Human Rights, 18 February 1999, para.57.

[162] *Matthews v UK*, Application no 24833/94, European Court of Human Rights, 18 February 1999.

[163] Council Decision No. 76/787/ECSC, EEC, EURATOM, and Act Concerning the Election of the Representatives of the European Parliament by Direct Universal Suffrage of 20 September 1976 and its Annexes.

in Gibraltar, a dependent territory of the UK, from having the right[164] to participate in the election.[165]

The UK Government contended, *inter alia*, that while there may be circumstances where a party to the European Convention on Human Rights might infringe its Convention obligations by entering into other treaty obligations that were incompatible with the Convention, they considered that in the present case the position was not the same since 'acts adopted by the Community or consequent to its requirements could not be imputed to the member States, together or individually, particularly when those acts concerned elections to a constitutional organ of the Community itself.'[166] Moreover, at the hearing the Government suggested that to engage the responsibility of a State under the Convention requires the State to have a power of effective control over the act complained of and that in the case of the Community provisions relating to the election of the European Parliament the UK Government had no such control.[167] This argument lacks cogency, however, since as noted above control is sufficient but not necessary for the purposes of establishing attribution. There is still in the case of full transfers the potential basis of attribution provided by Article 5 of the ILC Articles on State Responsibility. The Court in the *Matthews* case made several pronouncements in support of the application of Article 5 in cases of full transfers (*in casu*, to the EC). The Court found in its judgment that although the European Convention does not exclude States parties being able to confer powers on international organizations, it does require, however, that if such conferrals take place then Convention rights must continue to be 'secured'.[168] The Court went on to state: 'Member States' responsibility [under the European Convention] therefore continues even after such a transfer.'[169]

In the end, however, the Court did not have to deal directly with the issue of UK responsibility for a Community act since it found that the 1976 Act was not a ' "normal" act of the Community, but is a treaty within the Community legal order'.[170] Accordingly, the Court based the responsibility of the UK on its subsequent acceptance of the Act, being as it was an 'international instrument' which was 'freely entered into by the United Kingdom'.[171] In the

---

[164] Cf. Article 3 of Protocol No.1 to the European Convention on Human Rights which provides: 'The High Contracting Parties undertake to hold free elections at reasonable intervals by secret ballot, under conditions which will ensure the free expression of the opinion of the people in the choice of the legislature.'

[165] *Matthews v UK*, Application no.24833/94, European Court of Human Rights, 18 February 1999, para.18.

[166] *Matthews v UK*, Application no.24833/94, European Court of Human Rights, 18 February 1999, para.26.   [167] *Ibid.*

[168] *Ibid*, para.32.   [169] *Ibid.*

[170] *Ibid*, para.33. The Court found, moreover, that the Maastricht Treaty 'is not an act of the Community, but a treaty by which a revision of the EEC Treaty was brought about.' (*Ibid.*)

[171] *Ibid*, para.33. The Court went on to find that the applicant's right to vote, as guaranteed by Article 3 of Protocol No.1, was denied and there had therefore been a violation of that provision. For the terms of Article 3 of Protocol No.1, see *supra* n.164.

context of our discussion above this represents the commission by the UK of its own internationally wrongful act rather than having an internationally wrongful act of the EC attributed to the UK.

There is, finally, a potential secondary responsibility of States in the case of full transfers where States have actively pursued or supported within the organization the decision that mandates the commission of the internationally wrongful act. The considerations relating to this secondary responsibility are the same as those pertaining in the cases of delegations and partial transfers of powers considered above.[172]

---

[172] See *supra* n.160 and corresponding text.

7

Measures a State can take against
an International Organization on which
it has Conferred Powers

The broad range of measures being taken by international organizations in the exercise of conferred powers has led a variety of commentators and domestic political and judicial actors to question the constitutionality and propriety of continued conferrals of sovereign powers on organizations.[1] We have considered already in Chapter 6 the efforts by domestic arms of government to ensure the application of their sovereign values by international organizations when exercising governmental powers. The objective now of this chapter is to clarify what measures are available to a State under international law when it wants to try and change the way that an organization is exercising conferred powers.

There are a number of reasons why States may legitimately wish to take measures against an international organization on which they have conferred powers in addition to the issue of non-compliance with sovereign values already considered. States may consider that an organization's exercise of powers is *ultra vires* or—in the case where an organization has been conferred powers for a specific purpose—that its exercise of powers is *détournement de pouvoir.*[2]

---

[1] Among the academic commentators, see, for example, J. Ku, 'The Delegation of Federal Power to International Organizations: New Problems with Old Solutions', 85 *Minnesota Law Revue* (2000), p.71; C. Bradley, 'International Delegations, the Structural Constitution, and Non-Self-Execution', 55 *Stanford Law Review* (2003), p.1557; T. Schilling, 'The Anatomy of the Community Legal Order: An Analysis of Possible Foundations', 37 *Harvard International Law Journal* (1996), p.389; and P. Tangney, 'The New Internationalism: The Cession of Sovereign Competences to Supranational Organizations and Constitutional Change in the United States and Germany', 21 *Yale Journal of International Law* (1996), p.395.

[2] This concept of *détournement de pouvoir* (diversion of power from its true purpose) is originally known in French administrative law. In applying the concept to international organizations, James Fawcett contends that 'an international organization may commit a *détournement de pouvoir* if in the exercise of a discretionary power (a) it imposes conditions upon any of its member which are not necessary or appropriate to achieve the object for which the power was granted, or (b) takes any administrative action which, though not forbidden by the founding instrument, is inconsistent with or outside the scope of the objects of the organization.' (J. Fawcett, '*Détournement de Pouvoir* by International Organizations', 33 *BYBIL* (1957), p.311 at p.316.)

A good example of the application of *détournement de pouvoir* was by the ECJ in Case C-376/98 *Germany v Parliament and Council* (the 'Tobacco Advertising') case where the Court annulled Community Directive 98/34 on the basis that the regulation of tobacco advertising did not fall within the purpose of the relevant powers—Article 100a (now Article 95)—which conferred powers on the Community to adopt measures of harmonisation in order to build the EC's internal market. On this case, see, for example, D. Wyatt, 'Constitutional Significance of the *Tobacco Advertising* Judgment of the European Court of Justice' and G. de Búrca, 'The Tobacco

Then there is the rationale that the organization's exercise of conferred powers may be such that it places the State in breach of its other obligations under international law.[3] But there is also a less obvious reason here, identified by Vaughan Lowe, which is that the acts of the organization, or of member States within the organization, may contribute to the formation of customary international law and it is this which may lead, subsequently, to the State being bound in a certain way with which it disagrees.[4]

The number and type of measures that States may take against an organization will depend on the type of conferrals and the nature of the relationship that is established as a result of these conferrals between the States and the organization.[5]

I. AGENCY RELATIONSHIPS

It is in the case of agency relationships that the conferring States have the broadest range of measures available to them. These range from, on the one hand, being able in general to exercise direct control over the way in which powers are being exercised by the organization, to having, on the other, the competence to revoke or modify at any time their conferrals of powers on the organization.[6] These cases of agency are, however, not commonplace due to the operation of the presumption, discussed above in Chapter 4, which militates against the existence of agency relationships between States and organizations.[7]

In our other two types of conferrals, States have no direct control over the organization's exercise of powers outside the confines of the organization's decision-making processes[8] and they can as a result only try to influence the organization by participation in its decision-making processes, if the State is a member of the relevant organ, or by taking other measures against the

---

Advertising Saga: Political Aspirations and Constitutional Constraints', both contained in *The ECJ's Tobacco Advertising Judgment* (Cambridge Centre for European Legal Studies Occasional Paper, No 5, 2001); T. Hervey, 'Community and National Competence in Health after Tobacco Advertising', 38 *CMLRev* (2001), p. 1421.

[3] See, for examples, Section III(2) in Chapter 6.

[4] See V. Lowe, 'Can the European Community Bind the Member States on Questions of Customary International Law' in M. Koskenniemi, ed., *International Law Aspects of the European Union* (1998), p.149.
  On the practice of UN principal organs contributing to the formation of norms of customary international law, see R. Higgins, *Problems and Process: International Law and How We Use It* (1994), p.25; and in the specific case of UN General Assembly resolutions, see *Nicaragua* case, *ICJ Reports*, 1986, p.14 at p.100; M. Mendelson, 'The Formation of Customary International Law', 272 *Recueil des cours* (1998), p.155 at p.356 *et seq*; and J. Klabbers, *An Introduction to International Institutional Law* (2002), pp.207–210.

[5] On our typology of conferrals of powers, see Chapter 3.

[6] See Section II in Chapter 4.   [7] See Section III in Chapter 4.

[8] See Section II(2) in Chapter 3.

organization within their domestic legal systems. There are, however, four more general measures that States may take against an organization when it seeks to change the way in which delegated or transferred powers are being exercised.[9] The first measure is to seek to amend the terms of the treaty. The second is to take unilateral financial measures against the organization in respect of financial obligations that flow from the exercise of conferred powers. Third, is for a State to take the drastic step of withdrawing from the treaty altogether thereby terminating the conferral of powers. The fourth involves a State objecting on a persistent basis within the organization to try and prevent any emerging norm of customary international law resulting from the organization's—or indeed the State's own—practice from binding the State. The threat by a State of pursuing one of these measures may in itself lead to a change in approach by the organization which resolves the issue. If this is not, however, to the State's satisfaction then it may wish to act out its threat, but pursuit of these measures is not free from considerable difficulties in both law and practice. Let us now turn to examine more specifically the number and types of measures available to States in our categories of delegations and transfers.

II. DELEGATIONS OF POWERS

In the case of delegations of powers we recall from Chapters 3 and 5 that States retain the right to exercise powers on a unilateral basis and, importantly, they are not bound to comply with obligations flowing from the organization's exercise of conferred powers. Nonetheless, States that have delegated powers may still wish to take measures against a particular exercise by an organization of conferred powers which is considered to be *détournement de pouvoir, ultra vires*, or an internationally wrongful act with which the objecting States do not wish to be associated. Moreover, a State may wish to distance itself from the State practice of other member States within the organs of an organization which may contribute to the formation of customary international law that, in the absence of persistent objection, would otherwise bind the State.

1. *Treaty amendment*

The first measure of treaty amendment is often impossible to achieve in practice since it depends on obtaining the consent of all the States parties. Such consent is mandated by Articles 39–40 of the 1969 Vienna Convention on the

---

[9] There is the more specific measure that a State may, where there is provision, institute judicial review proceedings against the contested decision of the organ of the organization. See, for example, the case of the EU: *supra* n.2. For an argument in favour of the ICJ exercising such review for international organizations, see *infra* n.52 and corresponding text.

Law of Treaties ('Vienna Convention').[10] This consent may be obtained either by compliance with procedures for amendment specified in the treaty itself or by subsequent agreement among the States parties.[11] In the case of ad hoc conferrals[12] or in the case of a regional international organization such as the EC,[13] it may be a realistic option to obtain the consent of a limited number of States parties to amend the terms of the treaty. Where, however, conferrals of powers take place by constituent treaty of a large multilateral organization then formal amendment of conferred powers may well prove more problematic. Member States may, for example, take the opportunity to try and seek amendment of other aspects of the functioning of the organization with the likely result that no changes will be agreed.

2. *Unilateral financial measures*

The second measure available to a State is to take some form of unilateral financial measures against an organization. In practice such measures may either be general in nature or they may target more specifically the State's assessed contribution to the cost of the activity that the State is challenging. This measure may, depending on the proportion of the budget paid by the member State, be very effective as a means of changing the way an organization exercises conferred powers. This does not mean, however, that there are no legal difficulties that arise in such cases of unilateral withholding. These are well illustrated by the case of the UN and the practice of States withholding unilaterally their assessed contributions to the UN budget.

In the case of the UN, the ICJ in the *Expenses* case clearly established that the General Assembly has the sole right to decide upon and apportion the expenses of the Organization among its Member States with binding effect.[14] Despite this clear statement of the legal position, there has been a significant practice of States withholding payment of their assessed contributions to the UN budget.[15] There has been general condemnation of virtually all such

---

[10] On the amendment of treaties generally, see also I. Brownlie, *Principles of Public International Law* (2003, 6th edn), p.601; I. Sinclair, *The Vienna Convention on the Law of Treaties*, (1984, 2nd edn), pp.106–113; R. Jennings and A. Watts, *Oppenheim's International Law* (1992, 9th edn), pp.1254–1257; and R. Gardiner, 'Revising the Law of Carriage by Air: Mechanisms in Treaties and Contract', 47 *ICLQ* (1998), p.278.

[11] For a comprehensive review of amendment procedures in the constituent treaties of international organizations, see H. Schermers and N. Blokker, *International Institutional Law* (2003, 4th edn), pp.731–752. [12] On ad hoc conferrals of powers, see Section II in Chapter 2.

[13] For amendment in the case of the EC, see *infra* n.41 and corresponding text.

[14] *Expenses* case, *ICJ Reports*, 1962, p.151 at p.164.

[15] For further discussion of this practice, see, for example, Higgins, *supra* n.4, pp.178–180; F. Francioni, 'Multilateralism *à la Carte*: The Limits to Unilateral Withholdings of Assessed Contributions to the UN Budget', 11 *EJIL* (2000), p.43 at p.48; J. Alvarez, 'Financial Responsibility' in O. Schachter and C. Joyner, *United Nations Legal Order* (1995), vol.2, p.1091 at pp.1098–1099; E. Zoller, 'The "corporate will" of the United Nations and the Rights of the Minority', 81 *AJIL* (1987), p.610 at p.610; A. Gerson, 'Multilateralism *à la Carte*: The

withholdings as being unlawful,[16] with the possible exception of the US refusal to pay its assessed contribution under the UN budget for the Law of the Sea Preparatory Commission.[17] This Preparatory Commission was not part of the UN Organization nor a UN Specialized Agency, but rather was established under a separate treaty basis.[18] The US withholding in this case has a solid legal basis for the reason that the General Assembly's competence to decide and apportion the budget relates only to the UN Organization and thus a decision by the General Assembly that Member States must contribute on a compulsory basis to the financing of an entity with a separate legal basis—an entity not part of the Organization—would seem to lack a solid legal foundation.[19]

This case raises the more general question of what is the basis for a State being able to withhold its assessed financial contributions as a legal remedy against perceived breaches of the law or other unlawful acts by an organization in the exercise of conferred powers. The rationale for unilateral withholding by a State is that in the absence of a judicial body to test the lawfulness of acts of the organization, the practice of unilateral withholding is the only way that a minority of member States can ensure that the principle of legality[20] is upheld within the context of international organizations.[21] The consequence

Consequences of Unilateral 'Pick and Pay' Approaches', 11 *EJIL* (2000), p.61 at p.64; E. Cárdenas, 'UN Financing: Some Reflections', 11 *EJIL* (2000), p.67; Schermers and Blokker, *supra* n.11, pp.631–635; and R. Nelson, 'International Law and U.S. Withholding of Payments to International Organizations', 80 *AJIL* (1986), p.973 at pp.978–979.

[16] See, for example, Higgins, *supra* n.4, pp.178–180; Francioni, *ibid*, p.49, 55–56; Alvarez, *ibid*, pp.1098–1099; Zoller, *ibid*, p.633; E. Cárdenas, 'UN Financing: Some Reflections', 11 *EJIL* (2000), p.67; and R. Nelson, 'International Law and U.S. Withholding of Payments to International Organizations', 80 *AJIL* (1986), p.973 at pp.975, 978–979. For a defence of the U.S. position, see A. Gerson, 'Multilateralism *à la Carte*: The Consequences of Unilateral 'Pick and Pay' Approaches', 11 *EJIL* (2000), p.61 at p.64; and W.M. Reisman, 'The United States and International Institutions', 41(4) *Survival* (1999–2000), p.62 at p.66.

[17] See, eg., Alvarez, *ibid*, p.1102; and Francioni, *ibid*, p.55.

[18] On the Preparatory Commission and its work, see R. Churchill and V. Lowe, *The law of the sea* (1999, 3rd edn), pp.19, 236–237.

[19] On a similar possible issue arising in the context of the financing of the International Criminal Court, see D. Sarooshi, 'The Statute of the International Criminal Court', 48 *ICLQ* (1999), p.387 at p.394.

[20] The principle of legality was expressly applied by the ICJ to international organizations when in the *Conditions of Admission* case the Court stated: 'The political character of an organ cannot release it from the observance of the treaty provision established by the [UN] Charter when they constitute limitations on its powers or criteria for its judgment. To ascertain whether an organ has freedom of choice for its decisions, reference must be made to the terms of its constitution.' (*ICJ Reports*, 1948, p.57 at p.64.) For further consideration of the application of the principle of legality to the UN, see I. Brownlie, 'The Decisions of Political Organs of the United Nations and the Rule of Law' in R. St. J. Macdonald, ed., *Essays in Honour of Wang Tieya* (1993), p.91 at p.96.

[21] As the President of the ICJ, Judge Winiarski, stated in the *Expenses* case: 'a refusal to pay, as in the case before the Court, may be regarded by a Member State, loyal and indeed devoted to the Organization, as the only means of protesting against a resolution of the majority which, in its opinion, disregards the true meaning of the Charter and adopts in connection with it a decision which is legally invalid'. (*Expenses* case, *ICJ Reports*, 1962, p.151 at p.232.) See also Francioni, *supra* n.15, pp.52–53, 58; Alvarez, *supra* n.15, p.1108; and Zoller, *supra* n.15, pp.631–632.

of this rationale is that States do not have the right to withhold their assessed financial contributions in the case of international organizations, such as the EC, where there is a judicial body that has a compulsory jurisdiction to decide whether acts of the organization are unlawful.[22]

It is useful here to draw on the work of Francesco Francioni who has conducted a study of unilateral withholdings by States in the case of the UN and established three appropriate and reasonable conditions that a unilateral withholding must meet before it can be deemed lawful.[23] These are 'the principles of (i) specific necessity, (ii) integrity, and (iii) consistency'.[24]

The first of these, the 'principle of specific necessity', is explained in more detail by Francioni when he states that 'a challenge to the legality of a UN assessment must be necessitated by and related to a specific violation of the law of the Charter or of international law arising from the UN activity whose financing is contested. This principle excludes withholdings motivated by national interests or based on a generic complaint of illegality or on a breach unrelated to the activity whose financing is disputed.'[25] The problem though with this limitation is that it does not allow unilateral withholding by States in response to acts of an organization that do not have financial consequences. This position does not sit easily with the core of the justification for unilateral withholdings: that it is the lack of a compulsory judicial mechanism to test the legality of the acts of most international organizations that allows States to take unilateral financial measures against purported unlawful acts. The precondition for a unilateral withholding by a State should not be that there are financial obligations which flow from the contested act of an organization, but rather that an act is purportedly unlawful.

The problematic nature of this aspect of the principle of 'specific necessity' is borne out by a situation that arose before the Plenipotentiary Conference of the International Telecommunication Union (ITU) in 1982. A draft resolution was submitted to the Conference which aimed to suspend Israel's rights and privileges of ITU membership.[26] Several delegates questioned the legality of this draft resolution and in response the ITU's legal advisor stated that the Plenipotentiary Conference clearly does not possess such a power of suspension under the ITU constituent treaty in the case at hand.[27] If for the sake of argument the ITU Conference had gone ahead in this case and suspended

---

[22] See, for example, the decision of the European Court of Justice annulling an act of the Council: *supra* n.2.

[23] Francioni does, moreover, state that a unilateral withholding in response to an alleged *ultra vires* act is only a remedy of last resort. (Francioni, *supra* n.15, p.59.) See also Alvarez who states: 'If the majority opinion in the Expenses case is taken seriously, unilateral withholding in response to *ultra vires* action is, at most, an option of last resort, to be taken only after the complaining member has given the organization the opportunity to correct any error.' (Alvarez, *supra* n.15, p.1108.)   [24] Francioni, *supra* n.15, p.59.

[25] *Ibid*, p.54.

[26] There is a useful summary of this case in Schermers and Blokker, *supra* n.11, pp.916–917.

[27] Schermers and Blokker, *supra* n.11, pp.916–917.

Israel's membership then it would not be possible according to a narrow view of the 'principle of specific necessity' for dissenting Member States to protest against what is in their view, and that of the ITU legal advisor, an *ultra vires* decision by means of withholding part of their assessed contribution to the budget of the organization. Such a position surely runs counter to the very reason why States may have the right to withhold unilaterally their financial contributions as a last resort measure: to uphold the principle of legality within international organizations. It is for this reason that the 'principle of specific necessity', as stated by Francioni, should be modified to allow unilateral withholding by a State in all cases where an act of the organization is allegedly unlawful, thus also including those cases where there are no financial implications of the specific act of the organization. This broader approach may run the risk of impeding the effective functioning of an organization in certain cases, but this is arguably the justifiable cost of ensuring that States have available to them an effective means of challenging purportedly unlawful acts of international organizations.

Francioni's second principle of 'integrity' is essentially a requirement of good faith that 'has the advantage [as opposed to other more general claims of good faith] of being linked to an external referent, the prima facie breach in relation to which the challenge to withhold has to be evaluated. Under this criterion, the challenging state must at a minimum provide a plausible case to sustain the claim of illegality in order to reverse the general presumption in favour of the legality and validity of UN acts.'[28] Francioni's third principle of 'consistency' requires 'an attitude of the withholding state that is not contradicted over a period of time by positions that are incompatible with previous interpretations of the law or with previous objections to other members' view of the law.'[29] These second and third limitations on a State's right to withhold assessed contributions in response to an alleged unlawful act are both appropriate and reasonable, since they do not run contrary to the very rationale for the existence of a right to withhold and at the same time they seek to ensure a State's response is focused on an alleged unlawful act.

3. Termination of conferrals

The third measure available to a State is to terminate its conferral of powers. The existence of this measure in theory does not mean, however, that it will always be viable in practice. Its use will be particularly difficult in the case of delegations by constituent treaty where the State will have to terminate its membership of the organization in order to revoke its conferrals. There have, nonetheless, been instances where States have taken this extreme measure and withdrawn from the constituent treaty of an organization.[30] However, these

---

[28] Francioni, *supra* n.15, p.54.   [29] *Ibid*, p.55.
[30] For an account of this practice, see Schermers and Blokker, *supra* n.11, pp.82–91.

withdrawals mostly took place during the Cold War and were motivated at least in part by the adoption—or in some cases the lack of adoption—by an organization of a particular ideological approach to its mandate.[31] States today may be less willing to withdraw from international organizations for at least three general reasons.

First, a State's membership in an international organization may allow it to participate in the processes of decision-making concerning decisions which affect their vital interests to a greater degree than if they were not members.[32]

Second, the stigma attached to such an act in the current international climate where the emphasis is on more international co-operation rather than less may militate against withdrawal. Studies by Chayes and Chayes and others illustrate how the forces of 'social opprobrium' and 'the sense of shame or social disgrace' are factors that may also work to induce treaty compliance more generally.[33]

Third, unless there has been a significant change in the actual or perceived returns that a State enjoys by virtue of its membership in an organization then it is unlikely to withdraw over a disagreement with the way in which the organization is exercising a particular conferred power.[34] Moreover, a State's participation in the activities of an organization may well have seen a substantial investment both in terms of compromises made over the years in the conduct of its foreign policy in a number of cases but also in terms of possible adaptation of its domestic law. This also militates in favour of States continuing to participate in an organization even where the State disagrees with the way in which conferred powers are being exercised in a particular case. This may even be an understatement of the degree to which States consider as vital their continued participation as a member of important international organizations such as the UN.

4. Persistent objection

The fourth measure a State can take against an organization exercising delegated powers is to object on a persistent basis against an act or decision of an

---

[31] As Chayes and Chayes state: 'It is certainly true, for example, that the U.S. withdrawal from the UN Education, Scientific, and Cultural Organization... reflected a distaste not only for "wasteful spending" but also for the unwillingness of the secretary general to accept the policy priorities of the United States and the West.' (See A. Chayes and A. Chayes, *The New Sovereignty* (1995), p.282.)

[32] See R. Jennings, 'Sovereignty and International Law' in G. Kreijen, ed., *State, Sovereignty, and International Governance* (2002), p.27 at p.36.

[33] See, for example, Chayes and Chayes, *supra* n.31, pp.152, 232–233, 274; and O. Young, 'The Effectiveness of International Institutions: Hard Cases and Critical Variables' in J. Rosenau and E-O. Czempiel, eds., *Governance without Government: Order and Change in World Politics* (1992), p.160 at pp.176–177.

[34] A possible exception here is Indonesia's purported withdrawal from the United Nations in 1965 in response to the election of Malaysia as a non-permanent Member of the UN Security Council. On this purported withdrawal, see E. Schwelb, 'Withdrawal from the United Nations The Indonesian Intermezzo', 61 *AJIL* (1967), p.661; and Y. Blum, 'Indonesia's Return to the United Nations', 16 *ICLQ* (1967), p.522.

organization. The aim of these persistent objections is to prevent any subsequent rule of customary international law that is formed in part as a result
of decisions by the organization—and, more specifically, a State's participation
in these decisions—from binding the State. This is to avoid what occurred in
the *Nicaragua* case.[35] The International Court of Justice (ICJ) held in this case
that norms contained in certain General Assembly Resolutions had, subsequent
to their adoption, become part of the corpus of customary international law
and, moreover, that these norms were binding on the US because of its participation in the original adoption of the Resolutions.[36]

The 'persistent objector rule' in international law relies, arguably, on the
consent-based nature of custom[37] and provides that a State which objects on
a persistent basis to a practice before it has developed into a rule of customary international law can, by virtue of withholding its consent, exclude itself
from being bound by the new rule.[38] It should be made clear that a persistent
objection by a State to the practice of an organization—which meets the
requirements of the persistent objector exception[39]—would not of course
necessarily prevent the formation of a norm of customary international law,
but it would exempt the State from being bound by the practice once it had
become part of the corpus of custom.

To conclude, a State may wish to object in a persistent manner to the way in
which delegated powers are being exercised *within* an organization precisely
in order to prevent any future rule of custom that may result from the organization's acts binding the State and thus constraining its unilateral exercise of
powers *outside* the context of the organization.

III. TRANSFERS OF POWERS

In the case of transfers of powers, the measures that States can take against an
organization assume the most importance since in this type of conferral we

---

[35] *Nicaragua* case, *ICJ Reports*, 1986, p.14.

[36] The ICJ stated: 'The effect of [US] consent to the text of such resolutions cannot be understood as merely that of a "reiteration of elucidation" of the treaty commitment undertaken in the
Charter. On the contrary, it may be understood as an acceptance of the validity of the rule or set of
rules declared by the resolution by themselves.' (*Nicaragua* case, *ICJ Reports*, 1986, p.14 at p.100.)

[37] See, for example, Lowe, *supra* n.4, p.156. Cf., for example, I. Lobo de Souza, 'The Role
of State Consent in the Customary Process', 44 *ICLQ* (1995), p.521.

[38] See the *Anglo-Norwegian Fisheries* case, *ICJ Reports*, 1951, p.116 at p.131; I. Brownlie,
Principles of Public International Law (2003, 6th edn), p.11; and M. Mendelson, 'The Formation
of Customary International Law', 272 *Recueil des cours* (1998), p.155 at pp.227–244.

[39] If a State's objections are to have any consequence in law they would have to be made the
first time that the decision of the organization was taken and subsequently on a persistent basis
every time another such decision was taken: see G. Fitzmaurice, 'The Law and Procedure of the
International Court of Justice, 1951–1954: General Principles and Sources of Law', 30 *BYBIL*
(1953), p.1 at p.26; and H. Thirlway, 'The Law and Procedure of the International Court of
Justice 1960–1989, Part Two', 61 *BYBIL* (1990), p.1 at p.106.

recall that States are bound to comply with obligations that flow from the organization's exercise of powers.[40] The potential measures a State can take against an organization to which it has transferred powers are as follows.

1. Treaty amendment

The first is to seek amendment of the terms of the treaty, the general difficulties with this approach in practice having already been discussed above. Where, however, States disagree with the exercise by an organization of transferred powers, there is a stronger incentive to amend the terms of transfer due to the binding nature of obligations flowing from the organization's exercise of powers. An example of this is provided by the case of the EC where the Member States have amended the EC Treaties several times in response to contentious decisions of the European Court of Justice that would otherwise—in the absence of such amendment—have bound the Members.[41]

2. Unilateral financial measures

The second measure a State may wish to take against an organization in an attempt to change the way transferred powers are being exercised is for the State to withhold its assessed financial contributions to the organization. The lawful use of this measure would be, however, subject to the limitations already set out above.[42]

3. Termination of conferrals

The third measure potentially available is termination of the transfer of powers. This will run up against a legal problem in the case of most transfers since we recall that such conferrals powers are in general irrevocable.[43] There is,

---

[40] See Section II in Chapter 6.

[41] For example, as Joseph Weiler has stated: 'The most important example [of amendment] is the Protocol Concerning Article 119 of the Treaty Establishing the European Community, annexed to the EC Treaty which, according to Article 239 of the EC Treaty, is an "integral part" of it. This Protocol—the so-called "Barber" Protocol—was a reaction to the ECJ judgment in Case C-262/88, *Barber v. Royal Guardian Exchange Assurance Group* [1990] ECR 1, 889. Being the prototype of a consensus reaction of the Member States to a binding decision of the ECJ, the Barber Protocol is considered by some to be a warning to the ECJ.... Another example of the Member States altering the Treaties is the Protocol annexed to the Treaty on European Union and to the Treaties Establishing the European Union (the so-called "Irish Abortion" Protocol). Curtin submits that "the whole purpose of including the Protocol in the first place was to close the door that seemed to be left ajar...by the [ECJ] ruling in *SPUC v. Grogan* [Case C159/90 [1991] ECR I-4, 685]". Further examples—outside...[these] "special case" protocols—include the new provisions on culture (see Arts. 3(p) and 128 of the EC Treaty) and on public health (see Art.3(o) and Title X of the EC Treaty).' (J.H.H. Weiler, *The Constitution of Europe* (1999), p.291 (n.22).)   [42] See Section II(2).

[43] For discussion of this issue of revocability in the case of transfers, see Section I in Chapter 6.

however, the exceptional category of transfers, discussed above in Chapter 6,[44] which does allow the possibility of unilateral withdrawal. Moreover, we recall from Chapter 5 that where an organization changes the type of conferral of powers from a delegation to a transfer the State will have the competence to terminate its conferral.[45] The more general considerations relating to this decision will likely, however, be the same as pertains to the revocation of delegations of powers, discussed above.[46]

4. Persistent objection

The fourth measure a State may take is to object on a consistent basis against the way in which transferred powers are being interpreted or applied by the organization and thereby to attempt to exclude the application to itself of any obligations which may flow from a subsequent rule of custom that is formed in part by the practice of the organization. The issue of persistent objection in the case of transfers has two different facets as compared to cases of delegations of powers. The first is that in the case of transfers the exclusive competence of the organization to exercise conferred powers means that the *practice of the organization is the practice of the member States* for the purposes of the formation of customary international law,[47] unless a State goes on the record as objecting to the particular practice when the organization exercises its powers. The second difference is that in the case of transfers the conferring States are in any case bound by the organization's exercise of powers and as such the question of being bound in the same way under customary law appears at first glance as being moot. This does not mean, however, that persistent objection is without practical importance for States in the case of transfers. If for some reason the obligation on States pursuant to the organization's exercise of transferred powers no longer applied to the State—where, for example, the powers of the organization were amended, an objecting State withdrew from the organization, or indeed if the organization were dissolved—then the State which had persistently objected would not be constrained in the exercise of its newly regained powers by a norm of customary international law which had emerged from the previous practice of the organization.

IV. THE FUTURE

The general importance for States being able to pursue the above measures is reinforced by the reality that the organ of an organization whose acts are

---

[44] For discussion of this issue of revocability in the case of transfers, see Section I in Chapter 6.

[45] See *supra* nn.35–37 and corresponding text in Chapter 5.   [46] See Section II(3).

[47] This argument has been made by Vaughan Lowe in the context of the EC: Lowe, *supra* n.4, p.163. For discussion of the possibility and extent to which acts of the EC on questions of customary international law may bind member States, see Lowe, *ibid*, p.149.

being challenged will often be the very organ that has to decide on claims that its acts have been *détournement de pouvoir, ultra vires*, or otherwise unlawful. In any case, the vagaries of discussion and argument in the political organs of an organization are not particularly well-suited for such legal determinations.[48] Moreover, history teaches us that international organizations—as with most types of governments—seek to increase their relative power vis-à-vis other institutional actors (*in casu*, States) rather than voluntarily accepting constraints on their powers.[49] Viewed from this perspective the lawful measures available to States to challenge the way an organization exercises conferred powers of government appear inadequate.

A suitable legal remedy here—which does not adequately exist at present except in the case of the EC and its ECJ—would be the use or establishment of an international tribunal which could review the lawfulness of the exercise by international organizations of at least their expressly conferred powers. This approach may suffer, to an extent, from what Stern has expressed as the problem 'of constantly appealing to corrective justice through adjudication' instead of engaging in more 'preventative action'.[50] The point in our context, however, is that States have already had the opportunity to provide such safeguards in the decision-making processes of the organizations that exercise conferred powers and the issue, for our purposes, has now become whether the exercise of these conferred powers is lawful. This is a matter that fits squarely within the remit of adjudication. The use of the advisory—and possibly even contentious—jurisdiction of the ICJ may be of some use here, but only if changes were made to both sets of jurisdiction. At present it is only certain UN organs and authorized specialized agencies which can invoke the

---

[48] This is illustrated by the case of the International Civil Aviation Organization which, as Kirgis notes, 'has a procedure, set forth in the Chicago Convention, by which member states may submit their disputes regarding interpretation or application of the Convention [an adjudicative function] to the ICAO Council [a political body] for a decision. The Council consists of thirty-three representatives of member states.... Very few requests have been made, and none has been pursued to an adjudication on the merits. The ICAO procedure is generally regarded as unsatisfactory largely because the Council is ill-suited to playing an impartial adjudicative role notwithstanding its attempt to regularize the proceedings with rules.' (F. Kirgis, 'Claims Settlement and the United Nations Legal Structure' in R. Lillich, ed., *The United Nations Compensation Commission* (1995), p.103 at p.105.)

[49] See Chayes and Chayes, *supra* n.31, pp.274–275. The exception to this is where an organization's existence may be threatened due to misuse of powers or a perception by member States that an organization is consistently exceeding its powers. Cf. the resignation of the notorious 'Santer Commission' of the EC: see C. Harlow, *Accountability in the European Union* (2002), p.53 *et seq*, and A. Tomkins, 'Responsibility and Resignation in the European Commission', 62 *Modern Law Review* (1999), p.744.

[50] B. Stern, in *American Society of International Law Bulletin*, (November 1995), p.54 as cited in R. Jennings, 'The Role of the International Court of Justice', 68 *BYBIL* (1997), p.1 at pp.62–63. Or as Georges Abi-Saab eloquently states, recourse to international tribunals in all situations of international disputes between States cannot provide a 'panacée, un remède miracle à tous les maux et à toutes les faiblesses structurelles du système, une sorte de pierre philosophale du droit international'. (G. Abi-Saab, 'De l'évolution de la Cour International', 96 *Revue Générale de Droit International Public* (1992), p.273 at p.274.)

advisory jurisdiction of the Court under Article 96 of the UN Charter;[51] while the Court's contentious jurisdiction is only of course available to States that have consented, pursuant to Article 36 of the ICJ Statute, in a particular case.[52]

It is better that international courts fulfil this function of judicial review and give a single authoritative decision rather than domestic courts step in to fill this lacuna, since otherwise member States of an organization may well be placed under a domestic obligation to act in different ways in the organization depending on the decisions of their national courts, an issue considered above in Chapter 6.[53]

---

[51] This will of course depend on the ICJ being able to establish a basis for the exercise of its advisory jurisdiction in a particular case. The terms and conditions for the use of this jurisdiction are set out in Article 96 of the UN Charter and Article 65 of the ICJ Statute. A list of the UN organs and Specialized Agencies authorized to request advisory opinions of the Court is contained in the *Year Book of the International Court of Justice*.

[52] For a set of interesting articles which discuss a possible *jus standi* for international organizations before the ICJ see: J. Sztucki, 'International Organizations as Parties to Contentious Proceedings before the International Court of Justice' in A. Muller, D. Raic and J. Thuránszky, eds., *The International Court of Justice* (1997), p.141; P. Szasz, 'Granting International Organizations *Ius Standi* in the International Court of Justice' in Muller *et al.*, *ibid*, p.169; and I. Seidl-Hohenveldern, 'Access of International Organizations to the International Court of Justice' in Muller *et al.*, *ibid*, p.189. Similarly, see K. Wellens, *Remedies Against International Organizations* (2002), pp.224–261. But cf. the opinion of Judge Ferrari Bravo in his Declaration appended to the opinion of the International Court in the *Legality of the Use by a State of Nuclear Weapons in Armed Conflict (WHO Advisory Opinion)* case, *ICJ Reports*, 1996, p.66, Declaration of Judge Bravo at p.87.   [53] See Section II(1) in Chapter 6.

Concluding Remarks

The contestations between States over rival conceptions of sovereignty within international organizations are often the very same contestations of sovereignty that have been, and are still, occurring within nation-States. They are about the central problem of sovereignty: what powers are reserved to government; who exercises which of them, and how should they be exercised? In this respect, international organizations play an important role as a forum, transcendental to the State, where sovereign values that constrain the exercise of sovereign powers can be contested and developed. The challenge for international organizations exercising broad powers of government is to develop these values in conjunction with, rather than instead of, States and their organs of government.

The extent to which States and their organs of government are lawfully able to contest the exercise of sovereign powers by an international organization depends largely on the degree (or type) of conferrals of powers that have been made to the organization. The greater the degree of conferrals the less is the degree of direct control that States are allowed to exert over the organization's exercise of powers, outside the confines of the organization's decision-making processes; and yet, as a State confers powers to a greater degree on an organization there will often be more pressure exerted by the State—often as a result of increased domestic political pressures—to try and control the organization's decisions. This attempt to try and exercise greater control is often actively pursued not only by a State's executive branch, but also by its legislative and judicial branches who may seek either to direct the executive in its representation of the State in the organization or more simply threaten to exercise their own powers on the domestic plane to block the organization's decisions from having an effect within the State's legal system.

The extent to which the domestic arms of government contest sovereignty domestically is arguably a reliable indicator of the extent to which they may seek to contest the exercise of sovereign powers by an organization. This will in turn depend on a number of legal and political constraints that operate within different States. This leads us to question whether it should be left to the internal structure and decision-making processes of each State to determine the degree to which its domestic organs of government will in practice contest the formulation of sovereign values within international organizations. Instead, such contestations could be encouraged more generally. Instead of focusing on the seemingly intractable 'democratic deficit' of international organizations it may be more useful to focus on identifying and improving the 'contestability deficit' of international organizations: that is, to improve the extent to which the structures and decision-making processes of organizations promote substantive contestation by States and their arms of government in the formulation and application of sovereign values.

The necessity for such an enterprise is urgent: already the next issue in this area is beginning to loom large on the legal horizon: the relationship and interaction between international organizations that exercise sovereign powers. How will an *international organization* seek to ensure the observance of *its sovereign values* when dealing with other organizations that also exercise sovereign powers and what role will their respective member States (let alone their domestic arms of governments) play in these interactions? But that is a question for another day.

Bibliography

Aaronson, A., *Trade and the American Dream: A Social History of Postwar Trade Policy* (1996).

Abi-Saab, G., 'Cours Général de Droit International Public' 207 *Hague Recueil des cours* (1987-VII), p.9.

—— 'De l'évolution de la Cour International', 96 *Revue Générale de Droit International Public* (1992), p.273.

Adsera, A., Boix, C., and Payne, M., 'Are You Being Served? Political Accountability and Quality of Government', 19 *The Journal of Law, Economics, & Organization* (2003), p.445.

Akande, D., 'The Competence of International Organizations and the Advisory Jurisdiction of the International Court of Justice', 9 *EJIL* (1998), p.437.

Akehurst, M., 'Withdrawal from International Organizations', 32 *Current Legal Problems* (1979), p.143.

—— 'Decisions of the Court of Justice of the European Communities During 1971–1972', 46 *BYBIL* (1972–1973), p.439.

Allan, T., 'Parliamentary Sovereignty: Law, Politics, and Revolution', 113 *Law Quarterly Review* (1997), p.443.

Allison, J., *A Continental Distinction in the Common Law: A Historical and Comparative Perspective on English Public Law* (1996).

Allott, P., 'Intergovernmental societies and the idea of constitutionalism' in Coicaud, J-M., and Heiskanen, V., eds., *The Legitimacy of International Organizations* (2001), p.69.

—— *Eunomia: New Order for a New World* (2001, 2nd edn).

Angelet, N., 'Protest against Security Council decisions' in Wellens, K., *International Law: Theory and Practice: Essays in Honour of Eric Suy* (1998), p.277.

Alston, P., ed., *The EU and Human Rights* (1999).

—— and Weiler, J., 'An "Ever Closer Union" in Need of a Human Rights Policy: The European Union and Human Rights' in Alston, P., ed., *The EU and Human Rights* (1999), p.3.

—— and Bustelo, M., eds., *Whose New World Order: What Role for the United Nations* (1991).

Alter, K., 'Explaining National Court Acceptance of European Court Jurisprudence: A Critical Evaluation of Theories of Legal Integration' in Slaughter, A-M., Stone Sweet, A., Weiler, J., eds., *The European Court and National Courts—Doctrine and Jurisprudence: Legal Change in Its Social Context* (1998), p.227.

Aust, A., *Modern Treaty Law and Practice* (2000).

Alvarez, J., 'The New Treaty Makers', 25 *B.C. Int'l & Comp. L. Rev.* (2002), p.213.

—— 'Multilateralism and Its Discontents', 11 *EJIL* (2000), p.393.

—— 'Judging the Security Council', 90 *AJIL* (1996), p.1.

—— 'Financial Responsibility' in Schachter, O., and Joyner, C., eds., *United Nations Legal Order* (1995), vol.2, p.1091.

Amerasinghe, C., *Principles of the Institutional Law of International Organizations* (1996).

Amerasinghe, C., in 'Report by Rosalyn Higgins', 66-I *Annuaire de l'Institut de Droit International (AIDI)* (1995), p.353.

Anderson, D., 'Law-Making Process in the UN System', 2 *Max Planck Yearbook of United Nations Law* (1998), p.23.

Ando, N., ed., *Liber Amicorum Judge Shigeru Oda* (2002), vol.1.

Anthony, R., 'Which Agency Interpretations Should Bind Citizens and the Courts?', 7 *Yale Journal on Regulation* (1990), p.1.

Arangio-Ruiz, G., ' "The Federal Analogy" and UN Charter Interpretation: A Crucial Issue', 8 *EJIL* (1997), p.1.

Aznar-Gomez, M., 'The 1996 Nuclear Weapons Advisory Opinion and *Non Liquet* in International Law', 48 *ICLQ* (1999), p.3.

Baldwin, R., and Magee, C., 'Is trade policy for sale? Congressional voting on recent trade bills', 105 *Public Choice* (2000), p.79.

Bamforth, N., and Leyland, P., eds., *Public Law in a Multi-Layered Constitution* (2003).

Barcelo, J., 'Antidumping Laws as Barriers to Trade—The United States and the International Antidumping Code', 57 *Cornell Law Review* (1972), p.491.

Barendt, E., *An Introduction to Constitutional Law* (1998).

Barkin, J.S., and Cronin, B., 'The state and the nation: changing norms and the rules of sovereignty in international relations', 48 *International Organization* (1994), p.107.

Barron, D., and Kagan, E., 'Chevron's Nondelegation Doctrine', 2001 *Sup. Ct. Rev.* (2001), p.201.

Bartelson, J., *A Genealogy of Sovereignty* (1995).

Bausili, A., 'Rethinking the Methods of Dividing and Exercising Powers in the EU: Reforming Subsidiarity and National Parliaments', No. 9/02 *Jean Monnet Working Paper*, available at http://www.jeanmonnetprogram.org/papers/02/020901.html.

Beane, D., *The United States and GATT: A Relational Study* (2000).

Beatson, J., ' "Public" and "Private" in English Administrative Law', 103 *Law Quarterly Review* (1987), p.34.

Bekker, P., *The Legal Position of Intergovernmental Organizations: A Functional Necessity Analysis of Their Legal Status and Immunities* (1994).

Bell, J., and Eekelaar, J., eds., *Oxford Essays in Jurisprudence* (1987, 3rd Series).

Bergman, T., Müller, W., and Strøm, K., 'Introduction: Parliamentary democracy and the chain of delegation', 37 *European Journal of Political Research* (2000), p.255.

Berman, F., 'Community Law and International Law: How Far Does Either Belong to the Other?' in Markesinis, B., ed., *The Clifford Chance Lectures: Bridging the Channel* (1996), p.255.

Besanko, D., and Spulber, D., 'Delegation, Commitment, and the Regulatory Mandate', 8 *Journal of Law, Economics, and Organization* (1992), p.126.

Besson, S., 'Sovereignty in Conflict', 8(15) *European Integration online Papers* (2004), http://eiop.or.at/eiop/texte/2004-015.htm.

Bethlehem, D., 'International Law, European Community Law, National Law: Three Systems in Search of a Framework' in Koskenniemi, M., ed., *International Law Aspects of the European Union* (1998), p.169.

Blokker, N., and Schermers, H., *International Institutional Law* (2003, 4th edn).

—— 'Beyond "Dili": On the Powers and Practice of International Organizations' in Kreijen, G., ed., *State, Sovereignty, and International Governance* (2002).

—— and Muller, S., eds., *Towards More Effective Supervision by International Organizations: Essays in Honour of Henry Schermers* (1994).

Blum, Y., 'Indonesia's Return to the United Nations', 16 *ICLQ* (1967), p.522.

Boix, C., Adsera, A., and Payne, M., 'Are You Being Served? Political Accountability and Quality of Government', 19 *The Journal of Law, Economics, & Organization* (2003), p.445.

Bowett, D., 'The Court's role in relation to international organizations' in Lowe, V., and Fitzmaurice, M., eds., *Fifty Years of the International Court of Justice: Essays in Honour of Sir Robert Jennings* (1996), p.181.

—— 'Estoppel before International Tribunals and its Relation to Acquiescence', 33 *BYBIL* (1957), p.176.

Bradley, C., 'International Delegations, the Structural Constitution, and Non-Self-Execution', 55 *Stanford Law Review* (2003), p.1557.

—— 'The Treaty Power and American Federalism', 97 *Michigan Law Review* (1997–1998), p.390.

Brownlie, I., *Principles of Public International Law* (2003, 6th edn).

—— and Goodwin-Gill, G., *Basic Documents on Human Rights* (2002, 4th edn).

—— *The Rule of Law in International Affairs: International Law at the Fiftieth Anniversary of the United Nations* (1998).

—— 'State Responsibility: The Problem of Delegation' in Ginther, K., Hafner, G., Lang, W., Neuhold, H., and Sucharipa-Behrmann, L., eds., *Völkerrecht zwischen normativem anspruch und politischer Realität* (1994), p.299.

—— 'The Decisions of Political Organs of the United Nations and the Rule of Law' in Macdonald, R. St. J., ed., *Essays in Honour of Wang Tieya* (1993), p.91.

—— *Principles of Public International Law* (1990, 4th edn).

—— 'The Roles of International Law', 33 *Netherlands International Law Review* (1986), p.209.

Buergenthal, T., *Law-Making in the International Civil Aviation Organization* (1969).

Bustelo, M., and Alston, P., eds., *Whose New World Order: What Role for the United Nations* (1991).

Byers, M., ed., *The Role of Law in International Politics* (2000).

—— *Custom, Power and the Power of Rules: International Relations and Customary International Law* (1999).

Cane, P., 'Public Law and Private Law: a study of the analysis and use of a legal concept' in Eekelaar, J., and Bell, J., eds., *Oxford Essays in Jurisprudence* (1987, 3rd Series), p.57.

Cartabia, M., 'The Italian Constitutional Court and the Relationship Between the Italian legal system and the European Union' in Slaughter, A-M., Stone Sweet, A., and Weiler, J., eds., *The European Court and National Courts—Doctrine and Jurisprudence: Legal Change in Its Social Context* (1998), p.133.

Cárdenas, E., 'UN Financing: Some Reflections', 11 *EJIL* (2000), p.67.

Cassese, A., 'Modern Constitutions and International Law', 192 *Recueil des cours* (1985-III), p.331.

—— *United Nations Peace-Keeping: Legal Essays* (1978).

Chayes, A., and Chayes, A., *The New Sovereignty: Compliance with International Regulatory Agreements* (1995).

Cheng, B., *General Principles of Law as applied by International Courts and Tribunals* (1987).

Chilala, B., Mbirimi, I., and Grynberg, R., eds., *From Doha to Cancun: Delivering a Development Round* (2003).

Chimerine, L., Tonelson, A., von Schriltz, K., and Stanko, G., *Can the Phoenix Survive? The Fall and Rise of the American Steel Industry* (1994).

Chinkin, C., *Third Parties in International Law* (1993).

Churchill, R., and Lowe, V., *The law of the sea* (1999, 3rd edn).

Clapham, A., *Human Rights and the European Community: A Critical Overview* (1991), vol.1.

Cohen-Jonathan, G., 'Les Réserves dans les Traités Institutionnels Relatifs aux Droit de L'Homme. Nouveaux Aspects Européens et Internationaux', 100 *Revue Générale de Droit International Public* (1996), p.915.

Coicaud, J-M., and Heiskanen, V., eds., *The Legitimacy of International Organizations* (2001).

Collier, J., and Lowe, V., *The Settlement of Disputes in International Law* (1999).

Conforti, B., *The Law and Practice of the United Nations* (2000, 2nd edn).

Connolly, W., *The Terms of Political Discourse* (1993, 3rd edn).

Conway, G., 'Breaches of EC Law and the International Responsibility of Member States', 13 *EJIL* (2002), p.679.

Craig, P., 'Constitutional Process and Reform in the EU: Nice, Laeken, the Convention and the IGC', 10(4) *European Public Law* (2004), p.653.

—— 'Competence, Clarity, Conferral, Containment', 29(3) *European Law Review* (2004), p.323.

—— and Rawlings, R., eds., *Law and Administration in Europe* (2003).

—— and de Burca, G., *EU Law: text, cases and materials* (2003, 3rd edn).

—— 'Constitutions, Constitutionalism, and the European Union', 7 *European Law Journal* (2001), p.125.

—— 'Public Law and Control over Private Power' in Taggart, M., ed., *The Province of Administrative Law* (1997), p.196.

Craven, M., 'Legal Differentiation and the Concept of the Human Rights Treaty in International Law', 11 *EJIL* (2000), p.489.

Crawford J., *The International Law Commission's Articles on State Responsibility: Introduction, Text and Commentaries* (2002).

—— 'The Charter of the United Nations as a Constitution' in H. Fox, ed., *The Changing Constitution of the United Nations* (1997), p.3.

—— in 'Report by Rosalyn Higgins', 66-I *AIDI* (1995), p.334.

—— *The Creation of States in International Law* (1979).

Croley, S., and Jackson, J., 'WTO Dispute Procedures, Standard of Review, and Deference to National Governments', 90 *AJIL* (1996), p.193.

Cronin, B., and Barkin, J.S., 'The state and the nation: changing norms and the rules of sovereignty in international relations', 48 *International Organization* (1994), p.107.

Czempiel, E-O., and Rosenau, J., eds., *Governance without Government: Order and Change in World Politics* (1992).

de Búrca, G., and Craig, P., *EU Law: text, cases and materials* (2003, 3rd edn).

—— 'The Tobacco Advertising Saga: Political Aspirations and Constitutional Constraints' in *The ECJ's Tobacco Advertising Judgment* (Cambridge Centre for European Legal Studies Occasional Paper, No 5 (2001).

—— 'Fundamental Human Rights and the Reach of EC Law', 13 *Oxford Journal of Legal Studies* (1993), p.283.

Davey, W., Jackson, J., and Sykes, A., *Legal Problems of International Economic Relations: Cases, Materials and Text* (1995).

Decaux, E., Pettiti, L.-E., and Imbert, P.-H., eds., *La Convention européenne des droits de l'homme: Commentaire article par article* (1995).

Del Duca, P., and La Pergola, A., 'Community Law, International Law and the Italian Constitution', 79 *AJIL* (1985), p.598.

Denza, E., 'Two Legal Orders: Divergent or Convergent?', 48 *ICLQ* (1999), p.257.

De Smijter, E., and Lenaerts, K., 'The United Nations and the European Union: living apart together' in Wellens, K., ed., *International Law: Theory and Practice: Essays in Honour of Eric Suy* (1998), p.439.

Destler, I., *American Trade Politics* (1992, 2nd edn).

De Visscher; P., 'Remarques sur l'évolution de la jurisprudence de la cour internationale de justice relative au fondement obligatoire de certains actes unilatéraux' in Makarczyk. J., ed., *Essays in International Law in Honour of Judge Manfred Lachs* (1984).

Di Blase, A., 'The Role of the Host State's Consent with Regard to Non-Coercive Actions by the United Nations' in Cassese, A., ed., *United Nations Peace-Keeping: Legal Essays* (1978), p.55.

Dickinson, E., 'The Analogy between Natural Persons and International Persons in the Law of Nations', 26 *Yale Law Journal* (1916–1917), p.564.

Dinstein, Y., *War, Aggression and Self-Defence*, (1994).

Dupuy, R-J., ed., *Manuel sur les organisations internationales* (1988).

Dworkin, R., *Sovereign Virtue: The Theory and Practice of Equality* (2000).

Eagleton, C., *The Responsibility of States in International Law* (1928).

Eekelaar, J., and Bell, J., eds., *Oxford Essays in Jurisprudence* (1987, 3rd Series).

Effendi, S., *The World Order of Baha'u'llah* (1955).

Evans, M., ed., *Remedies in International Law* (1998).

Fassbender, B., *UN Security Council Reform and the Right of Veto: A Constitutional Perspective* (1998).

Fawcett, J., '*Détournement de Pouvoir* by International Organizations', 33 *BYBIL* (1957), p.311.

Feinberg, N., 'Unilateral Withdrawal from an International Organization', 39 *BYBIL* (1963), p.189.

Finger, J., 'The meaning of "Unfair" in United States import policy', 1 *Minnesota Journal of Global Trade* (1992), p.35.

Fiorina, M., 'Legislator Uncertainty, Legislative Control, and the Delegation of Legislative Power', 2 *Journal of Law, Economics, and Organization* (1986), p.33.

Fisher, L., 'Sidestepping Congress: Presidents Acting under the UN and NATO', 47 *Case Western Reserve Law Review* (1996–1997), p.1237.

Fisler Damrosch, L., ' "Sovereignty" and International Organizations', 3 *U.C. Davis J. Int'l L. & Policy* (1997), p.159.

Fitzmaurice, G., 'The Law and Procedure of the International Court of Justice, 1951–1954: General Principles and Sources of Law', 30 *BYBIL* (1953), p.1.

Fitzmaurice, M., and Sarooshi, D., *Issues of State Responsibility Before International Judicial Institutions* (2004).

—— and Lowe, V., eds., *Fifty Years of the International Court of Justice: Essays in Honour of Sir Robert Jennings* (1996).

Flaherty, M., 'History Right?: Historical Scholarship, Original Understanding, and Treaties as "Supreme Law of the Land" ', 99 *Columbia Law Review* (1999), p.2095.

Foot, R., Gaddis, J., and Hurrell, A., eds., *Order and Justice in International Relations* (2003).

Fox, H., 'The International Court of Justice's Treatment of Acts of the State, and in Particular the Attribution of Acts of Individuals to the State' in Ando, N., ed., *Liber Amicorum Judge Shigeru Oda* (2002), vol.1, p.147.

—— ed., *The Changing Constitution of the United Nations* (1997).

—— 'UK Implementation of UN Economic Sanctions', 42 *ICLQ* (1993), p.945.

—— and Wickremasinghe, C., 'British Implementation of UN Sanctions Against Iraq', 41 *ICLQ* (1992), p.920.

Francioni, F., 'Multilateralism *à la Carte*: The Limits to Unilateral Withholdings of Assessed Contributions to the UN Budget', 11 *EJIL* (2000), p.43.

Franck, T., ed., *Delegating State Powers: The Effect of Treaty Regimes on Democracy and Sovereignty* (2000).

—— *The Empowered Self: Law and Society in the Age of Individualism* (1999).

—— 'Can the United States Delegate Aspects of Sovereignty to International Regimes?' in Franck, T., ed., *Delegating State Powers: The Effect of Treaty Regimes on Democracy and Sovereignty* (2000), p.1.

—— 'The "Powers of Appreciation": Who is the Ultimate Guardian of UN Legality', 86 *AJIL* (1992), p.519.

Fridman, G., *The Law of Agency* (1996, 7th edn).

Friel, R., 'Providing a Constitutional Framework for Withdrawal from the EU: Article 59 of the Draft European Constitution', 53 *ICLQ* (2004), p.407.

Fries, S.C., and Weiler, J., 'A Human Rights Policy for the European Community and Union: The Question of Competences' in Alston, P., ed., *The EU and Human Rights* (1999), p.147.

Frowein, J., 'Das *Maastricht*—Urteil und die Grenzen der Verfassungsgerichtsbarkeit' ('The *Maastricht* Judgment and the Limits of Constitutional Jurisdiction'), 54 *ZaöRV* (1994).

Gaddis, J., Foot, R., and Hurrell, A., eds., *Order and Justice in International Relations* (2003).

Gallie, W. B., 'Essentially Contested Concepts', LVI *Proceedings of the Aristotelian Society* (1956), p.167.

Gaja, G., 'A "New" Vienna Convention on Treaties between States and International Organizations or between International Organizations: A Critical Commentary', 58 *BYBIL* (1987), p.253.

Garcia de Enterria, E., and Ortega, L., 'European influences on the national administrative laws from the point of view of the Member States: Spanish Report' in Schwarze, J., ed., *Administrative Law under European Influence: on the Convergence of the Administrative Law of the EU Member States* (1996), p.695.

Gardiner, R., 'Revising the Law of Carriage by Air: Mechanisms in Treaties and Contract', 47 *ICLQ* (1998), p.278.

Garver, E., 'Rhetoric and Essentially Contested Arguments', 11 *Philosophy and Rhetoric* (1978), p.156.

Garvey, J., 'United Nations Peacekeeping and Host State Consent', 64 *AJIL* (1970), p.241.

Gazzini, T., 'NATO Coercive Military Activities in the Yugoslav Crisis (1992–1999)', 12 *EJIL* (2001), p.391.

Germer, P., 'European influences on the national administrative laws from the point of view of the Member States: Danish Report' in Schwarze, J., ed., *Administrative Law under European Influence: on the convergence of the administrative law of the EU Member States* (1996), p.377.

Gerson, A., 'Multilateralism *à la Carte*: The Consequences of Unilateral "Pick and Pay" Approaches', 11 *EJIL* (2000), p.61.

Giddens, A., *The Nation-State and Violence* (1985).

Ginther, K., Hafner, G., Lang, W., Neuhold, H., and Sucharipa-Behrmann, L., eds., *Völkerrecht zwischen normativem anspruch und politischer Realität* (1994).

Golove, D., 'The New Confederalism: Treaty Delegations of Legislative, Executive, and Judicial Authority', 55 *Stanford Law Review* (2003), p.1697.

—— 'From Versailles to San Francisco: The Revolutionary Transformation of the War Powers', 70 *University of Colorado Law Review* (1999), p.1491.

Goodman, R., and Jinks, D., 'Toward an Institutional Theory of Sovereignty', 55 *Stanford Law Review* (2003), p.1749.

Goodwin-Gill, G., 'State Responsibility and the "Good Faith" Obligation in International Law' in Fitzmaurice, M., and Sarooshi, D., *Issues of State Responsibility Before International Judicial Institutions* (2004), p.75.

—— and Brownlie, I., *Basic Documents on Human Rights* (2002, 4th edn).

Gowlland-Debbas, V., 'The functions of the United Nations Security Council in the international legal system' in M. Byers, ed., *The Role of Law in International Politics* (2000).

—— *Collective Responses to Illegal Acts under International Law: United Nations Action in the Case of Southern Rhodesia* (1990).

—— 'The Relationship between the International Court of Justice and the Security Council in the Light of the *Lockerbie* case', 88 *AJIL* (1994), p.643.

—— 'Security Council Enforcement Action and Issues of State Responsibility', 43 *ICLQ* (1994), p.55.

Grabenwarter, C., 'The Austrian Federal Constitution and Peace between States', 51 *Zeitschrift für öffentliches Recht* (1996), p.61.

Grané, P., and Jackson, J., 'The Saga Continues: An Update on the Banana Dispute and Its Procedural Offspring', 4 *JIEL* (2001), p.581.

Gray, C., 'Regional Arrangements and the United Nations Collective Security System' in Fox, H., ed., *The Changing Constitution of the United Nations* (1997), p.91.

Gray, J., 'On the Contestability of Social and Political Concepts', 5 *Political Theory* (1977), p.331.

Greenwood, C., 'State Responsibility for the Decisions of National Courts' in Fitzmaurice, M., and Sarooshi, D., *Issues of State Responsibility Before International Judicial Institutions* (2004), p.55.

Greenwood, C., 'The United Nations as Guarantor of International Peace and Security: Past, Present and Future—A United Kingdom View' in Tomuschat, C., *The United Nations at Age Fifty: A Legal Perspective* (1995), p.69.
—— 'The International Tribunal for Former Yugoslavia', 69 *International Affairs* (1993), p.641.
Gregory, W., *The Law of Agency and Partnership* (2001, 3rd edn).
Greig, D., 'The Advisory Jurisdiction of the International Court and the Settlement of Disputes between States', 15 *ICLQ* (1966), p.325.
Gross, L., *Essays on International Law and Organization* (1984).
—— 'States as Organs of International Law and the Problem of Autointerpretation' in Gross, L., *Essays on International Law and Organization* (1984), vol.I, p.367.
Grynberg, R., Mbirimi, I., and Chilala, B., eds., *From Doha to Cancun: Delivering a Development Round* (2003).
Gunther, K., 'The Legacies of Injustice and Fear: A European Approach to Human Rights and their Effects on Political Culture' in Alston, P., ed., *The EU and Human Rights* (1999), p.117.
Guyénot, J., *The French Law of Agency and Distributorship Agreements* (1976).
Hafner, G., Ginther, K., Lang, W., Neuhold, H., and Sucharipa-Behrmann, L., eds., *Völkerrecht zwischen normativem anspruch und politischer Realität* (1994).
Hahn, H., 'La Cour Constitutionnelle Federale D'Allemagne et le Traite de Maastricht', 98 *Revue Générale de Droit International Public* (1994), p.107.
Harck, S., and Olsen, H., 'International Decisions: Decision Concerning the Maastricht Treaty', 93 *AJIL* (1999), p.209.
Harlow, C., *Accountability in the European Union* (2002).
—— ' "Public" and "Private" Law: Definition without Distinction', 43 *Modern Law Review* (1980), p.241.
Hathaway, O., 'Positive Feedback: The Impact of Trade Liberalization on Industry Demands for Protection', 52 *International Organization* (1998), p.575.
Heiskanen, V., and Coicaud, J-M., eds., *The Legitimacy of International Organizations* (2001).
Helfer, L., and Slaughter, A-M., 'Toward a Theory of Effective Supranational Adjudication', 107 *Yale Law Journal* (1997–1998), p.273.
Hendry, I., Macleod, I., and Hyett, S., *The External Relations of the European Communities* (1996).
Henkin, L., *Foreign Affairs and the Constitution* (1996, 2nd edn).
—— 'International Organization and the Rule of Law', 23 *International Organization* (1969), p.656.
Herman, A., 'The WTO Dispute Settlement Review Commission: An Unwise Extension of Extrajudicial Roles', 47 *Hastings Law Journal* (1995–1996), p.1635.
Hervey, T., 'Community and National Competence in Health after Tobacco Advertising', 38 *CMLRev* (2001), p.1421.
Higgins, R., 'Issues of State Responsibility before the International Court of Justice' in Fitzmaurice, M., and Sarooshi, D., *Issues of State Responsibility Before International Judicial Institutions* (2004), p.1.
—— 'The Responsibility of States Members for the Defaults of International Organizations: Continuing the Dialogue' in Schlemmer-Schulte, S., and Tung, K., eds., *Liber Amicorum Ibrahim F.I. Shihata: International Finance and Development Law* (2001), p.442.

—— 'The International Court of Justice and human rights' in Wellens, K., ed., *International Law: Theory and Practice: Essays in Honour of Eric Suy* (1998), p.691.

—— 'Final Report of the Legal Consequences for Member States of the Non-Fulfilment by International Organizations of their Obligations Towards Third Parties', *Report of the Institut de droit International*, 66-I *AIDI* (1995), p.251.

—— 'The United Nations 50 Years On, Part III: Achievements and Failures', *European Journal of International Law*, Special Issue, (1995), Chapter 6, p.14.

—— *Problems and Process: International Law and How We Use It* (1994).

—— 'International Law and the Avoidance, Containment and Resolution of Disputes', 230 *Hague Recueil des Cours* (1991-V), p.9.

—— 'Human Rights: Some Questions of Integrity', 52 *MLR* (1989), p.1.

—— *United Nations Peacekeeping 1946–1967* (1969), vol.1.

—— 'Policy Considerations and the International Judicial Process', 17 *ICLQ* (1968), p.58.

Hinsley, F.H., *Sovereignty* (1986, 2nd edn).

Hirschl, R., *Towards Juristocracy: The Origins and Consequences of the New Constitutionalism* (2004).

—— 'The Political Origins of Judicial Empowerment through Constitutionalization: Lessons from Four Constitutional Revolutions', 25 *Law & Social Inquiry* (2000), p.91.

Hirsh, J., and Oakley, R., *Somalia and Operation Restore Hope: Reflections on Peacemaking and Peacekeeping* (1995).

Ho, B., *Hong Kong Agency Law* (1991).

Hohfeld, W., 'Some Fundamental Legal Conceptions as Applied in Judicial Reasoning', 23 *Yale Law Journal* (1913–1914), p.16.

Holland, T., *Elements of Jurisprudence* (1906).

Howse, R., 'From Politics to Technocracy—and Back Again: The Fate of the Multilateral Trading Regime', 96 *AJIL* (2002), p. 94.

—— and Nicolaidis, K., 'Introduction: The Federal Vision, Levels of Governance, and Legitimacy' in Nicolaidis, K., and Howse, R., eds., *The Federal Vision: Legitimacy and Levels of Governance in the United States and the European Union* (2001), p.1.

Hudec, R., *Essays on the Nature of International Trade Law* (1999).

Hurrell, A., Foot, R., and Gaddis, J., eds., *Order and Justice in International Relations* (2003).

Hyett, S., Macleod, I., and Hendry, I., *The External Relations of the European Communities* (1996).

Imbert, P.-H., Pettiti, L.-E., and Decaux, E., eds., *La Convention européenne des droits de l'homme: Commentaire article par article* (1995).

Jackson, J., 'Sovereignty-Modern: A New Approach to an Outdated Concept', 97 *AJIL* (2003), p. 782.

—— and Grané, P., 'The Saga Continues: An Update on the Banana Dispute and Its Procedural Offspring', 4 *JIEL* (2001), p.581.

—— 'The WTO "Constitution" and Proposed Reforms: Seven "Mantras" Revisited', 4 *JIEL* (2001), p.60.

—— *The Jurisprudence of GATT and the WTO* (2000).

—— and Salas, M., 'Procedural Overview of the WTO-EC Bananas Dispute', 3 *JIEL* (2000), p.145.

Jackson, J., 'The Great 1994 Sovereignty Debate: United States Acceptance and Implementation of the Uruguay Round Results', 36 *Columbia Journal of Transnational Law* (1998), p.157.

—— and Grané, P., 'The WTO Dispute Settlement Understanding— Misunderstandings on the Nature of Legal Obligation', 91 *AJIL* (1997), p.60.

—— and Sykes, A., eds., *Implementing the Uruguay Round* (1997).

—— and Croley, S., 'WTO Dispute Procedures, Standard of Review, and Deference to National Governments', 90 *AJIL* (1996), p.193.

—— and Davey, W., and Sykes, A., *Legal Problems of International Economic Relations: Cases, Materials and Text* (1995).

—— 'United States law and implementation of the Tokyo Round negotiation' in Jackson, J., Louis, J., and Matsushita, M., eds., *Implementing the Tokyo Round: national constitutions and international economic rules* (1984), p.139.

—— and Louis, J., and Matsushita, M., eds., *Implementing the Tokyo Round: national constitutions and international economic rules* (1984), p.139.

Jacobson, H., and Ku, C., 'Using military forces under international auspices and democratic accountability', 1 *International Relations of the Asia-Pacific* (2001), p.21.

James, A., *Sovereign Statehood: The Basis of International Society* (1986).

Jennings, R., 'Book review of *The Spirit of International Law*', 97 *AJIL* (2003), p.725.

—— 'Sovereignty and International Law' in Kreijen, G., ed., *State, Sovereignty, and International Governance* (2002), p.27.

—— 'The Role of the International Court of Justice', 68 *BYBIL* (1997), p.1.

—— and Watts, A., *Oppenheim's International Law* (1992, 9th edn).

Jessup, P., *A Modern Law of Nations* (1968).

Jinks, D., and Goodman, R., 'Toward an Institutional Theory of Sovereignty', 55 *Stanford Law Review* (2003), p.1749.

Jowell, J., Smith, S. de and Woolf, H., *Judicial Review of Administrative Action* (1995).

Joyner, C., and Schachter, O., eds., *United Nations Legal Order* (1995), vol.2.

Kagan, E., and Barron, D., 'Chevron's Nondelegation Doctrine', 2001 *Sup. Ct. Rev.* (2001), p.201.

Kalshoven, F., Kuyper, J., and Lammers, J., eds., *Essays on the Development of the International Legal Order: in Memory of Haro F. Van Panhuys* (1980).

Kaniel, M., *The Exclusive Treaty-Making Power of the European Community up to the Period of the Single European Act* (1996).

Katzenstein, P., Keohane, R., and Krasner, S., '*International Organization* at Its Golden Anniversary' in Katzenstein, P., Keohane, R., and Krasner, S., eds., *Exploration and contestation in the study of world politics* (1999), p.1.

—— and Keohane, R., and Krasner, S., eds., *Exploration and contestation in the study of world politics* (1999).

Keith, K., *The Extent of the Advisory Jurisdiction of the ICJ* (1971).

Kekes, J., 'Essentially Contested Concepts: A Reconsideration', 10 *Philosophy and Rhetoric* (1977), p.71.

Kelsen, H., *The Law of the United Nations: a critical analysis of its fundamental problems* (1950).

Kennedy, D., *International Legal Structures* (1987).

Keohane, R., Katzenstein, P., and Krasner, S., '*International Organization* at Its Golden Anniversary' in Katzenstein, P., Keohane, R., and Krasner, S., eds., *Exploration and contestation in the study of world politics* (1999), p.1.

—— and Katzenstein, P., and Krasner, S., eds., *Exploration and contestation in the study of world politics* (1999),

Kingsbury, B., 'Sovereignty and Inequality', 9 *EJIL* (1998), p.599.

Kingston, J., 'External Relations of the European Community—External Capacity Versus Internal Competence', 44 *ICLQ* (1995), p.659.

Kirgis, F., 'Fuzzy Logic and the Sliding Scale Theorem', *53 Ala. L. Rev.* (2002), p.421.

—— 'Security Council Governance of Postconflict Societies: A Plea for Good Faith and Informed Decisionmaking', 95 *AJIL* (2001), p.1.

—— 'Aviation' in O. Schachter and C. Joyner, eds., *United Nations Legal Order* (1995), vol.2, p.825.

—— 'Claims Settlement and the United Nations Legal Structure' in Lillich, R., ed., *The United Nations Compensation Commission* (1995), p.103.

—— *International Organizations in their Legal Setting* (1993, 2nd ed.).

—— 'Custom on a Sliding Scale', 81 *AJIL* (1987), p.146.

Klabbers, J., *An Introduction to International Institutional Law* (2002).

—— 'The Life and Times of the Law of International Organizations', 70 *Nordic Journal of International Law* (2001), p.287.

—— *The Concept of Treaty in International Law* (1996).

Klein, P., and Sands, P., eds., *Bowett's Law of International Institutions* (2001, 5th edn).

—— *La responsabilité des organisations internationales dans le ordres juridiques internes et en droit des gens* (1998).

Koh, H., 'The Globalization of Freedom', 26 *Yale Journal of International Law* (2001), p.305.

—— 'Transnational Legal Process', 75 *Nebraska Law Review* (1996), p.181.

Kolb, R., 'The Jurisprudence of the Yugoslav and Rwandan Criminal Tribunals on their Jurisdiction and on International Crimes', 71 *BYBIL* (2000), p.259.

König, D., 'Das Urteil des Bundesverfassungsgerichts zum Vertrag von Maastricht—ein Stolperstein auf dem Weg in die europäische Integration?' ('The Judgment of the Bundesverfassungsgerichts (Federal Constitutional Court) on the Maastricht Treaty—An Obstacle On the Way to European Integration?'), 54 *ZaöRV* (1994), p.17.

Koskenniemi, M., *The Gentle Civilizer of Nations: The Rise and Fall of International Law 1870–1960* (2001).

—— 'The Effects of Rights on Political Culture' in Alston, P., ed., *The EU and Human Rights* (1999), p.99.

—— ed., *International Law Aspects of the European Union* (1998).

—— 'The Future of Statehood', 32 *Harvard International Law Journal* (1991), p.397.

—— *From Apology to Utopia: The Structure of International Legal Argument* (1989).

Krasner, S., *Sovereignty: Organized Hypocrisy* (1999).

—— and Keohane, R., and Katzenstein, P., '*International Organization* at Its Golden Anniversary' in Katzenstein, P., Keohane, R., and Krasner, S., eds., *Exploration and contestation in the study of world politics* (1999), p.1.

Kreijen, G., ed., *State, Sovereignty, and International Governance* (2002).

Krisch, N., 'More equal than the rest? Hierarchy, equality and U.S. predominance in international law' in Byers, M., and Nolte, G., eds., *United States Hegemony and the Foundations of International law* (2003), p.135.

Ku, C., and Jacobson, H., 'Using military forces under international auspices and democratic accountability', 1 *International Relations of the Asia-Pacific* (2001), p.21.

Ku, J., 'The Delegation of Federal Power to International Organizations: New Problems with Old Solutions', 85 *Minnesota Law Review* (2000–2001), p.71.

Kumm, M., and Ferreres Comella, V., 'The Future of Constitutional Conflict in the European Union: Constitutional Supremacy after the Constitutional Treaty', 5(4) *Jean Monnet Working Paper* (2004), available at http://www.jeanmonnetprogram.org/papers/04/040501-15.html.

Kuyper, J., Kalshoven, F., and Lammers, J., eds., *Essays on the Development of the International Legal Order: in Memory of Haro F. Van Panhuys* (1980).

Lacroix, J., and Nicolaidis, K., 'Order and Justice Beyond the Nation State: Europe's Competing Paradigms' in Foot, R., Gaddis, J., and Hurrell, A., eds., *Order and Justice in International Relations* (2003), p.125.

La Pergola, A., and Del Duca, P., 'Community Law, International Law and the Italian Constitution', 79 *AJIL* (1985), p.598.

Lamb, S., 'The Powers of Arrest of the International Criminal Tribunal for the former Yugoslavia', 69 *BYBIL* (1999), p.165.

Lammers, J., 'General Principles of Law Recognized by Civilized Nations' in Kalshoven, F., Kuyper, J., and Lammers, J., eds., *Essays on the Development of the International Legal Order: in Memory of Haro F. Van Panhuys* (1980), p.53.

Lang, W., Ginther, K., Hafner, G., Neuhold, H., and Sucharipa-Behrmann, L., eds., *Völkerrecht zwischen normativem anspruch und politischer Realität* (1994).

Lauterpacht, H., *International Law: Being the Collected Papers of Hersch Lauterpacht*, vol.3, *The Law of Peace*, Parts II–VI (1970–2004).

—— *Private Law Sources and Analogies of International Law* (1927).

Lee, R., ed., *The International Criminal Court: The Making of the Rome Statute* (1999).

Leebron, D., 'Implementation of the Uruguay Round Results in the United States' in Jackson, J., and Sykes, A., eds., *Implementing the Uruguay Round* (1997), p.175.

Leino, P., 'All Dressed Up and Nowhere to Go: The Debate on the EU Charter of Fundamental Rights', 11 *Finnish Yearbook of International Law* (2000), p.37.

Lenaerts, K., and De Smijter, E., 'The United Nations and the European Union: living apart together' in Wellens, K., ed., *International Law: Theory and Practice: Essays in Honour of Eric Suy* (1998), p.439.

Lenaerts, K., 'Constitutionalism and the Many Faces of Federalism', 38 *American Journal of Comparative Law* (1990), p.205.

—— 'Fundamental Rights to be Included in a Community Catalogue', 16 *European Law Review* (1991), p.367.

Lenway, S., Morck, R., and Young, B., 'Rent Seeking, Protectionism, and Innovation in the American Steel Industry', 106 *The Economic Journal* (March 1996), p.410.

Lindahl, H., 'Sovereignty and the Institutionalization of Normative Order', 21 *Oxford Journal of Legal Studies* (2001), p.165.

Lindseth, P., 'Democratic Legitimacy and the Administrative Character of Supranationalism: the example of the European Community', 99 *Columbia Law Review* (1999), p.628.

Lobo de Souza, I., 'The Role of State Consent in the Customary Process', 44 *ICLQ* (1995), p.521.

Louis, J., Jackson, J., and Matsushita, M., eds., *Implementing the Tokyo Round: national constitutions and international economic rules* (1984).

Loughlin, M., *The Idea of Public Law* (2003).
—— *Public Law and Political Theory* (1992).
Low, P., *Trading Free: The GATT and US Trade Policy* (1993).
Lowe, A.V., 'Responsibility for the Conduct of Other States', *Japanese Journal of International Law* (2002), p.1.
—— 'The Politics of Law-Making: Are the Method and Character of Norm Creation Changing?' in Byers, M., ed., *The Role of Law in International Politics* (2000), p.207.
—— and Churchill, R., *The law of the sea* (1999, 3rd edn).
—— and Collier, J., *The Settlement of Disputes in International Law* (1999).
—— 'Precluding Wrongfulness or Responsibility: A Plea for Excuses', 10 *EJIL* (1999), p.405.
—— 'Can the European Community Bind the Member States on Questions of Customary International Law?' in Koskenniemi, M., ed., *International Law Aspects of the European Union* (1998), p.149.
—— and Fitzmaurice, M., eds., *Fifty Years of the International Court of Justice: Essays in Honour of Sir Robert Jennings* (1996).
Lupia, A., and McCubbins, M., 'Representation or abdication? How citizens use institutions to help delegation succeed', 37 *European Journal of Political Research* (2000), p.291.
MacCormick, N., *Questioning Sovereignty: Law, State, and Nation in the European Commonwealth* (1999).
—— 'Beyond the Sovereign State', 56 *Modern Law Review* (1993), p.1.
Macdonald, R. St. J., ed., *Essays in Honour of Wang Tieya* (1993).
Macleod, I., Hendry, I., and Hyett, S., *The External Relations of the European Communities* (1996).
Magee, C., and Baldwin, R., 'Is trade policy for sale? Congressional voting on recent trade bills', 105 *Public Choice* (2000), p.79.
Mancini, G., 'The Making of a Constitution for Europe', 26 *Common Market Law Review* (1989), p.595.
Markesinis, B., ed., *The Clifford Chance Lectures: Bridging the Channel* (1996).
Martinez, M., *National Sovereignty and International Organizations* (1996).
Matheson, M., 'United Nations Governance of Postconflict Societies', 95 *AJIL* (2001), p.76.
Matsushita, M., Schoenbaum, T., and Mavroidis, P., *The World Trade Organization: Law, Practice, and Policy* (2003).
—— and Jackson, J., and Louis, J., eds., *Implementing the Tokyo Round: national constitutions and international economic rules* (1984).
Mattli, W., and Slaughter, A-M., 'The Role of National Courts in the Process of European Integration: Accounting for Judicial Preferences and Constraints' in Slaughter, A-M., Stone Sweet, A., and Weiler, J., eds., *The European Court and National Courts—Doctrine and Jurisprudence: Legal Change in Its Social Context* (1998), p.253.
Mavroidis, P., Matsushita, M., and Schoenbaum, T., *The World Trade Organization: Law, Practice, and Policy* (2003).
—— '*Amicus Curiae* Briefs Before The WTO: Much Ado About Nothing', 2(1) *Jean Monnet Working Paper* (2001), available at: http://www.jeanmonnetprogram.org/papers/01/010201.rtf.
Mbirimi, I., Chilala, B., and Grynberg, R., eds., *From Doha to Cancun: Delivering a Development Round* (2003).

McBride, S., 'Dispute Settlement in the WTO: Backbone of the Global Trading System or Delegation of Awesome Power', 32 *Law & Pol'y Int'l Bus.* (2001), p.643.

McCubbins, M., and Lupia, A., 'Representation or abdication? How citizens use institutions to help delegation succeed', 37 *European Journal of Political Research* (2000), p.291.

McGoldrick, D., *International Relations Law of the European Union* (1997).

—— *The Human Rights Committee* (1991), p.151.

McNair, A., *The Law of Treaties* (1961).

—— 'The General Principles of Law Recognized by Civilized Nations', 33 *BYBIL* (1957), p.1.

Melchior, M., 'La procédure de conclusion des accords externes de la Communauté Économique Européenne', 2 *Revue Belge de Droit International* (1966), p.187.

Mendelson, M., 'State Responsibility for Breach of Interim Protection Orders of the International Court of Justice' in Fitzmaurice, M., and Sarooshi, D., *Issues of State Responsibility Before International Judicial Institutions* (2004), p.35.

—— 'The Formation of Customary International Law', 272 *Recueil des cours* (1998), p.155.

—— 'The Subjective Element in Customary International Law', 66 *BYBIL* (1995), p.177.

—— 'The Impact of European Community Law on the Implementation of the European Convention on Human Rights', 3 *Yearbook of European Law* (1983), p.99.

Merills, J., *International Dispute Settlement* (1998, 3rd edn).

Merrill, T., 'Judicial Deference to Executive Precedent', 101 *Yale Law Journal* (1992), p.969.

Molyneux, C., *Domestic Structures and International Trade: The Unfair Trade Instruments of the United States and European Union* (2001).

Moravcsik, A., 'The Origins of Human Rights Regimes: Democratic Delegation in Postwar Europe', 54 *International Organization* (2000), p.217.

Morck, R., Lenway, S., and Young, B., 'Rent Seeking, Protectionism, and Innovation in the American Steel Industry', 106 *The Economic Journal* (March 1996), p.410.

Muller, A., Raic, D., and Thuránszky, J., eds., *The International Court of Justice* (1997).

Müller, W., Bergman, T., and Strøm, K., 'Introduction: Parliamentary democracy and the chain of delegation', 37 *European Journal of Political Research* (2000), p.255.

Müllerson, R., 'The interplay of objective and subjective elements in customary international law' in Wellens, K., ed., *International Law: Theory and Practice: Essays in Honour of Eric Suy* (1998), p.161.

Mundo, P., *National Politics in a Global Economy: The Domestic Sources of US Trade Policy* (1999).

Murphy, S., 'Contemporary practice of the United States relating to international law', 94 *AJIL* (2000).

Nelson, R., 'International Law and U.S. Withholding of Payments to International Organizations', 80 *AJIL* (1986), p.973.

Neuhold, H., Ginther, K., Hafner, G., Lang, W., and Sucharipa-Behrmann, L., eds., *Völkerrecht zwischen normativem anspruch und politischer Realität* (1994).

Neuwahl, N., and Rosas, A., eds., *The European Union and Human Rights* (1995).

Nicolaidis, K., and Lacroix, J., 'Order and Justice Beyond the Nation State: Europe's Competing Paradigms' in Foot, R., Gaddis, J., and Hurrell, A., eds., *Order and Justice in International Relations* (2003), p.125.

——and Howse, R., 'Introduction: The Federal Vision, Levels of Governance, and Legitimacy' in Nicolaidis, K., and Howse, R., eds., *The Federal Vision: Legitimacy and Levels of Governance in the United States and the European Union* (2001), p.1.

Nolte, G., 'Constitutional Implications of German Participation in Treaty Regimes' in Franck, T., ed., *Delegating State Powers: The Effect of Treaty Regimes on Democracy and Sovereignty* (2000), p.261.

Oakley, R., and Hirsh, J., *Somalia and Operation Restore Hope: Reflections on Peacemaking and Peacekeeping* (1995).

O'Keeffe, D., and Twomey, P., eds., *Legal Issues of the Maastricht Treaty* (1994).

Oliver, D., *Common Values and the Public-Private Divide* (1999).

——'The Underlying Values of Public and Private Law' in Taggart, M., ed., *The Province of Administrative Law* (1997), p.217.

Oliver, P., 'The French Constitution and the Treaty of Maastricht', 43 *ICLQ* (1994), p.1.

Olsen, H., and Harck, S., 'International Decisions: Decision Concerning the Maastricht Treaty', 93 *AJIL* (1999), p.209.

Oppenheimer, A., ed., *The Relationship between European Community Law and National Law: The Cases* (1994).

Ortega, L., and Garcia de Enterria, E., 'European influences on the national administrative laws from the point of view of the Member States: Spanish Report' in Schwarze, J., ed., *Administrative Law under European Influence: on the Convergence of the Administrative Law of the EU Member States* (1996), p.695.

Pace, W., and Thieroff, M., 'Participation of Non-Governmental Organizations' in Lee, R., ed., *The International Criminal Court: The Making of the Rome Statute* (1999), p.391.

Parry, C., 'The Treaty-Making Power of the United Nations', 26 *BYBIL* (1949), p.108.

Pavoni, R., 'UN Sanctions in EU and National Law: The *Centro-Com* Case', 48 *ICLQ* (1999), p.582.

Payne, M., Adsera, A., and Boix, C., 'Are You Being Served? Political Accountability and Quality of Government', 19 *The Journal of Law, Economics, & Organization* (2003), p.445.

Pellet, A., 'A French Constitutional Perspective on Treaty Implementation' in Franck T., ed., *Delegating State Powers: The Effect of Treaty Regimes on Democracy and Sovereignty* (2000), p.279.

Pettiti, L.-E., Decaux, E., and Imbert, P.-H., eds., *La Convention européenne des droits de l'homme: Commentaire article par article* (1995).

Philpott, D., 'Sovereignty' in Zalta, E., ed., *The Stanford Encyclopedia of Philosophy* (2003).

Pierce, R., 'Chevron and its Aftermath: Judicial Review of Agency Interpretations of Statutory Provisions', 41 *Vanderbilt Law Journal* (1988), p.301.

Plötner, J., 'Report on France' in Slaughter, A-M., Stone Sweet, A., and Weiler, J., eds., *The European Court and national courts: doctrine and jurisprudence: legal change in its social context* (1998), p.41.

Pomerance, M., 'The Advisory Role of the International Court of Justice and its "Judicial" Character?' in Muller, A., Raic, D., and Thuránszky, J., eds., *The International Court of Justice* (1997), p.271.

Pratap, D., *The Advisory Jurisdiction of the International Court* (1972).

Prechel, H., 'Steel and the State: Industry Politics and Business Policy Formation, 1940–1989', 55 *American Sociological Review* (1990), p.648.

Presley, M., 'Sovereignty and Delegation Issues Regarding U.S. Commitment to the World Trade Organization's Dispute Settlement Process', 8 *J. Transnat'l L. & Pol'y* (1998), p.173.

Raftopoulos, E., *The Inadequacy of the Contractual Analogy in the Law of Treaties* (1990).

Rahimi-Laridjani, E., 'The Instance of Commercial Regimes' in T. Franck, ed., *Delegating State Powers: The Effect of Treaty Regimes on Democracy and Sovereignty* (2000), p.61.

Raic, D., Muller, A., and Thuránszky, J., eds., *The International Court of Justice* (1997).

Ratner, S., 'The Cambodia Settlement Agreements', 87 *AJIL* (1993), p.1.

Raustiala, K., 'Sovereignty and Multilateralism', 1 *Chicago Journal of International Law* (2000), p.401.

Raz, J., *The Authority of Law* (1979).

Rawlings, R., and Craig, P., eds., *Law and Administration in Europe* (2003).

Redgwell, C., 'Reservations to Treaties and Human Rights Committee General Comment No.24(52)', 46 *ICLQ* (1997), p.390.

——'Universality or Integrity? Some Reflections on Reservations to General Multilateral Treaties', 64 *British Year Book of International Law* (1993), p.245.

Reich, N., 'Judge-made "Europe à la carte": Some Remarks on Recent Conflicts between European and German Constitutional Law Provoked by the Banana Litigation', 7 *EJIL* (1996), p.103.

Reinisch, A., *International Organizations before National Courts* (2000).

Reisman, W.M., 'The United States and International Institutions', 41 *Survival* (1999–2000), p.62.

——'The Constitutional Crisis in the United Nations', 87 *AJIL* (1993), p.83.

——'Sovereignty and Human Rights in Contemporary International Law', 84 *AJIL* (1990), p.866.

Reynolds, F., *Bowstead and Reynolds on Agency* (2001, 17th edn).

Rosas, A., and Neuwahl, N., eds., *The European Union and Human Rights* (1995).

Rosenne, S., *The World Court: What it is and how it works* (1995, 5th edn).

Rosenau, J., and Czempiel, E-O., eds., *Governance without Government: Order and Change in World Politics* (1992).

Rubin, A., 'Dole, Clinton Compromise Greases Wheels for GATT', *Congressional Quarterly Weekly Report*, 26 November 1994, Vol.52, No.46, p.3405.

Saarbrücken, G., 'The Interpretation of the Charter' in Simma, B., ed., *The Charter of the United Nations* (2002, 2nd edn), p.25.

Salas, M., and Jackson, J., 'Procedural Overview of the WTO-EC Bananas Dispute', 3 *JIEL* (2000), p.145.

Salzberger, E., and Voigt, S., 'Economic Analysis of Constitutional Law: On Constitutional Processes and the Delegation of Power, with Special Emphasis on Israel and Central and Eastern Europe', 3 *Theoretical Inq. L* (2002), p.207.

Sands, P., and Klein, P., eds., *Bowett's Law of International Institutions* (2001, 5th edn).
―― ' "Unilateralism", Values, and International Law', 11 *EJIL* (2000), p.291.
Sarooshi, D., and Fitzmaurice, M., *Issues of State Responsibility Before International Judicial Institutions* (2004).
―― 'Reform of the WTO Dispute Settlement Understanding' in Mbirimi, I., Chilala, B., and Grynberg, R., eds., *From Doha to Cancun: Delivering a Development Round* (2003), p.105.
―― 'The United Nations Collective Security System and the Establishment of Peace', 53 *Current Legal Problems* (2000), p.621.
―― 'The Role of the United Nations Secretary-General in United Nations Peace-Keeping Operations', 20 *Australian Yearbook of International Law* (1999), p.279.
―― 'The Statute of the International Criminal Court', 48 *ICLQ* (1999), p.387.
―― *The United Nations and the Development of Collective Security: the Delegation by the UN Security Council of its Chapter VII Powers* (1999).
―― 'The Legal Framework Governing United Nations Subsidiary Organs', 67 *BYBIL* (1996), p.413.
Sato, T., *Evolving Constitutions of International Organizations* (1996).
Schachter, O., and Joyner, C., eds., *United Nations Legal Order* (1995), vol.2.
Schermers, H., and Blokker, N., *International Institutional Law* (2003, 4th edn).
Schilling, T., 'The Autonomy of the Community Legal Order: An Analysis of Possible Foundations', 37 *Harvard International Law Journal* (1996), p.389.
Schlemmer-Schulte, S., and Tung, K., eds., *Liber Amicorum Ibrahim F.I. Shihata: International Finance and Development Law* (2001).
Schoenbaum, T., Matsushita, M., and Mavroidis, P., *The World Trade Organization: Law, Practice, and Policy* (2003).
Schwarze, J., ed., *Administrative Law under European Influence: on the Convergence of the Administrative Law of the EU Member States* (1996).
Schwarzenberger, G., *Power Politics: A Study of International Society* (1951).
Schwelb, E., 'Withdrawal from the United Nations The Indonesian Intermezzo', 61 *AJIL* (1967), p.661.
Seavey, W., 'The Rationale of Agency', 29 *Yale Law Journal* (1919–1920), p.859.
Seidl-Hohenveldern, I., 'Access of International Organizations to the International Court of Justice' in Muller, A., Raic, D., and Thuránszky, J., eds., *The International Court of Justice* (1997), p.189.
―― 'Constitutional Problems involved in Austria's Accession to the EU', 32 *CMLRev* (1995), p.727.
Sereni, A., 'Agency in International Law', 34 *AJIL* (1940), p.638.
Seyersted, F., 'Is the International Personality of Intergovernmental Organizations valid *vis-à-vis* Non-members?', 4 *Indian Journal of International Law* (1964), p.233.
Shachor-Landau, C., 'The International Legal Personality of the EEC and its Treaty-Making Power', 20 *Israel Law Review* (1985), p.341.
Shahabuddeen, M., 'Municipal law reasoning in international law' in Lowe, V., and Fitzmaurice, M., eds., *Fifty Years of the International Court of Justice: Essays in Honour of Sir Robert Jennings* (1996), p.90.
Shaw, M., 'The International Court, Responsibility and Remedies' in Fitzmaurice, M., and Sarooshi, D., *Issues of State Responsibility Before International Judicial Institutions* (2004), p.19.

Shaw, M., *International Law* (2003, 5th edn).
—— 'A Practical Look at the International Court of Justice' in Evans, M., ed., *Remedies in International Law* (1998), p.11.
Simma, B., *The Charter of the United Nations* (2002, 2nd edn).
—— 'From Bilateralism to Community Interest in International Law', 250 *Recueil des cours* (1994-VI), p.209.
—— 'Self-Contained Regimes', 16 *Netherlands Yearbook of International Law* (1985), p.111.
Sinclair, I., *The Vienna Convention on the Law of Treaties*, (1984, 2nd edn).
Skubiszewski, K., 'Law-Making by International Organizations', 19 *Thesaurus Acroasium, Sources of International Law* (1992).
Slaughter, A-M., Tulumello, A., and Wood, S., 'International Law and International Relations Theory: A New Generation of Interdisciplinary Scholarship', 92 *AJIL* (1998), p.367.
—— and Stone Sweet, A., and Weiler, J., *The European Court and national courts: doctrine and jurisprudence: legal change in its social context* (1998).
—— and Mattli, W., 'The Role of National Courts in the Process of European Integration: Accounting for Judicial Preferences and Constraints' in Slaughter, A-M., Stone Sweet, A., and Weiler, J., eds., *The European Court and National Courts—Doctrine and Jurisprudence: Legal Change in Its Social Context* (1998), p.253.
—— and Helfer, L., 'Toward a Theory of Effective Supranational Adjudication', 107 *Yale Law Journal* (1997–1998), p.273.
Sloan, B., 'General Assembly Resolutions Revisited (Forty Years Later)', 58 *BYBIL* (1987), p.39.
Smith, S. de, Woolf, H., and Jowell, J., *Judicial Review of Administrative Action* (1995).
Snyder, F., 'The Origins of the "Nonmarket Economy": Ideas, Pluralism, and Power in EC Anti-dumping Law about China', 7 *European Law Journal* (2001), p.369.
Sorensen, G., 'Sovereignty: Change and Continuity in a Fundamental Institution', 47 *Political Studies* (1999), p.590.
Spulber, D., and Besanko, D., 'Delegation, Commitment, and the Regulatory Mandate', 8 *Journal of Law, Economics, and Organization* (1992), p.126.
Stanko, G., Chimerine, L., Tonelson, A., and von Schriltz, K., *Can the Phoenix Survive? The Fall and Rise of the American Steel Industry* (1994).
Staubach, F., *The German Law of Agency and Distributorship Agreements* (1977).
Stein, E., 'International Integration and Democracy: No Love at First Sight', 95 *AJIL* (2001), p.489.
Stewart, T., ed., *The GATT Uruguay Round: A Negotiating History (1986–1994)*, Volumes I, IV.
Steyger, E., *Europe and its Members* (1995).
Stone, A., *The Birth of Judicial Politics in France: the Constitutional Council in Comparative Perspective* (1992).
Stone Sweet, A., Slaughter, A-M., and Weiler, J., *The European Court and national courts: doctrine and jurisprudence: legal change in its social context* (1998).
Strøm, K., Bergman, T., and Müller, W., 'Introduction: Parliamentary democracy and the chain of delegation', 37 *European Journal of Political Research* (2000), p.255.

Sucharipa-Behrmann, L., Ginther, K., Hafner, G., Neuhold, H., and Lang, W., eds., *Völkerrecht zwischen normativem anspruch und politischer Realität* (1994).

Sugihara, T., 'The Advisory Function of the International Court of Justice', 18 *Japanese Annual of International Law* (1974), p.23.

Swaine, E., 'The Constitutionality of International Delegations', 104 *Columbia Law Review* (2004), p.1492.

Suy, E., *Les Actes juridiques unilatéraux en droit international public* (1962).

Szasz, P., 'Granting International Organizations *Ius Standi* in the International Court of Justice' in Muller, A., Raic, D., and Thuránszky, J., eds., *The International Court of Justice* (1997), p.169.

Sztucki, J., 'International Organization as Parties to Contentious Proceedings before the International Court of Justice' in Muller, A., Raic, D., and Thuránszky, J., eds., *The International Court of Justice* (1997), p.141.

Sykes, A., and Jackson, J., eds., *Implementing the Uruguay Round* (1997).

—— and Davey, W., and Jackson, J., *Legal Problems of International Economic Relations: Cases, Materials and Text* (1995).

Taggart, M., ed., *The Province of Administrative Law* (1997).

Tangney, P., 'The New Internationalism: The Cession of Sovereign Competences to Supranational Organizations and Constitutional Change in the United States and Germany', 21 *Yale Journal of International Law* (1996), p.395.

Thieroff, M., and Pace, W., 'Participation of Non-Governmental Organizations' in Lee, R., ed., *The International Criminal Court: The Making of the Rome Statute* (1999), p.391.

Tierney, S., and Warbrick, C., eds., *The Sovereignty of States and the Sovereignty of International Law* (forthcoming: 2005).

Thirlway, H., 'The Law and Procedure of the International Court of Justice 1960–1989, Part Eight', 67 *BYBIL* (1996), p.1.

—— 'The Law and Procedure of the International Court of Justice 1960–1989, Part Four', 63 *BYBIL* (1992), p.1.

—— 'The Law and Procedure of the International Court of Justice 1960–1989, Part Two', 61 *BYBIL* (1990), p.1.

—— 'The Law and Procedure of the International Court of Justice 1960–1989, Part One', 60 *BYBIL* (1989), p.1.

Thuránszky, J., Muller, A., and Raic, D., eds., *The International Court of Justice* (1997).

Tomkins, A., 'Responsibility and Resignation in the European Commission', 62 *Modern Law Review* (1999), p.744.

Tomuschat, C., ed., *The United Nations at Age Fifty: A Legal Perspective* (1995).

Tonelson, A., Chimerine, L., von Schriltz, K., and Stanko, G., *Can the Phoenix Survive? The Fall and Rise of the American Steel Industry* (1994).

Trachtman, J., 'The Domain of WTO Dispute Settlement', 40 *Harvard International Law Journal* (1999), p.333.

Tridimas, T., *The General Principles of EC Law* (1999).

Tulumello, A., Slaughter, A-M., and Wood, S., 'International Law and International Relations Theory: A New Generation of Interdisciplinary Scholarship', 92 *AJIL* (1998), p.367.

Tung, K., and Schlemmer-Schulte, S., eds., *Liber Amicorum Ibrahim F.I. Shihata: International Finance and Development Law* (2001).

Twomey, P., and O'Keefe, D., eds., *Legal Issues of the Maastricht Treaty* (1994).

Usher, J., *European Community Law and National Law—The Irreversible Transfer* (1981).

Vallat, F., 'The Competence of the United Nations General Assembly', 97 *Recueil des cours* (1959-II), p.207.

Van Panhuys, J., 'The Netherlands Constitution and International Law', 58 *AJIL* (1964), p.88.

Vazquez, C.M., 'Laughing at Treaties', 99 *Columbia Law Review* (1999), p.2154.

—— 'The Four Doctrines of Self-Executing Treaties', 89 *AJIL* (1995), p.695.

Voigt, S., and Salzberger, E., 'Economic Analysis of Constitutional Law: On Constitutional Processes and the Delegation of Power, with Special Emphasis on Israel and Central and Eastern Europe', 3 *Theoretical Inq. L* (2002), p.207.

von Schriltz, K., Chimerine, L., Tonelson, A., and Stanko, G., *Can the Phoenix Survive? The Fall and Rise of the American Steel Industry* (1994).

Wade, W., 'Sovereignty—Reduction or Evolution?', 112 *Law Quarterly Review* (1996), p.568.

Waldron, J., 'Is the rule of law an essentially contested concept?', 21 *Law and Philosophy* (2002), p.137.

Warbrick, C., and Tierney, S., eds., *The Sovereignty of States and the Sovereignty of International Law* (forthcoming: 2005).

Watts, A., and Jennings, R., *Oppenheim's International Law* (1992, 9th edn).

J.H.H. Weiler, 'Federalism Without Constitutionalism: Europe's *Sonderweg*' in K. Nicoladis and R. Howse, eds, *The Federal Vision: Legitimacy and Levels of Governance in the United States and the European Union* (2001), p.54.

—— *The Constitution of Europe* (1999).

—— and Fries, S.C., 'A Human Rights Policy for the European Community and Union: The Question of Competences' in Alston, P., ed., *The EU and Human Rights* (1999), p.147.

—— and Stone Sweet, A., and Slaughter, A-M., *The European Court and national courts: doctrine and jurisprudence: legal change in its social context* (1998).

—— 'The Transformation of Europe', 100 *Yale LJ* (1991), p.2403.

—— 'Alternatives to withdrawal from an international organization: the case of the European Economic Community', 20 *Israel Law Review* (1985), p.282.

Weiss, F., 'Greenland's withdrawal from the European Communities', 10 *European Law Review* (1985), p.173.

Wellens, K., *Remedies Against International Organizations* (2002).

—— ed., *International Law: Theory and Practice: Essays in Honour of Eric Suy* (1998).

—— 'The Court's Judgment in the case concerning the Gabcikovo-Nagymaros project (Hungary/Slovakia): some preliminary reflections' in Wellens, K., ed., *International Law: Theory and Practice: Essays in Honour of Eric Suy* (1998), p.765.

—— *Resolutions and Statements of the United Nations Security Council (1946–1989)* (1993, 2nd edn).

White, N., *The Law of International Organisations* (1996).

Wickremasinghe, C., and Fox, H., 'British Implementation of UN Sanctions Against Iraq', 41 *ICLQ* (1992), p.920.

Widdows, K., 'The Unilateral Denunciation of Treaties Containing No Denunciation Clause', 53 *BYBIL* (1982), p.83.

Wilde, R., 'From Danzig to East Timor and Beyond: the Role of International Territorial Administration', 95 *AJIL* (2001), p.583.

Wood, S., Slaughter, A-M., and Tulumello, A., 'International Law and International Relations Theory: A New Generation of Interdisciplinary Scholarship', 92 *AJIL* (1998), p.367.

Woolf, H., Smith, S. de and Jowell, J., *Judicial Review of Administrative Action* (1995).

Wright, Q., 'Treaties and the Constitutional Separation of Powers in the United States', 12 *AJIL* (1918), p.64.

WTO, *The Legal Texts: The Results of the Uruguay Round of Multilateral Trade Negotiations* (1999).

Wyatt, D., 'Constitutional Significance of the *Tobacco Advertising* Judgment of the European Court of Justice' in *The ECJ's Tobacco Advertising Judgment* (Cambridge Centre for European Legal Studies Occasional Paper, No 5 (2001).

—— 'New Legal Order, or Old?', 7 *European Law Review* (1982), p. 147.

Yataganas, X., 'The Treaty of Nice: The Sharing of Power and the Institutional Balance in the European Union—A Continental Perspective', 1/01 *Jean Monnet Working Paper* (2001), available at http://www.jeanmonnetprogram.org/ papers/ 01/ 010101.html.

Yoo, J., 'Globalism and the Constitution: Treaties, Non-Self-Execution, and the Original Understanding', 99 *Columbia Law Review* (1999), p.1955.

—— 'The New Sovereignty and the Old Constitution: The Chemical Weapons Convention and the Appointments Clause', 15 *Constitutional Commentary* (1998), p.87.

Young, B., Lenway, S., and Morck, R., 'Rent Seeking, Protectionism, and Innovation in the American Steel Industry', 106 *The Economic Journal* (March 1996), p.410.

Young, O., 'The Effectiveness of International Institutions: Hard Cases and Critical Variables' in Rosenau, J., and Czempiel, E-O., eds., *Governance without Government: Order and Change in World Politics* (1992), p.160.

Zalta, E., ed., *The Stanford Encyclopedia of Philosophy* (2003).

Zemanek, K., 'The Legal Foundations of the International System: General Course on Public International Law', 266 *Recueil des Cours* (1997), p.9.

—— in 'Report by Rosalyn Higgins', 66-I *AIDI* (1995), p.327.

Zoller, E., 'The "corporate will" of the United Nations and the Rights of the Minority', 81 *AJIL* (1987), p.610.

Index

accountability
    exercise of powers at domestic level 14
    sovereign values 9, 14
Acts of Parliament
    EC law, conformity with 7
    judicial review 7
administrative law
    international organization,
        application to 14–17
    appropriate use 16
    United States
        judicial deference to agency
            decisions 17
Africa
    Italian colonies in 21
agency relationships
    acceptance of ad hoc conferral of
        powers 46
    implied consent 46
    attribution distinguished 38
    attribution of acts
        effective control test 38–39, 40, 46
        overall control test 40, 46
    changing legal relations of principal,
        agent 50
    conditions for recognition 33, 46
    consent
        attribution of acts of State 37–38
        implied consent 37–41
        prerequisite for agency relationship
            35–37
        role of State control 37–41
    consequences of establishment 50–53
        changing legal relations of principal,
            agent 50
        fiduciary duty of agent to act in interests
            of principal 51–53
        responsibility of principal for acts of
            agent 50–51
    delegation of powers distinguished 54
    distinct legal concept 33
    establishment 33, 42–53
        consequences 50–53
        member states 42, 43–49
        non-member states 42, 49–53
        presumption against establishment 43

fiduciary duty of agent to act in interests
    of principal 51–53
ICJ recognition of relationships 33
ILC recognition of relationships 33,
    35–36
measures available to States 109–110
member states 42, 43–49
NATO and member states 46–49
non-member states 42, 49–53
recognition of relationships 33
representation 34
responsibility of principal for acts of
    agent 50–51
revocability 29–30, 41–42
separate legal entities, principal and agent
    as 34
termination 41–42
typology of conferrals of powers, place
    in 29
use of concept 35
autonomy
    sovereign values 9

Bahá'u'lláh 1
Baranja 23–25
Belgium 73

Cambodia 21
    Paris Peace Accords 26–27
ceding
    typology of conferrals of powers 28
Charter of Fundamental Rights of the
    Union 74–75
Chemical Weapons Convention 77
China 10
    Tiananmen Square massacre 10
conferrals of powers
    acceptance by organization 20
    ad hoc basis 19–27
    consent of organization to 20
    constituent treaty, by 18–19
    constraints accepted by 22, 25–26
    declaration accepting 21
    general competence to accept conferral
        25–26
    importance of ability 18

conferrals of powers (*cont.*)
  intention of organization to accept 21
  jurisdiction of or organ 22
  powers not possessed under constituent
    treaty 25
  process 19–27
    ad hoc basis 19–27
    constituent treaty, by 18–19
    generally 18
    treaty 18–19
  reaction of organization to conferrals of
    powers 20–27
  resolution accepting 21
  revocability 29–30
  scope of powers, determination of 22
  treaties
    ad hoc basis 19–27
    constituent 18–19
    powers not possessed under constituent
      treaty 25
    separate power, by 18–19
  typology 13–14, 28–32
    see also typology of conferrals of
      powers
  unilateral act accepting 21
  United Nations 22–25
  Vienna Convention on the Law of
    Treaties 20
constituent treaty
  complexity 18
  conferrals of powers by 18–19
  function 18
Constitution for Europe, Draft Treaty
  Establishing 12, 68, 75
corporate economic autonomy
  General Agreement on Tariffs and Trade
    (GATT) 8
  World Trade Organization (WTO) 8
Croatia 23–25
Cuba 10
customary international law 20

Dayton Peace Agreement 22, 23
delegation of powers by States 54–64
  agency relationships distinguished 54
  concurrent exercise of powers by
    organization 54, 58–62
  consequences for State-organization
    relationship 62–64
    fiduciary issues 62–63
    responsibility issues 63–64
  fiduciary issues 62–63

  generally 54
  measures available to States 110–116
    persistent objection 115–116
    termination of conferrals 114–115
    treaty amendment 110–111
    unilateral financial measures 111–114
  responsibility issues 63–64
  revocability 29–30, 54–58
    competence 55
    express provision in treaty 55–56
    intention of parties 56, 57
    legal basis 55
    notice periods 55–56
    unilateral withdrawal 56
    Vienna Convention on the Law of
      Treaties 55
  transfer of powers distinguished 54
  typology of conferrals of powers,
    place in 28
democratic deficit 6, 121
Denmark 74, 75
détournement de pouvoir, exercise of powers
  measures available to States 108–109, 119
direct effect
  European Communities (EC) 70
dispute settlement system
  World Trade Organization (WTO) 13
    contestation of decisions 13
    establishment 95–97
    rationale of US push for 98–100
divisible sovereignty 4

Eastern Slavonia 23–25
equality
  sovereign values 9, 78, 79
essentially contested concept
  continual contestation 5
  exemplar, original 5
  Gallie's formulation 5
  meaning 4
  original formulation 5
  rule of law 5
  sovereignty as 3–5, 11
    consequence of 6–7
estoppel 104
ethnicity 12
European Communities (EC)
  competence to conclude treaties 101
  conferrals of powers by States on 67
  contestation of sovereign values by
    domestic courts 5–6
  direct effect 70

transfer of powers 65, 66–68, 72–76
European Convention on Human Rights
      105–106
European Court of Human Rights 105–106
European Court of Justice (ECJ)
      jurisprudence 15
European Monetary Union
      opt-outs 13
European Union
      withdrawal from 68–69
exclusive control of territory 9
exemplar
      contestations of sovereignty 6
      essentially contested concept 5
      Gallie's notion of 5, 6
      nation-State as 5–6
external sovereignty 4

Federal Republic of Yugoslavia (FRY)
      North Atlantic Treaty Organization
          (NATO) and 47–49
fiduciary duties
      agency relationships 51–53
      delegation of powers, consequences
          of 62–63
      transfers of powers 100–101
Four Powers 19
France 73
freedom
      sovereign values 9

General Agreement on Tariffs and Trade
      (GATT) 81
      see also World Trade Organization (WTO)
      corporate economic autonomy 8
      members 17
Germany
      conferred powers of EC, exercise of 11
      Constitutional Court 15, 67–68
      legislature 15
governmental sovereignty 4

history
      sovereignty and 11

identity
      sovereignty and 11
ILC *see* International Law Commission
indivisible sovereignty 4
Indonesia 115
interdependence sovereignty 4
internal affairs of other States

non-intervention in 9
internal sovereignty 4
International Civil Aviation Organization
      59, 119
International Court of Justice
      advisory jurisdiction, role of 119–120
      agency relationships, recognition of 33
      jus standi of international organizations
          before 120
      legality, application of principle of 112
International Covenant on Civil and Political
      Rights (ICCPR) 60
International Criminal Tribunal for the
      former Yugoslavia (ICTY) 39–40
International Labour Organization
      notice of withdrawal from 56
International Law Commission
      agency relationships, recognition of
          33, 35–36
      State Responsibility, Articles on 63–64,
          102–104, 105–107
      withdrawal from treaties, draft Article
          on 57–58
international legal sovereignty 4
international organizations
      administrative and domestic public law
          principles, application of 14–17
      agency relationships *see* agency
          relationships
      contestability deficit 121
      democratic deficit 121
      general principles of law, application
          of 16
      international law, application of 20
      ontological function 12–13
      private law analogies, application of 15
International Telecommunication Union
      (ITU) 113
International Tin Council litigation 43–45
International Trade Organization
      Charter 91
Italy 73

judicial review
      Acts of Parliament 7

language
      philosophy of 4
Law of the Sea Preparatory Commission
      UN budget for 112
legal journals
      literature on sovereignty 3

legal sovereignty 4
legitimacy
  sovereign values 9
liberal tradition 9
Liechtenstein 33

measures available to States 108–120
  agency relationships 109–110
  breach of obligations under international
    law 109
  customary international law 109
  delegation of powers 110–116
    persistent objection 115–116
    termination of conferrals 114–115
    treaty amendment 110–111
    unilateral financial measures 111–114
  détournement de pouvoir, exercise of
    powers 108–109, 119
  future 118–120
  generally 108–109
  persistent objection
    delegation of powers 115–116
    transfer of powers 118
  reasons for taking 108–109
  termination of conferrals
    delegation of powers 114–115
    transfer of powers 117–118
  transfer of powers 116–118
    persistent objection 118
    termination of conferrals 117–118
    treaty amendment 117
    unilateral financial measures 117
  treaty amendment
    delegation of powers 110–111
    transfer of powers 117
  ultra vires exercise of powers 108, 119
  unilateral financial measures
    delegation of powers 111–114
    transfer of powers 117
modernity 12
Morocco 21
Most Favoured Nation 78

nation-State
  economic autonomy 8, 79–91
  exemplar, as 5–6
  reference point, as 6
National Treatment 78
nationality 12
NATO *see* North Atlantic Treaty
    Organization (NATO)
Nauru 34

Administering Authority 34
Netherlands 73
non-discrimination principles
  World Trade Organization (WTO) 78
North Atlantic Treaty Organization (NATO)
  agency relationship with members 46–49
  Federal Republic of Yugoslavia (FRY)
    and 47–49

ontological function of sovereignty 11–14
Organization of American States
  notice of withdrawal from 56

Paris Peace Accords 26–27
persistent objector rule 115–116
political sovereignty 4
popular sovereignty 4
powers
  conferrals *see* conferrals of powers
  delegation *see* delegation of powers
  exercise of powers at domestic level 14
  transfer *see* transfer of powers
preclusion 104
public law principles
  international organization,
    application to 14–17
    appropriate use 16
    sub-delegation of powers 17
  sub-delegation of powers 17

Queen Victoria, letter of Bahá'u'lláh to 1

responsibility
  see also fiduciary duties
  issues 104–107
  principal for acts of agent, of 50–51
  state 63–64, 102–104, 105–107
revocability
  agency relationships 29–30
  conferrals of powers 29–30
  delegation of powers 29–30, 54
    competence 55
    express provision in treaty 55–56
    intention of parties 56, 57
    legal basis 55
    notice periods 55–56
    unilateral withdrawal 56
    Vienna Convention on the Law of
      Treaties 55
  independent legal personality, retention
    of 29–30
  legality 30

transfer of powers 54, 65, 66–69
typology of conferrals of powers 29–30
withdrawal from organization 30
Rhodesia 10
Romania 10
rule of law
  essentially contested concept 5

Santer Commission 119
security
  sovereign values 9
self-determination
  sovereign values 9
Somalia 47
sovereign values
  accountability 9, 14
  autonomy 9
  contestation of
    European Community, within 5–6,
      72–75
    WTO, within 13, 76–94
  differing approaches 10
  economic autonomy 8, 79–91
  equality 9, 78, 79
  examples 9
  exclusive control of territory 9
  exercise of public powers of government
    9–10
  exercise of sovereign powers in accordance
    with 14
  freedom 9
  incorporation 9–10, 14–15
  integral part of concept of sovereignty 10
  international organizations and 10–11
  legitimacy 9
  non-intervention in internal affairs of other
    States 9
  normative character 9–11
  protection of sovereignty 10
  rival concepts 121
  security 9
  self-determination 9
sovereignty
  concept 3–4
    contestation 5–6
    initial content 6
  contested elements 4, 121
  core criteria 4–5
  domestic 4
  domestic arms of government
    contesting 7–8
  essentially contested concept, as 3–5, 11

  concept of 6–7
  ontological decisions 11–12
  external *v* internal 4
  governmental *v* popular 4
  history and 11
  identity and 121
  importance of concept 3
  indivisible *v* divisible 4
  inequality of states, management of 11
  interdependence 4
  international legal 4
  international organizations and 6–8
  lack of definition, implication of 7
  legal *v* political 4
  'loss' of 3
  meaning of concept 3
  normative character of 9–11
  ontological function 11–14
  typology 3–4
  values *see* sovereign values
  Westphalian 4
state responsibility 63–64, 102–104,
    105–107
sub-delegation of powers
  domestic public law principles 17
Switzerland 33

territory
  exclusive control 9
transfer of powers 65–107
  consequences of transfers 100–107
    fiduciary issues 100–101
    responsibility issues 101–107
  contestation of sovereign values *see*
    sovereign values
  delegation of powers distinguished 54
  European Communities (EC) 65, 66–68,
    72–76
  examples 65
  fiduciary issues 100–101
  full 69
    consent 71
    European Community (EC) 72–76
    example 70
    legitimacy to exercise transferred
      powers 71
    meaning 70
    responsibility issues 104–107
  generally 65–66
  irrevocability 54, 65, 66–69
  measures available to States 116–118
    persistent objection 118

transfer of powers (*cont.*)
  termination of conferrals 117–118
  treaty amendment 117
  unilateral financial measures 117
  partial 69, 76–100
  meaning 70
  responsibility issues 102–104
  US transferring powers to the WTO
    76–100; *see also* World Trade
    Organization (WTO)
  responsibility issues 101–107
  full transfers 104–107
  partial transfers 102–104
  sovereign powers, exercise of 71
  State's consent to be bound by obligations
    flowing from exercise of conferred
    powers 69–100
  typology of conferrals of powers,
    place in 28
  US transferring powers to the WTO
    76–100
  see also World Trade Organization
    (WTO)
  World Trade Organization (WTO) *see*
    World Trade Organization (WTO)
treaties
  conferrals of powers
    constituent treaty, by 18–19
    separate treaty, by 19
  unilateral withdrawal 56–57
  withdrawal 55–58
typology of conferrals of powers 13–14,
    28–32
  agency 29
  see also agency relationships
  authorization 28
  concurrent competence to exercise
    conferred powers 31–32
  conflation of terminology 28
  control by States over the organization
    30–31
  delegation of powers 28
  see also delegation of powers
  exclusive competence to exercise
    conferred powers 31–32
  inconsistent usage of terms 28
  measurement of degree to which powers
    have been given away 29–32
  revocability 29–30
  sole right to exercise conferred
    powers 31–32

spectrum of conferrals 29
transfer 28
  see also transfer of powers

ultra vires exercise of powers
  measures available to States 108, 119
United Kingdom 73
United Nations
  expenses 111–112
  Human Rights Committee (HRC) 60
  Paris Peace Accords 26–27
  peace-keeping forces 25
  Security Council
    own powers used instead of purported
      conferrals 22–23
    resolutions 21
  Transitional Authority for Eastern
    Slavonia, Baranja and Western
    Sirmium 23–25
  Transitional Authority in Cambodia 26–27
  treaty making powers 59
United States
  administrative law
    judicial deference to agency
      decisions 17
  Advisory Committee for Trade Policy and
    Negotiations (ACTPN) 85
  agency interpretation of Statutes 17
  Congress-Executive relationship 82–91
  contestation of economic sovereignty
    within 82–91
  countervailing measures 86–87
  economic autonomy as value of US
    sovereignty 79–82
  fast-track authority of Executive 84–85
  International Antidumping Code 84
  Omnibus Trade and Competitiveness
    Act 1988 93
  protectionism 81
  R&D investment 89–90
  Reciprocal Trade Agreements Act 1934
    82–83
  self-execution of treaties 77
  Smoot-Hawley legislation 82
  Special Representative for Trade
    Negotiations 83
  'Super 301' trade measures 93
  Trade Act 1974 92
  Trade Expansion Act 1962 83, 92
  trade policy control 82–91
  Trade Promotion Authority 85

Trade Representative 83
transfer of powers to WTO *see under*
    World Trade Organization (WTO)
Uruguay Round Agreements Act 86
Universal Postal Union 59
UNOSOM II 47

values *see* sovereign values
Vienna Convention on the Law of Treaties
    consent 110–111
    treaty obligations, effect of 20
    unilateral termination, right of 42
    withdrawal from treaty 55–56

Westphalian sovereignty 4
World Health Organization 59
World Trade Organization (WTO)
    Agreement on Subsidies and
        Countervailing Measures 86
    Agreements 78
    Appellate Body 16, 69, 70, 78, 79
    corporate economic autonomy and 8,
        91–94
    Dispute Settlement Body 69
    dispute settlement system 13
        contestation of decisions 13
        establishment 95–97

    rationale of US push for 98–100
    Dispute Settlement Understanding 69
    equality, value of 78
    Most Favoured Nation principle 78
    National Treatment principle 78
    non-discrimination principles 78
    Panels 16, 69, 70, 78, 79
    reports 69
    termination of membership 30
    transfer of powers 65
    transfers by States of powers to dispute
        settlement organs of 69
    US transfer of powers to 76–100
        see also United States
        Congress 76–78
        corporate economic autonomy, efforts
            by Congress to protect 91–95
        dispute settlement system, establishment
            of 95–97
        economic autonomy as value of
            US sovereignty 79–82
        General Accounting Office study of
            96–97
        partial transfer 78–100
WTO *see* World Trade Organization (WTO)

Zimbabwe 10